**Order, Legitimacy, and Wealth in Ancient States**

This volume delineates a new comparative approach to civilizations centered around three terms, order, legitimacy, and wealth. This approach was initially developed in 1992 in an influential paper by John Baines and Norman Yoffee, comparing and contrasting the nature of social and political power in Egypt and Mesopotamia, and it was the first analysis of the impact of wealth and high culture on the development of states. Following an introductory essay on the concept of 'civilization' by the editors, contributors to the present book apply the Baines/Yoffee model to the range of ancient states around the world, providing documentary and archaeological evidence on the production and uses of 'high culture', literature, and monumental architecture. There are chapters on Mesoamerica, the Andes, the Indus Valley, the Han Dynasty of China, and Greece during the Roman empire, while others expand on the original Egypt–Mesopotamia comparison.

# NEW DIRECTIONS IN ARCHAEOLOGY

## Order, Legitimacy, and Wealth in Ancient States

# Order, Legitimacy, and Wealth in Ancient States

*Edited by*
JANET RICHARDS
*University of Michigan*
and
MARY VAN BUREN
*Colorado State University*

CAMBRIDGE
UNIVERSITY PRESS

CAMBRIDGE UNIVERSITY PRESS
Cambridge, New York, Melbourne, Madrid, Cape Town,
Singapore, São Paulo, Delhi, Mexico City

Cambridge University Press
The Edinburgh Building, Cambridge CB2 8RU, UK

Published in the United States of America by Cambridge University Press, New York

www.cambridge.org
Information on this title: www.cambridge.org/9780521776714



First published 2000

*A catalogue record for this publication is available from the British Library*

*Library of Congress Cataloguing in Publication Data*
Order, legitimacy, and wealth in ancient states / edited by
Janet Richards and Mary Van Buren.
p. cm. – (New directions in archaeology)
Includes bibliographical references and index.
ISBN 0 521 77212 5 (hb) – ISBN 0 521 77671 6 (pb)
1. Civilization, Ancient. 2. Wealth.
I. Richards, Janet. II. Van Buren, Mary. III. Series.
CB311.O734 2000
930–dc21 99–056316

ISBN 978-0-521-77212-9 Hardback
ISBN 978-0-521-77671-4 Paperback

**For our parents**

**Nicholas and Betty Dowdal**
**and**
**Ed and Donya Van Buren**

# Contents

# Figures

# Contributors

SUSAN E. ALCOCK
Department of Classical Studies
University of Michigan

JOHN BAINES
Griffith Institute
Oxford University

BENNET BRONSON
Field Museum of Natural History, Chicago, Illinois

ELIZABETH M. BRUMFIEL
Department of Sociology and Anthropology
Albion College, Albion, Michigan

ROSEMARY A. JOYCE
Department of Anthropology
University of California, Berkeley

JONATHAN MARK KENOYER
Department of Anthropology
University of Wisconsin, Madison

DAVID O'CONNOR
Institute of Fine Arts
New York University

JANET RICHARDS
Department of Near Eastern Studies
Kelsey Museum of Archaeology
University of Michigan

MARY VAN BUREN
Department of Anthropology
Colorado State University

NORMAN YOFFEE
Department of Near Eastern Studies and Department of Anthropology, University of Michigan

# Acknowledgements

We would like to thank the following friends, family, and colleagues who helped throughout the production of this volume: Stuart Kirsch and Dimitris Stevis for support and productive debate; Jessica Kuper for encouragement and expert insights from the beginning; Amanda Sprochi for invaluable, tireless, and substantial work on all technical aspects of the final editing process; Terry Wilfong and Carla Sinopoli for helpful suggestions and editorial advice; Geoff Compton for assistance with maps; and Christina McIntosh for work in the early stages. Last but certainly not least, we thank John Baines and Norm Yoffee for writing the essay which inspired both the project and key points of our discussion in the introductory chapter; and our contributors for their thoughtful exploration of the themes laid out in the original paper.

PART I

# Order, legitimacy, and wealth in ancient states

# 1
# Introduction: ideology, wealth, and the comparative study of "civilizations"

MARY VAN BUREN AND
JANET RICHARDS

Over the last decade critiques of processual archaeology have generated renewed interest in the role of ideology in the development and organization of ancient states. While such a perspective provides an important counterpoint to scholarship that focuses exclusively on demographic and economic factors, it usually leads to an emphasis on the unique configurations of specific cultures, reiterating the division between humanist and social-scientific understandings of past societies. The purpose of this volume is to develop an approach that bridges this dichotomy by using the same conceptual categories to simultaneously examine both the distinctive and common features of ancient civilizations. This is accomplished by applying three analytical concepts – order, legitimacy, and wealth (ideologies of domination and the economic tools with which they are materialized) – to the textual and archaeological records of ancient states as a means of understanding how "high culture," and thus civilization itself, was created and maintained over time.

This approach was initially developed by John Baines and Norman Yoffee in their paper "Order, legitimacy, and wealth in ancient Egypt and Mesopotamia" (Baines and Yoffee 1998), which was produced for a School of American Research seminar on archaic states (Feinman and Marcus 1998). In 1994, Janet Richards and Norman Yoffee convened a symposium entitled "Order, Legitimacy, and Wealth in Early States" at the annual meeting of the American Anthropological Association, in order to examine that approach from a cross-cultural perspective. Seven scholars with expertise in Old World and New World states employed the concepts proposed by Baines and Yoffee as a platform for a comparative method that allows for contrasts as well as commonalities to be identified and explained.[1] How do the concepts of order, legitimacy, and wealth play out in Mesoamerica, in the Andes, in the Indus, in China, or in Greece? What organizational principles are shared? What is truly "unique" in different contexts and why?

The results of the 1994 symposium form the basis of this volume. The model proposed by Baines and Yoffee is summarized here in their chapter "Setting the terms," followed by contributions exploring the central concepts of that debate through a series of case studies that span the ancient world. Elizabeth Brumfiel's final chapter summarizes the findings, evaluates the model from a comparative perspective, and introduces a further illustrative example from the Aztec state. Many of the contributors, in evaluating the operation of the principles of order, legitimacy, and wealth in their own research areas, take a multi-dimensional approach, addressing textual, archaeological, and iconographic data in their discussions, thereby highlighting the interpretive richness in a synthesis of these often disparate sources of data. All touch on issues of discourse and communication in ancient societies, attempting to understand possible points of interaction between elites and the populations they ruled, and the latter's opportunities for and strategies of resistance to ideological and political hegemony.

## Order, legitimacy, and wealth in ancient Egypt and Mesopotamia: the initial debate

In their initial discussion of Mesopotamia and Egypt, Baines and Yoffee carried out a controlled comparison of these two civilizations (Baines and Yoffee 1998). They considered the commonalities and differences, the relationship between archaeological and historical data, and finally, issues of continuity and change, all viewed through an integrated lens of order, legitimacy, and wealth. Throughout, their interest lay not in the emergence of civilizations, but in their operation and articulation, and the ways in which the monopoly and deployment of social and political power was effected, materialized, and maintained.

Baines and Yoffee approached this problem by identifying and focusing on a nexus of elements that distinguishes civilizations from states and other complex social forms: the distinctive corpus of art, thought, and elite practice that is unique to each. They argue that civilization is, in fact, coincident with high culture, which they define as "the production and consumption of aesthetic items under the control, and for the benefit of, the inner elite" (Baines and Yoffee 1998: 235). These products, which range from architecture and sculpture to exotic foods and zoological gardens, are meant for the most elite sector of society, comprised of the highest-ranking individuals in addition to the rulers and the gods. While the specific content of high culture distinguishes one civilization from another, it appears to be created for similar purposes and under comparable conditions. Baines and Yoffee identify three themes that pervade the development and maintenance of high culture and that can be used as terms of comparison to clarify the differences and similarities among early civilizations.

Ideologies of **order** and hierarchy within that order were of fundamental importance to early states in which large populations were organized by novel means, and rulers attempted to maintain control during periods of rapid political and economic change. Civic order resulted from the creation of new institutions, the imposition of laws, and the use of coercion, but worldly order was also generated by incorporating society into a broader, more perfectly ordered cosmological whole. Elites played a critical role in this endeavor as they occupied the point of articulation between society, the gods, and the privileged dead.

Order is distinctively embodied and expressed – materialized (De Marrais *et al.* 1996) – in the high cultural complex surrounding the institutions and lives of the ruling group. High culture is a realm that valorizes the exclusive and expensive, and affirms the necessity of this ruling group to the maintenance of the cosmos. It thus absorbs much of the surplus extracted from commoners, which is used to concretize and inscribe order in a way that may be meaningful only to inner elites. Although elites may assert the opposite, order is fragile, as is the high cultural complex. Both need constant support and ideally expansion. Nonetheless, they can be sustained and recreated through periods of political and economic collapse, but only via the continued existence of an elite cognoscenti. According to Baines and Yoffee, order is threatened primarily by the emergence of a competing order, together with the withering of its predecessor.

**Legitimacy** underpins order in social and political terms. Legitimacy results from the acceptance of order and the elite's role in it. It is attained in part through the maintenance and manipulation of central cultural symbols, particularly those that represent and integrate the differentiated groups within states, and is thus closely tied to high culture and the defining elements of a civilization. Legitimacy depends on some level of consensus, even if incomplete, but Baines and Yoffee propose that the primary audience for most of the aesthetic items that express and negotiate order is, in fact, the inner elite itself. It is on this particular point that many of the volume contributors offer different perspectives.

**Wealth** plays a critical role in this process, and effectively sustains both order and legitimacy. It is of course an integral part of all civilizations, and its deployment is a clear indication of the high degree of social stratification that characterizes such societies. However, the embodiment of order and its use in legitimation require wealth, and it is usually expended on these sorts of projects. Under such circumstances the amassment of wealth cannot be understood merely as an end in itself, but also as a means of expressing and maintaining order.

The unreliability of directly equating material wealth with status is much discussed in the archaeological literature (see, for instance, Kus 1982; M. Smith 1987; Cowgill 1992a). However, understood as an expression of unequal access to labor and to key resources (Webster 1980; Costin and Earle 1989; Paynter 1989), the relationship of wealth to processes of social and political power emerges more clearly (Mann 1986; Paynter and McGuire 1991). Differential access to commodities, especially those envalued and restricted as symbols of power and authority (Appadurai 1986a), affects the ability on the part of different groups to embody either that power or a competing ideology, placing these groups at a disadvantage both within the political arena, and in terms of their visibility in the archaeological record.

## "Civilizations"

These three main terms of analysis – order, legitimacy, and wealth (discussed in more detail by Baines and Yoffee in chapter 2) – thus address intertwined aspects of a civilization's core. Examining the relationship of inner elites to high culture in light of these categories, and, further, the role of competing groups and non-elites within that same nexus, provides a clearer understanding of how civilizations are sustained over long periods of time and vast amounts of space, despite the demise of individual polities. This use of the term "civilization" and consideration of the functioning of civilizational complexes through the lens of order, legitimacy, and wealth, is a rhetoric continued in the contributors' chapters. All of the papers deal with complex societies judged to have attained and/or maintained a "state" level of political organization, and which have traditionally been and continue to be categorized as "civilizations" in the literature (see, for instance, Sasson 1995; Trigger 1993), despite the negative connotations of that term. Like the concept of "culture," "civilization" has had a checkered history in the discipline; yet, again like "culture", it persists in archaeological discourse.

Our own uneasiness with this term has led us to an interest in its genealogy within anthropological and historical study, and to an attempt at formulating a working definition based on its use by the different scholars who have contributed to this volume. Such a definition might be that civilizations are ideological phenomena, typically associated with complex societies, that endure for relatively long periods of time and cover large geographical regions, frequently persisting despite the emergence or destruction of individual polities. Their large scale and lack of congruence with specific institutions makes them especially difficult to characterize, but one recurrent feature is the presence of distinctive and persistent features, both material and ideological.

Why is the term "civilization," uncomfortably reminiscent of imperialist and colonialist rhetoric, itself so persistent? And why perpetuate its use? Part of our own answer, parallel to that of Baines and Yoffee, has lain in a fascination with the longevity of these entities, and a desire to track the components of recurrent and successful strategies in place over time. What makes a complex like ancient Egyptian civilization – embodied in extremely longlived notions of cosmos, kingship and social order – thrive in such a way that it is deployed and contested and redeployed, yet still recognizable in form over thousands of years? "Civilization" as an analytical category transcends the temporal and spatial limits of individual states. Its utility may lie in that quality, as it permits the discussion of the considerable time depth of complex societies; and its persistence may be due at least in part to the increasing interest by modern political groups in controlling the past as a strategic resource (Layton 1988; Meskell 1998), echoing its earlier role in the search for the forerunners of modern "civilization."

## Studying civilizations

The study of entities categorized as civilizations has been a part of archaeological research since its inception in the nineteenth century and has been pursued with varying degrees of effort by every subsequent generation of archaeologists. From a disciplinary perspective this preoccupation is due, in part, to the ability of archaeologists to examine the temporal and geographic sweep of civilizations over the last 5,000 years, an interest shared only with historians. Describing and explaining the large-scale patterns associated with complex societies has thus remained central to archaeological investigations, despite sharp differences in theoretical outlook. However, academic concern with the identification and study of ancient civilizations has also been fueled by public fascination with the monuments and treasures they left behind; more subtly, by the role they play in the ongoing discourse over the relationship of Western nations to the societies they have historically dominated; and increasingly by the role which manipulation of the past has come to play in the legitimizing strategies of current political regimes within the territories they occupy. Comparison has been employed in almost all cases, ranging from straightforward applications of the comparative method to identify common processes or historical connections, to its implicit use in framing contrasts and commonalities among ancient and contemporary cultures.

## Evolutionary approaches

These concerns are, perhaps, most salient in the work of nineteenth-century cultural evolutionists who attempted to order growing bodies of ethnographic and archaeological information by categorizing and arranging cultures in a developmental sequence. Cross-cultural comparison was crucial to the reconstruction of the successive steps from savagery to civilization, but differences among societies within the same state were not really addressed; instead, it was the contrast between stages as well as the overall unity of the process that was emphasized. Civilization was regarded as the final step in a unilineal process propelled largely by the law of progress, which in its crudest form was defined in Darwinian terms. Only the fittest survived, and the fit were by definition the wealthiest, most powerful, and most "civilized" segments of the world's population. Classical evolutionary theory thus provided a scientific underpinning for the grand narrative of the historical development and expansion of western states. It is this imperialist and capitalist driven understanding that still permeates popular thought and makes the very term "civilization" somewhat suspect among contemporary scholars.

The demise of nineteenth-century evolutionary theory in academic discourse reshaped, but did not eliminate, archaeological interest in civilizations, or in the use of comparison to better understand these phenomena. V. Gordon Childe's work (e.g., 1936, 1944) most clearly carried these concerns into the twentieth century. His ability to synthesize enormous amounts of data was facilitated by an evolutionary perspective that drew more from Marx and Engels than from Darwin or Tylor. Childe (1951) rejected biological determinism and instead attributed progress to the accumulation of knowledge which leads to greater technical control over nature and the expansion of both human possibilities and populations. Explicitly countering the nationalism of his time, he argued that all people benefit from knowledge developed over the ages as a result of diffusion – both geographic and across generations. Unlike the evolutionists of the previous century or the neo-evolutionists who succeeded him, Childe viewed societies as permeable and susceptible to external stimuli, or, phrased more broadly, open to historical forces generated by interaction with other groups. He also argued that while the comparison of civilizations – such as Egypt and Sumer – could point to common processes and results, most details of economic as well as religious and political systems varied tremendously; thus the histories of individual civilizations could not be subsumed by a single narrative of social change.

Childe (1950) equated the emergence of civilization with the development of urbanism and a series of concomitants such as writing, monumental architecture, and specialized craft production. He believed that progress, or the accumulation of practical knowledge, accelerated with the initial emergence of civilization; periods of arrested cultural growth he attributed, not to racial deficiencies, but to internal and external contradictions generated by the urban revolution itself. Of particular importance in this regard was that neither the producers – who had been reduced to lower status – nor the elites – who relied heavily on religion and superstition for legitimation – were motivated to pursue practical inventions that would lead to further growth.

Childe's explication of the urban revolution has been criticized for its reliance on a trait list that is heavily biased towards the Near East, perceived as the antecedent of European civilization. The latter charge is undoubtedly true, but while contemporary scholars often reduce his characterization of urban development to a list of discrete traits, Childe systematically interrelated most of these variables in a model that stressed the role played by surplus accumulation in the development of dense populations, economic specialization, and class formation, emphases that he occasionally attributed to Marxist theory.

In 1952 Robert Redfield delivered six lectures at Cornell in which he responded to Childe's ideas regarding the emergence of civilization, and specifically objected to his focus on economic factors. These talks were part of a series entitled the "Messenger Lectures on the Evolution of Civilization," established in 1923 "for the special purpose of raising the moral standard of our political, business, and social life" (Hiram Messenger quoted in Redfield 1953: 180). Redfield's argument was explicitly grounded in contemporary Western concerns with the disintegration of the moral order, as well as the potential of civilized societies to shape their own futures. Like Childe, he identified cities as hallmarks of civilization; unlike Childe, he saw them as agents of continuing change, instead of end products of the Urban Revolution. In Redfield's view, cities transform traditional peoples into peasants and constitute one of the key links between urban elites and rural communities. Such a perspective was clearly shaped by his ethnographic study of acculturation among the Yucatec Maya and his use of ethnological data to model prehistoric change.

Redfield's delineation of the interdependence of the "little" tradition of the peasantry and the "great" tradition of the elites (Redfield 1956: 70) – both of which comprise civilizations – is directly relevant to the concerns raised by a number of contributors to this volume who examine the roles played by commoners, literati, and other social "types" in the generation and negotiation of high culture. His work provides insight into the disparate positions voiced by these scholars, on the one hand, and Baines and Yoffee on the other. Redfield argued that:

> Civilization is, of course, things added to society: cities, writing, public works, the state, the market, and so forth. Another way of looking at it is from the base provided by the folk society . . . If we do adopt this way of conceiving civilization, we shall think of Toynbee's twenty-one civilizations as different developments away from the folk society. We see then that civilizations do not depart from the nature of the folk society evenly or in the same way. (Redfield 1953: 22)

Thus the precise nature of the relationship between inner elites and others may be a source of variability among archaic states, rather than a characteristic common to all civilizations as Baines and Yoffee suggest.

The message that Redfield derived from the study of civilizations, like the one promoted by Childe (1936) was one of hope and progress. However, in contrast to Childe's vision of betterment through the practical knowledge produced by economic change, Redfield contended that the ethical perspective which distinguishes civilized from traditional society is the impetus for improvement. He argued that the emergence of civilization resulted in the creation of a new moral order forged in urban contexts; the development of political and religious elites, as well as the presence of people with varied traditions, gave rise to self-conscious creativity and the possibility of universalizing ethical programs. Only in these circumstances, Redfield believed, could the great ideas that shape history develop, a process akin to the emergence of axial age civilizations described by Eisenstadt (1986) and others.

The notion that ideas determine the development of humankind was forcefully rejected by the neo-evolutionists of the second half of the twentieth century. As Trigger (1989) has clearly shown, the "new" archaeologists of this generation excluded most historical processes, such as diffusion or internally generated change, as possible sources of social transformation. They also differed from nineteenth-century conceptions in the development of a dual approach to the study of evolution and the rejection of racism as an explanation for cultural differences. However, stage models persisted under the rubric of general evolution, with the schema developed by Service and Fried providing the descriptive framework employed by most archaeologists of the 1960s and 1970s. The notion of civilization was first eclipsed by a narrower focus on individual states, and then by increasingly abstract concepts such as differentiation and centralization. The overwhelming interest was in change, specifically the development of social complexity and the emergence of pristine states. The goal of comparison was to identify universal laws that could account for all such cases, or at least general processes that were commonly associated with them. Multilineal or specific evolution was more concerned with the diversity of cultures than with uniform processes, and relied more heavily on the concept of adaptation. However, as a number of archaeologists have noted (e.g, Flannery and Marcus 1983; Yoffee 1993), archaeologists were often preoccupied with classifying societies according to the categories proposed by Service, rather than with examining and explaining their differences.

Despite the optimism engendered by archaeologists such as Binford regarding the possibility of reconstructing all aspects of prehistoric societies, the focus of neoevolutionists was squarely on ecological factors. Explanations for the development of social complexity almost invariably relied on environmental or demographic variables as well. Surprisingly, despite their ties to functionalism and the extensive use of systems theory, processual archaeologists produced few comparisons of how past civilizations actually operated. They were primarily interested in comparing processes that resulted in state formation, rather than the mature results of those developments.

Research on the origin of the state has declined precipitously over the last two decades. As models of the development of social complexity themselves became more complex, the notion propelling such research – that the causes of social evolution could be clearly identified – lost its attraction. On the one hand, archaeological investigations of these processes indicated that they were complicated, multivariate, and subject to specific historical conditions (e.g., Flannery and J. Marcus 1983; J. Marcus and Flannery 1996; Fowler 1989). At the same time, the positivist program, and neoevolutionary theory especially, was under attack for being a handmaiden to American imperialism (Trigger 1998).

Post-processualists, the primary critics of the "new" archaeology, may recognize the importance of addressing long-term trends (Hodder 1987), but their methods are primarily ethnographic in origin and scope. More than earlier archaeologists, they are concerned with reconstructing whole cultures and understanding them within a contextual, or emic, framework. Furthermore, they reject the notion of a smoothly functioning social system, and examine, instead, the continual contestation of power within cultures (e.g., D. Miller 1989). Ideology, and its role in maintaining and transforming social relations, is thus of particular interest. A holistic approach with an emphasis on ideology creates a possible point of convergence between post-processualists and scholars with an interest in civilizations. However, more than any of the earlier schools of thought, interpretive versions of post-processualism eschew comparison because meaning – which is viewed as the source of all social action – is culture specific.

### Culture history and civilizationist studies

Another intellectual current in the study of ancient civilizations flows from history, but occasionally intersects with anthropological work on the same subject. Most famous, of course, are the comparative historians Arnold Toynbee (1934–1961) and Oswald Spengler (1922). Both of these scholars conceived of civilizations in organic terms and emphasized their unique qualities, while at the same time analyzing them comparatively in order to uncover underlying similarities in their development and decline. Their interest in the internal dynamics of civilizations has been carried on by scholars such as William Eckhardt, Matthew Melko, and David

Wilkinson (Sanderson 1995) as well as other participants in the International Society for the Comparative Study of Civilizations.

Less well known, perhaps, is that a number of anthropologists, including Alfred Kroeber (1957, 1962) and Philip Bagby (1958), are also identified as "civilizationists." Kroeber (1957), for example, touched on many of the issues being raised today with regard to the study of civilizations, including the distinction between civilization and society, the processes underlying cultural continuity and change, and the systematic comparison of whole cultures rather than parts. His main focus, however, was always on style. Kroeber defined civilization as a collection of styles, and believed that it was best understood in terms of the creative and cultural activities – ranging from visual arts to fashion – that are stylistically distinct. He argued that since these creative products express values, and values allow civilizations to cohere, style would be the most appropriate way to delimit, characterize, and even compare civilizations.

This thesis is in some ways comparable to the argument advanced by Baines and Yoffee. One of the most important differences, however, is that Kroeber understood style almost exclusively in terms of creativity, rather than as the product of social interaction. Like Spengler (1922), he employed an organic analogy to describe and explain the growth and death of civilizations, which he attributed to "creative exhaustion." Kroeber's understanding of culture as transcending individual action left little room for social agency of any kind; accordingly, for the archaeologists inspired by him, artifact patterning was completely conflated with historical process. Bennett (1948), for example, promoted the concept of the co-tradition for characterizing distinctive, long-lived cultural traditions that were shared by interacting groups, a definition that included, but was not limited to the civilizations associated with complex societies. Co-traditions could be compared in terms of their centers, size, complexity, and rate of change, and also in order to determine specific historical relationships among them. However, the absence of a model relating material culture to social practices led to the treatment of such traditions as associations of unconnected traits, and the objects themselves, rather than the underlying social relations, became the focus of study. This virtually complete separation of material culture from human behavior was one of the primary criticisms of the subsequent generation of archaeologists.

### World-systems approaches

The most prevalent archaeological approach to the study of civilizations today is the world-systems perspective elaborated by Immanuel Wallerstein (see Trigger 1993 for an important exception). Wallerstein (1974) sought to utilize Fernand Braudel's notion of the *longue durée* (Braudel 1994) to explicate the development and long-term characteristics of capitalism. Archaeologists have directly applied ideas from the Annales school (Bintliff 1991; Knapp 1992) as well as world-systems theory in their studies of ancient states and civilizations, but the most common strategy is the use of a world-systems perspective that has been modified to accommodate the analysis of pre-capitalist social formations (e.g., Peregrine 1996).

The world-systems perspective emerged, in part, from a critique of development models that were predicated on evolutionary theory and that attributed the lack of economic progress in some countries to the inertia of national elites, the traditionalism of peasant cultures, or other internal problems. Instead, Frank, Wallerstein, Amin, and others regard underdevelopment as the result of a nation's historically constituted role in a global economic system. This fundamental shift in the unit of analysis is one of the primary advantages of the world-systems approach, and something that archaeologists have attempted on a more modest scale with interaction sphere and peer-polity models (Renfrew and Cherry 1986; Rowlands *et al.* 1987). World-systems, of course, are not entirely coincident with civilizations, but often substantially overlap with them. Hall and Chase-Dunn (1996: 12–13), for instance, define world-systems as "intersocietal networks in which the interactions (e.g., trade, warfare, intermarriage, information) are important for the reproduction of the internal structures of the composite units and importantly affect changes which occur in these local structures." They go on to propose that these interactions can involve political or military relations, as well as the exchange of bulk or prestige goods, and information.

Such a definition differs from the concept of a civilization as used in this volume in two important ways. First, networks are not always associated with complex societies, and second, civilizations are usually conceived in terms of the last type of exchange, information, broadly construed to include ideology, religion, and culture. Civilizations, then, are a subset of the larger and more diverse class of world-systems. In recognition of this fact, attempts have recently been made to establish explicit conceptual links between world-systems theory and the work produced by civilizationists (Sanderson 1995). While civilizationists tend to focus on the cultural aspects of early civilizations, and world-systems researchers on the linkages underpinning the modern global economy, the two approaches do have points of convergence. These relate primarily to broad-scale features of these networks, such as size, developmental patterns, and internal settlement hierarchies, all of which can be systematically compared (Chase-Dunn and Hall 1995). However, many of the phenomena which interest civilizationists have been largely ignored by world-systems scholars: the latter have been criticized for their inattention to culture as well as the role of ideology in the hegemonic relations that characterize the modern world system.

### Civilized discourse

Most approaches to the study of civilizations, then, have focused on their emergence, growth, or decline, taking change, either linear or cyclical, as the primary object of investigation. Baines and Yoffee's work (1998), however, raises a different question: what accounts for the relative continuity of civilizations through time and across space, despite the fact that they encompass diverse groups who are potential sources of competing ideologies and alternative world views? Part of the answer lies in the way in which past civilizations are perceived in the present, both contemporary times and previous "presents." Civilized elites often attempt to create a legitimizing cultural genealogy, even in the face of variation and discontinuity, in order to generate the illusion of great antiquity (Helms 1993). So, for example, ancient Egyptian literature was rarely set in a contemporary "present"; rather, stories or didactic texts not infrequently recounted events in the past, which deftly foreshadowed or legitimized shifts in political power (Baines 1989; Parkinson 1997). Thus this strategy of a call to archaism entails, at times, the self-conscious rewriting of history and the erasure of competing views – but more often a less conscious emphasis on events or objects that are conceived as signposts to the present. Such processes acting in the past would have obscured archaeological and textual evidence for ruptures of various sorts; acting in the present they inhibit the ability of scholars to perceive or describe such discontinuities (see Richards, chapter 2 in this volume).

Baines and Yoffee recognize that such processes occurred, but offer a different, if related, answer to the question of continuity. They identify inner elites, and their role as the exclusive carriers of high culture, as key to the maintenance of civilization in Mesopotamia and ancient Egypt, arguing that "in most cases, a civilization's style . . . is more or less coterminous with its extent in space and time. The style is created in a high-cultural context, is sustained by an elite that commissions and consumes the works that transmit the stylistic tradition, and incorporates fundamental values . . . This value-laden stylistic complex is crucial to the transmission of the civilization's essence through time" (Baines and Yoffee 1998: 237). While Baines and Yoffee explicitly characterize high culture as a communicative complex, they argue that this discourse is restricted almost entirely to the inner elites, their rulers, and gods. People outside this small circle play little if any role in the creation or consumption of high culture, even as audiences for legitimizing performances:

> The division of elite and the rest leaves open the question of whether the rest have a different culture or values from those of the elite . . . So far as relevant archaeological and epigraphic evidence in Egypt and Mesopotamia goes, that does not seem to be the case. Rather elite high culture appears to stand in contrast to a poverty or an absence of distinctive materialized ideology for others . . . Essential factors favoring the persistence of high culture in Egypt and Mesopotamia seem to lie in the lack of available effective alternatives within the same culture and, until the first millennium BC, even in neighboring cultures. (Baines and Yoffee 1998: 45–46)

In contrast to the highly exclusionary position asserted by Baines and Yoffee, the importance of communication between inner elites and others can be argued on logical as well as empirical grounds. Emergent elites had a limited array of strategies available to them in order to maintain their class position: they could actively convince their subordinates of the legitimacy of their demands for labor and goods; their subordinates could share such beliefs already; elites could engage in a limited reallocation of resources; or they could use coercion. While the latter certainly occurred (although, interestingly, not a factor addressed in depth by any of the contributors to this volume), it is neither cost effective nor a sustainable means of surplus extraction when used alone. The complete separation of elites and non-elites posited by Baines and Yoffee is thus unlikely to have persisted for long periods.

In fact, the majority of contributors to this volume emphasize that inner elites constitute only one set of actors in the broad arena in which civilizations emerged and endured. In the societies examined by these authors, the creation and maintenance of civilization involved a diverse array of players and processes. These cases indicate that while ancient civilizations are not entirely comparable to modern ideological or socio-political phenomena, non-elites were more important, and communication among different groups more intensive, than Baines and Yoffee propose. However, neither the participation of diverse actors, nor resistance by them, necessarily resulted in gross spatial or temporal discontinuities in the high cultural complexes that distinguish civilizations.

Attention to the communicative aspects of high culture, its link to legitimation, and to ideological and social discourse in general, encourages a more complete understanding of the dynamics of early civilizations, and particularly how challenges to the status quo could result in continuity of style or world view, if not political substance. This occurred, in part, because of the discursive nature of ideological transformations, the need to engage or at least address current belief systems in the course of promoting new ones. Such a process must have been present even during the rise of civilizations, when ruptures with previous conceptions of order and aesthetic principles are most apparent. While the development of extreme inequality was associated with the advent of novel ideologies and associated aesthetic principles, the disjuncture between new and previous world views was not complete. Extant beliefs and practices would have formed the raw materials from which emergent inner elites constructed a new order. For instance, it has been suggested that the cosmologically charged pyramidal form associated with the graves of ancient Egyptian rulers from the third and second millennia BC had its origins in the folk traditions and mortuary practices of non-elites (Hawass and Lehner 1994).

At the start of this process, the selective and exclusive arrogation of such concepts would have been critical to legitimizing the elite's novel role in society (D. Miller *et al.* 1989b). However, as Baines and Yoffee note, elites sometimes had a vested interest in obscuring the connection between civilization and the "chaos" which preceded it, and of that between high culture and folk tradition, thus rendering such continuity archaeologically ambiguous or invisible. Exclusionary ideological control of these concepts was also subject to repeated challenge over time, potentially obscuring even further the origins of key ideological elements.

The last several years have seen an increasing emphasis in the literature on the concept of social negotiation, and all it implies regarding communication, resistance, factionalism, and the role of diverse groups in the functioning of complex societies, and the effect of these factors on dominant ideologies (e.g., D. Miller *et al.* 1989b; Brumfiel 1989, 1994; Chase and Chase 1992; De Marrais *et al.* 1996). One focus is the consideration of factions within elites, subgroups competing for power within political, religious or social arenas, leading more often to the usurpation or capture of ideology, rather than its complete replacement (Brumfiel 1989). In the context of empire or state, such competition could lie at the level of dynasties, cities, or states; or among provincial or lower elites emulating inner elites in attempts to gain status or grace through imitation.

Another strong current has been a call to recontextualize elites within society as a whole, considering their interactions with "the masses" in discussions of power and ideology (Kowalewski *et al.* 1992; G. Marcus 1992; Cowgill 1992a; De Marrais *et al.* 1996). Alternative world views almost certainly existed among non-elites, alongside the "state" formulations. In a recent volume on sorcery in modern day Sri Lanka, Kapferer points out that subordinate groups, while aware of the hegemonizing ideology of the elite, "do not necessarily internalize the themes stressed by those who command dominant institutions . . . subordinated groups are far from duped by controlling ideas and practices and are able to penetrate them" (cf. Scott 1985: 314–350). In Sri Lanka, local sorcery shrines "can become places . . . that are vital centers for the expression and formulation of a resistant consciousness" (Kapferer 1997: 256). In fact, he suggests, "the persons who are hegemonized are the ruling classes themselves" (*Ibid.*). In the study of past societies, alternative ideologies are inevitably difficult to track given the inability of poorer or marginalized groups to materialize ideology in a lasting form; but the reality of multiple arenas for action (Brumfiel 1998), the crucial role of oral communication in these diverse arenas (see Heyer 1988; Lasswell *et al.* 1979; Goody 1986), the issue of differential literacy and access to power (e.g., Bowman and Woolf 1994), and the potential for contestation of hegemonic ideologies, reminds us that commoners as well as elites were active participants in social negotiation.

### The case studies

The case studies which follow Baines and Yoffee's "Setting the terms" essay (chapter 2) employ the concepts of order, legitimacy, and wealth as an interrelated medium within which to consider the functioning of several different civilizations. Additionally, a number of the themes discussed in the preceding sections crosscut these discussions, complementing those set forth by Baines and Yoffee: the notion of a "civilization" and what causes it to endure; the power of archaism as a legitimizing tool; the role of actors and factions other than inner elites, including provincial elites, artisans, tradesmen, scholars, and non-elites; the crucial issue of communication and points of articulation between different levels of society, and of resistance and negotiation; and the tantalizing relationship between archaeological and textual evidence in reconstructing these patterns.

The case studies begin with a series of papers which debate or expand upon Baines and Yoffee's original Egypt–Mesopotamia comparison. Two papers on Egypt explore the interplay of order, legitimacy, and wealth in the Egyptian Nile Valley from the early third through the mid-second millennia BC. David O'Connor explores the ambiguity of the ideology of order in early Egypt (the Early Dynastic and Old Kingdom periods, 3100–2260 BC), arguing that it may have been a society-wide preoccupation as opposed to a strictly elite concern. Through general consideration of the range of archaeological data present for the period, and detailed analysis of a provincial elite monument erected during a centralized period of ancient Egyptian civilization, he considers the role of the individual actor within the ideology of cosmological order (*ma'at*) promulgated by early elites, and contests the notion that maintenance of this order was presented or perceived as completely exclusive. Rather, he suggests, every individual had a part to play in the maintenance of cosmic order, in regional and local landscapes.

Working within a later time span than that considered by O'Connor, Janet Richards examines the changing patterns of access to key symbols, commodities, and ritual landscapes in the First Intermediate and Middle Kingdom periods in Egypt (2250–1650 BC), and the concomitant effect on legitimizing strategies of the inner elite. Also questioning the notion of uncontested domination and completely exclusive high cultural ideology, she considers archaeological and textual evidence for the communicative interplay over time between ruling elites and other social groups, and the effects of shifting access to symbolic and material resources on the discourse of inequality and power.

In a paper on law courts, social conflict, and the institution of *nadītu*s (female testators assigned to temples and forbidden to marry) in Mesopotamia, Norman Yoffee considers the instability of Mesopotamian political systems in the perspective of the struggle to produce wealth, to maintain symbols and systems of knowledge, and to construct order. Instituted during a time of unprecedented economic and social mobility, this strategy was one way in which elites mediated potential dislocations of "cosmic" order, and reaffirmed traditional ideologies through deliberate archaism, a call to the most venerable symbols.

Subsequent chapters move beyond the spatial and chronological framework of the original comparison. For the New World, Rosemary Joyce examines the construction of categories of value in Mesoamerica and their relationship, over time, to the definition of wealth and order. Focusing on the elite's creation of an aesthetic of beauty, she addresses the social process by which value was assigned not only to materials used to communicate status and exclusivity, but the different contexts within which these high cultural forms were consumed, and the contribution of these forms to the continuation of a "civilizational order" of Mesoamerica.

Within the framework of an empire incorporating multicultural groups and diverse territories, Mary Van Buren investigates the relationship between inner elites and the production of high culture in the Andes, suggesting that provincial elites and commoners played important roles in the creation and transmission of Andean civilization. In delineating the political strategies of imperial expansion by the Inka, she considers the co-existence within the empire of both coercive and ideological control (the latter manipulating existing concepts both of the sun cult, and of envalued technologies relating to textiles and metal), and of indigenous resistance to that control. Through the use of ethnohistorical data she is able to track the persistence of specific "civilizational traits" into the present, examining issues of transmission and change in meaning over time.

Additional case studies of Old World civilizations include the Indus Valley, the Roman Empire, and Han Dynasty China. Jonathan Mark Kenoyer, working from a substantial fund of archaeological data, examines the creation of wealth and its role in the legitimation of power as reflected in material culture and technology during the rise of cities in the Indus Valley traditions. Tracking the development of order, legitimacy, and wealth from the Neolithic through the Harappan periods, a time span of nearly six thousand years, his contribution provides a telling contrast to patterns in Mesopotamia and Egypt, against which the Indus has been either traditionally or unconsciously measured. In highlighting the roles of merchants and artisans in the development and control of technology and craft production, Kenoyer stresses the importance of looking at non-exotic goods, and of considering the different arenas within which a discourse of status and power exists, both public or private. He concludes, contrary to most approaches to wealth and its relationship to status, that in the Indus wealth was explicitly equated with status, and with a legitimizing ideology of authority.

Susan Alcock discusses the uses of power and nostalgia in negotiating order and legitimacy in the Roman revival and use of Greek "high culture," and the strategies used by Greeks of the imperial age to create an alternative framework which allowed both the accommodation and rejection of Roman rule. Highlighting the importance of ideological inversion and its use in contestation, she uses the evidence of both material culture and literary works to argue that the Greeks, despite a transformed political order and cultural identity following their incorporation into the Roman empire, were able to actively negotiate notions of order and legitimacy through the retrospective use of classical "high culture."

Finally, Bennet Bronson discusses order, legitimacy, and wealth in early Han China, highlighting contrasts in these principles to the early states of the Mediterranean world. Specifically, he explores the role of the intelligentsia in constructing and regulating the dominant ideology of rule, and their potential, through the power of privileged knowledge, to resist hegemony, and to affect the legitimacy and efficacy of the elite wielding political power. What is particularly intriguing in Bronson's contribution is the self-consciousness of the discourse regarding order and what constituted appropriate legitimizing strategies, an insight not salient in the various contemporary and ethnohistorical sources bearing on other discussions in the volume.

In her closing discussion, Elizabeth Brumfiel synthesizes and broadens the themes addressed throughout the volume. She considers the preceding papers within the general context of the study of complex societies and the specific advantages of returning to the topic of "high culture," and supplies a further example of the political uses of high culture to manage factional competition within the Aztec elite stratum. She considers the concept of *tonalli*, a crucial heat–light–energy force, its relationship to an ideology of cosmic warfare, and its materialization in objects of skilled craftsmanship. Finally, she demonstrates that Aztec rulers, by manipulating these factors, averted contestation among young nobles and transformed them into political allies, providing a vignette of a functioning arena in which power was built and resistance managed and negotiated.

## Conclusion

The spectrum of complex societies represented in this volume ranges from nonliterate arenas such as the Andes and the Indus Valley, where reliance on archaeological or ethnohistorical data is pronounced, to literate states such as the Roman empire or ancient Egypt, for which scholarship has been traditionally dominated by humanistic or historical approaches. In the multidimensional approach taken by the various contributors, and their use of the order–legitimacy–wealth platform as a point of departure from which to consider the functioning of "civilization" in their particular research areas, they have offered fresh perspectives and questioned long held assumptions. Especially fruitful is the recurrent stress in the volume on communication within social and political networks, and on all of the various groups between which communicative discourse takes place, whether or not they are archaeologically visible. In this volume, the concept of "civilization" is used in its most inclusive and dynamic sense, as a complex of ideologies and arenas created, perceived, inhabited, and negotiated by living people of all different social, economic, and political levels.

## Note

1 Jonathan Mark Kenoyer joins the session participants in this volume with his chapter on the Indus Valley.

# 2
# Order, legitimacy, and wealth: setting the terms

JOHN BAINES AND
NORMAN YOFFEE

### Introduction

This chapter recapitulates briefly the main theoretical points of our earlier essay "Order, legitimacy, and wealth in ancient Egypt and Mesopotamia," composed in 1992 (hereafter OLW; Baines and Yoffee 1998). The history of the composition and publication of that essay is given in the introduction to this volume. Here we do not repeat or expand upon the examples from Egypt and Mesopotamia that are presented in the original OLW essay, but we do add a further linking example below under the heading "An extreme illustration." We limit our bibliographic references in this chapter and simply refer readers to the more detailed treatment in the 1998 publication of OLW (to which we were able to add only very few references to material published after 1992). We do not respond to criticisms and new perspectives in other chapters in the present volume; such a discussion can come later.

### Preliminaries

Our problematic in OLW lies first in the method of comparing two early civilizations, ancient Egypt and Mesopotamia, which arose at about the same time and in more or less the same region of the world, and then in the larger epistemological issues of how one employs or builds a comparative method in which the evolution of ancient states and civilizations can be generally investigated.

In brief, we reviewed the extraordinarily different institutions in the two ancient civilizations: kingship and government, urbanization, writing systems and the nature of diverse types of sources, the economy, and elites. Given these contrasting institutions, we went on to posit that the elements of similarity between the two civilizations did not lie in specific socioeconomic formations, on which most of the social evolutionary literature concentrates, but in the nature of order, legitimacy, and wealth and the interrelations among these (we are pleased to note the comparable strategy of Bruce Trigger's quite separate 1993 study of a broad range of civilizations). We see the interplay of these three as focusing in, and being exemplified by, the distinctive complex of "high culture." Through an investigation of the instrumental principles of hierarchization, of the restriction and display of certain kinds of wealth and the devaluation of other kinds of symbols, and of constitutive institutions of legitimation that emphasize the dispersive ties between rulers and ruled we argue that a comparative method can be pursued. This method, we also strongly insist, must incorporate both humanistic and social scientific domains and styles of research. By seeking to understand the commonalities in ancient states (political systems) and civilizations we ask what it is that makes each civilization unique – what makes Egypt Egypt and/or Mesopotamia Mesopotamia, for example – as well as what makes civilizations comparable. We also want to move social evolutionary theory from a dominant concern with what states and civilizations are to research about what they do.

### An extreme illustration

Thus, in addressing fundamental aspects of early civilizations, both in their comparability and their particularity, our prime concern is not the political and socioeconomic terms of the examples. Of course, the material bases of these civilizations are necessary preconditions for their existence, and this is for the most part what archaeologists have successfully defined in social evolutionary studies. Our focus on order, legitimacy, and wealth, however, takes us to different questions about the self-identity of civilizations. In many studies, extremes of inequality are not only noted (and occasionally deplored) and are now often analyzed as "political economy"; we consider additionally what it is that elites take to be their own *raison d'être* and how non-elites accept, negotiate, or struggle against these terms. By focusing as far as possible on the actors' terms, we can see what it is that lies within a civilization over against what lies outside.

Certain of these points, including that of boundaries, can be illustrated in a first, perhaps marginal example.

Correspondence and gifts happen to be well documented between Egypt and Mesopotamia (and other parts of the ancient Near East) in the middle third of the second millennium BC (Liverani 1990; see Yoffee 1995b). The gifts had material economic significance in the sending and receiving countries, which belonged to different civilizations. Insofar as one side did not cheat the other, the items exchanged were culturally central, since they consisted of prize products of their countries, ones that incorporated the meanings they valued most. All this was as true for the recipient as for the donor. But the recipient might burn a gold-inlaid throne to recover its gold: he wanted the product of the work of his own civilization, not something from outside. Yet the exchange retained its value through and beyond the destruction and recycling of the goods: its purpose was ultimately communication rather than any specific enaction, a communication that was maintained whatever the destiny of the gift.

Whereas the gifts were in general reciprocal, the Egyptians sent grain in time of famine to the Hittites, with whom they were allied by treaty. The system of diplomatic exchange, which was the apex of interconnections across civilizations in the Near Eastern Late Bronze Age, lasted some centuries, but the famine aid came at its end. The famine was part of a breakdown in normal conditions, and any economic aid there may have been received little emphasis in times of prosperity. The high-cultural world of which this exchange was a crowning element was fragile and required constant nurturing, as well as being both a product of and a factor in prosperity. That applies just as strongly to the individual orders of ancient states and civilizations. Order is threatened and fragile. The carriers of a civilization, principally its elite, both define it and are engrossed in the task of maintaining it. Whereas our focus is on order, this approach offers diagnostic pointers also for periods of formation or collapse, since it is the establishment of a new order and its failure that also define these phenomena. Understanding the nature of order, legitimacy, and wealth also allows us to investigate how and whether a civilization can survive as recognizably the same entity through periods of political and economic collapse and of wholesale takeover from outside.

## Order

Order in ancient civilizations necessarily encompasses more than just human beings, and includes the gods and the dead; it also crucially includes the king as a special category and the specialized governmental apparatus we call the state. The gods and the dead are real, but their reality is of a different kind from that of the king and humanity. They often absorb a large proportion of the surplus flowing to the state.

Order in ancient civilizations implies the creation of a new ideology, by which we mean the ascribed set of meanings about social, political, and economic relations and events, and specifically about who has power and how it is got. The ruling elite, who have access to the gods and the privileged dead, must present themselves as worthy participants in this process. The new ideologies assert that there should be a state, centralized leadership, powerful elites, and their dependants (see Yoffee, this volume). These ideologies must be communicated through tangible vehicles that accompany and constitute them. The artifactual embodiments of order, therefore, from small objects to cities and landscapes, materialize it (in the sense of De Marrais, Castillo, and Earle 1996) in a form that may be given from on high, from the deities who participate in it and inform it, but is made present by human labor. However massive and durable an embodiment, it cannot be of the scale of the surrounding physical world, and this discrepancy cannot but draw attention to order's fragility and need of support. These embodiments also create a distancing between ideal order and the present. In this way they display time and draw attention to its problematic, while also creating much of the enduring subject matter of civilization.

These are mainly the ideological aspects of order and its instrumentalization. States and civilizations structure the universe more tightly than do social forms that precede them and often surround them, and they may bear hard on nonconformity. Order is expensive, and there are those who are at the harsh receiving end of its effects. It does not follow, however, that the order proclaimed at the center is rejected by those outside. They may accept it as legitimate (see below), or resist oppression under the rules of order, or simply have no alternative to it. In certain cases order may bring with it a reduction in the level of violence in a civilization and hence overlap in a straightforward way with the everyday sense of the term, including the "order" imposed by totalitarian regimes.

Order in civilizations is characterized by a variety of kin-based structures, non-kin-based structures, ethnic groups, economic groups, and/or a variety of social orientations which are, however differentially constituted, overarched in such a way that all are encompassed within one societal umbrella. Order emphatically does not require any particular form of basic social organization.

It is this definition of order in an ancient differentiated and stratified society with a specialized governmental center that makes a civilization. Order circumscribes a dominant way of meaning and becomes axiomatic in the socialization of members of society. It may weaken or may change subtly, and it may be abrogated and subsequently reaffirmed. For early civilizations, perhaps unlike more recent ones, the disappearance or replacement of a recognized style of order betokens their end.

### Legitimacy

In the case of a regional state such as Egypt, whatever combination of elements legitimized its original formation could in theory have endured to do the same for its continuation. In practice the transformations embodied in new social and symbolic forms hardly allow such a possibility, and hence there are systematic reformulations and commentaries throughout the existence of the state, all taking as given that the state is distinct from what lies temporally or spatially outside. But the complex nature of legitimation is much more evident in "galactic" civilizations like Mesopotamia or the Maya, whose definition applies across a range of polities that are hardly ever politically unified. Legitimacy is vested in shared perceptions that transcend the individual polities.

In essence legitimacy is the institutionalization of people's acceptance of, involvement in, and contribution towards order. The two cannot be imagined without each other. Order, however, could not survive the frequent shocks it suffers if people were not able to make play with legitimacy and illegitimacy. Legitimacy frequently invokes the past as something absolute that acts as a point of reference for the present, normally by transmuting the past into some form of the present.

What is distinctive for early civilizations is the complexity of the vehicles through which legitimacy is projected. These civilizations incorporate legitimacy into the normal constitutive relations between people, and on a larger scale inscribe legitimacy in the landscape. Through specialization and unprecedented forms of inequality, ruling elites acquire the capacity to embody their legitimacy in objects and to alter the environment.

The embodiments of legitimacy relate both to elites and to the wider society. Order and legitimacy are the concern of elites, and only they may fully comprehend them. Legitimacy is thus an internal matter for the elite. At the same time it encompasses the society as a whole, as well as offering to the elite themselves a rationale for inequality that goes beyond simple privilege. But that is not the chief power of legitimacy. Rather, the entire society must accept, however variably and with whatever degree of coercion, that its order is the only one and the right one, and must work to maintain that order or contest those who are delinquent in, or incapable of, preserving order.

### Wealth

Wealth is an essential feature of early – of any – civilization. A striking feature is the extent to which most early civilizations multiplied the productive potential of their predecessor societies, both demographically and in the creation and institutionalization of surpluses. Surpluses might be in labor or in goods – and in any case each implies the other – and might be applied to a vast range of purposes. An emblem of several early civilizations, from the Inka to Egypt, is the architectural provision of enormous or hugely extravagant storage spaces, both for this world and for the next. Another obvious emblem, visible more or less everywhere, is the display and consumption of vastly expensive and generally rarefied artifacts dedicated to the gods, the dead, the ruler, and the elite.

All this amassing, retention, and harnessing of wealth was achieved without great technological advance – as against differences in scale and refinement – from predecessor societies, and much continuity in basic material culture is visible across the transformations of civilization. If we look to comprehend wealth, we should therefore see it as a social and civilizational phenomenon rather than a technological or simply economic one.

This is not the place for detailed economic analysis, although it is clear that in economic and related legal terms early civilizations show a marked complexity and stratification, and the absence of "money" was no significant impediment to them. Nevertheless, the scale of productive institutions, the extent to which labor would be deployed, and the level of specialized training and expertise have profound implications for a civilization's character and need for legitimation. Wealth makes a reversion to what went before almost unthinkable.

What is particularly important is the focus of wealth. The public and archaeologists, too, tend to place great weight on the wealth generated in early civilizations, its display, and the competition for resources. Models of this sort, however, may depend on unexamined assumptions. Just as wealth is important, it seems equally clear that its exploitation and display are often subject to strong controls, and its most extravagant forms may be realized in contexts where such control is – at least in theory – easiest, such as the tomb. Wealth should not be seen as an end in itself, but rather as an essential enabling factor whose potential is released, but also harnessed and contained, by societies and civilizations.

But wealth cannot be fully contained. It tends to expose the weakness of the system, while also allowing it the potential to change. The obvious example of wealth's disruptive character is in the extravagant discarding of wealth – in material perspective but not that of the actors – in burial. The world's second oldest profession may be tomb robbery, a practice that exists on the periphery of order and allows wealth to be recycled and perhaps indirectly to sustain the system's continuation. Tomb robbery has obvious parallels in the looting of temple treasures and other such practices. What these latter expose rather more disruptively, by revealing that people may be interested in the material goods rather than their significance in context, is order's fragility. Ideologies and legitimations are not completely persuasive or coercive. Potentially they leave both central symbols and the material forms in which they are embodied open to reincorporation in other forms.

A final aspect of wealth relates strongly to order and legitimacy. Wealth helps to celebrate and reenact an order that may not be fully itself without such celebration. In joyfully reaffirming order and legitimacy, the actors use wealth to counter fragility, often addressing celebration beyond their own group and involving much of the wider society. Without celebration, order may be threatened; with it, everyone may internalize its significance.

## High culture

In order to take these analyses further we must ask how the ruling elites organize and structure their lives by exploiting wealth in the service of a legitimacy that sustains the order of a society, and ultimately a civilization, in which they are the supreme beneficiaries. It is this intersection of order, legitimacy, and wealth that we term "high culture." This high culture is enacted and celebrated, and it sets early civilizations off from the culture of their forerunners. Our notion of the high cultures of the earliest civilizations also sets them off from diverse successor empires and civilizations of the "axial age" (a term proposed by Karl Jaspers and explored by Shmuel Eisenstadt and colleagues [1986]). In these axial age civilizations (which include Han China, ancient Greece, ancient Israel, Brahman India, and later developments in Christianity, Buddhism, and Islam) ideologies arose

> which strive to present a comprehensive view of the world, not merely of any particular group, and argue that humanity's main task is to remake present reality, corrupt and imperfect as it is, in accordance with the dictates of a higher moral order. Socially, Axial civilizations come to be pervaded by new kinds of groups, labeled by Eisenstadt "autonomous elites," because their existence, recruitment, and legitimacy do not depend finally on the political establishment, nor on individual kinship ties, but on individual qualifications, especially intellectual ability. It is the *raison d'être* of these groups, in turn, to create, promulgate, and refine the new ideologies. (Machinist 1986: 183)

These later "autonomous elites" are very different from the ruling groups of the earliest civilizations, which we characterize by the term "inner elite". An inner elite consists of a very small percentage of people, certainly less than one percent, and constitutes both the cultural and the administrative and executive core of a society. The inner elite is deeply involved in cultural matters, whether or not any of its members have the technical training or roles to be executants, either in artistic or in ritual productions. Dependent on the inner elite is a larger "sub-elite" of qualified people such as scribes, administrators, and artisans. Nevertheless, the inner elite is the group that carries and transmits the central meanings of the civilization.

A crucial and uncomfortable question is that of whom the communications of order and legitimacy addressed. This is often presented in modernist terms of propaganda for the masses. That idea is problematic because of the content and context of many high cultural products, which require deep immersion in their genres to be comprehended. Additionally, many such products could not have been seen at all once they had been created, or had the most restricted possible audiences. The conclusion seems inescapable that the principal focus of high culture was the very elites themselves, at whose behest it was created and for whom it was sustained, and the great gods. The inner elites made themselves into the focus and repository of civilizational meanings in such a way that the rest of society was excluded from the development and maintenance of those meanings. There must have been a delicate balance between elite participation in core concerns and communication with broader groups. Central symbols may have implicitly or explicitly addressed all of society and intermediate groups may have mediated them more widely, but the gulf between the inner elite and the rest remained profound and the elite's small size was accepted as being natural in the order of things.

High culture does not consist in any one phenomenon but varies from civilization to civilization, also enlarging its repertory within single civilizations. A striking aspect of it is that it coincides so well with categories and objects of humanistic study that have built up in Western and other scholarship, from architecture and the various visual arts, through music, dance, and performing arts, to such domains as textiles and body ornamentation, as well as oral and written literature. Many of these are hard to see from the archaeological record, since the visual arts include aspects of material culture that are perishable or verbal arts which are not materials at all. Archaeologists, furthermore, are not usually trained in the analysis of such phenomena or, as natural materialists, are suspicious of the analytical power and importance of such exemplifications of high culture.

Part of the life conducted within the bounds of high culture is that of the gods. Rituals performed for the gods include the most costly objects and elaborate performances and are located in the most significant and highly formed spaces. Religious rituals also present the gods to people outside – albeit often invisibly since the deity may remain enclosed in a shrine – and in the inclusiveness of some festivals celebrations may span all social groups. Many festivals are celebrated, however, within the elite realm, or they reach out to connect and communicate in an exceptional, brief, and marginal moment.

One core of high culture is cosmological. The ruling elite together sustains the cosmos, whose demanding divine and human members require – and glory in – vast investments, from the dedication of precious objects and the construction of large temples to the sacrifice of victims of war. In detail, moreover, high cultural artifacts of many types mimic and celebrate the cosmos. Such cosmological and cosmographic material is powerfully incorporated into visual media. Verbal arts exercise persuasion on behalf of the order celebrated in visual forms while tempering celebration with complexities for which those forms offer little place. Literature, like high culture in general in the earliest states, was the preserve of the elite. In its complexity literature was part of their legitimacy, a mechanism through which they addressed, tempered, and extended their moral position.

An essential feature is the high-cultural products' requirement of commitment, expertise, and expense, a requirement that is typically related to maintaining a tradition and hence to the negotiation of the past. As often uneasy protagonists of our own high culture, many archaeologists should be able to identify with these preoccupations, even while retaining some detachment. High culture was desperately important for the ancient actors. Here the modern public that is excited by "treasures" of ancient civilizations may be nearer to the carriers of these civilizations – and indeed to those outside the ancient elites – than are archaeologists who rightly seek a broader view of the constituent societies.

## Conclusion

To end this brief essay – a digest of the longer, original paper with a new illustration – we note that high culture can often endure through political and economic collapse into subsequent periods of revival (e.g., Yoffee 1988b). The high-cultural frame that includes independent states or groups of city-states also is crucial in showing the insufficiency of political and economic analysis alone in understanding the formation and nature of early civilizations. People – the elite and in this case no doubt also the rest – knew what it was to be Egyptian or Maya, for example, and this commitment is a presupposition for their lives. The elite express "what it is" in complex high-cultural terms.

Apart from their ability to revive, civilizations, and with them high culture, may also survive political conquest and absorption into larger empires or other overarching polities. Their final disappearance is as often marked by the eclipse of high culture and attendant loss of legitimacy as by the suppression of leaders. Into the place of one order comes another. At this point, analysis in the terms we have set up has to end, because the successor civilizations differ from their earlier predecessors in many ways, especially in the nature of elites (as briefly noted above in connection with axial age civilizations). Even if the later civilizations can be seen in terms of order, legitimacy, and wealth, the meanings of those aspects have changed, and they may have no longer the same centrality.

PART II

# Civilizations in comparative perspective

# 3
# Society and individual in early Egypt

DAVID O'CONNOR

Baines and Yoffee's persuasive demonstration that "matters of similarity" between early high civilizations lie "in the nature of order, legitimacy, and wealth and the interrelations among these" (Baines and Yoffee, in chapter 2 in this volume; Baines and Yoffee 1998) provides us with an important and new theoretical approach. While enriched with specific examples, their theory is, however, necessarily presented at a fairly high level of abstraction and generalization, and especially so in their chapter in this volume. What happens when we apply the interpretive model they propose to specific and complex examples, and what kind of modifications or qualifications then arise with regard to the model?

To address these issues with reference to early Egypt, I focus on two aspects of Old Kingdom Egypt (3rd to 6th Dynasties, *c.* 2750–2260 BC). First, I move beyond the elite to examine whether the broader society and its archaeology reveal the characteristics predicted for them by the Baines/Yoffee model. Two questions are addressed: is the evidence necessary to test the model available, and, to the extent that it is, does it display characteristics predicted by the model?

Second, I consider the interplay between the societal and the individual dimensions of a representative monument, the tomb and attached mortuary chapel of Pepyankh, a provincial governor of the 6th Dynasty (2407–2260 BC). To what extent can such monuments be persuasively interpreted in terms of the Baines/Yoffee model, and how does that model relate to others that might seem more powerful in explaining the form and functions of the monument?

**Beyond the elite**

Baines and Yoffee's (1998) interpretation of the relationships between elites and the broader society in early Egypt needs to be tested by reference to whatever relevant evidence exists. They assert that by the 3rd and 4th Dynasties (*c.* 2750–2544 BC) an exclusive elite dominated Egypt and produced a distinctive form of "high culture." The latter's particular vision of cosmos legitimized the elite's "massive appropriation of material resources" (Baines and Yoffee 1998: 234) and curtailed the freedoms of the broader society. In turn, the ruler dominated the elite, which itself was internally hierarchized and competitive, and the wealth that supported "high culture." The earlier social forms and principles of exchange of the broader society had thus been transformed, to that society's severe disadvantage.

This broader society was provincial, distinct from the population of the Memphite region (the center of royal and elite power), and Baines and Yoffee's approach requires the following trends to be evident in it.

1. Settlement sizes and locations change as large-scale, elite imposed resettlement occurs.
2. Socioeconomic structures and trade patterns change, due to the transformation of older social forms and principles of exchange.
3. "City" development does not occur.
4. Living standards deteriorate.
5. The broader society, excluded from concepts and symbols monopolized by the elite, lacks a distinctive material culture. It does not display an aestheticized, ritualized life-style, or even the "proper burials" which guarantee a privileged afterlife.
6. Links with the elite are hard to locate and define. However, Baines and Yoffee observe that additional values and interests must have bound societies together in goals pursued by the elite, and that the "cohesiveness and potency of [high culture] are compromised if it is divorced from the culture of the rest of society" (Baines and Yoffee 1998: 240).

Insofar as early Egypt is concerned, Baines and Yoffee's focus is mainly on the royal and elite cemeteries clustered around Memphis; however, to check the validity of the points listed above we must move beyond the elite and to the larger society. Here, our best evidence is archaeological, for relevant documents of societal and economic interactions have survived poorly. In theory, archaeological data should be abundant, as Old Kingdom Egypt may have had 1,200,000 inhabitants (Hassan 1993: 56), possibly concentrated largely

| | |
|---|---|
| **Predynastic Period** | |
| Badarian | 4800–4200 BC |
| Naqada I | 4200–3700 BC |
| Naqada II | 3700–3250 BC |
| Naqada III | 3250–3100 BC |
| **Early Dynastic Period** | |
| 1st Dynasty | 3100–2900 BC |
| 2nd Dynasty | 2900–2750 BC |
| **Old Kingdom** | |
| 3rd Dynasty | 2750–2680 BC |
| 4th Dynasty | 2680–2544 BC |
| 5th Dynasty | 2544–2407 BC |
| 6th Dynasty | 2407–2260 BC |
| **First Intermediate Period** | |
| 7th–10th Dynasties | 2260–2035 BC |
| 11th Dynasty (1st half) | 2035–2040 BC |
| **Middle Kingdom** | |
| 11th Dynasty (2nd half) | 2040–1991 BC |
| 12th Dynasty | 1991–1783 BC |
| 13th Dynasty | 1783–1650 BC |
| **Second Intermediate Period** | |
| 14th–17th Dynasties | 1720–1570 BC |
| **New Kingdom** | |
| 18th Dynasty | 1570–1293 BC |
| 19th Dynasty | 1293–1185 BC |
| 20th Dynasty | 1185–1070 BC |
| **Third Intermediate Period** | |
| 21st Dynasty | 1070–946 BC |
| 22nd Dynasty | 946–712 BC |
| 23rd Dynasty | 828–665 BC |
| 24th Dynasty | 718–685 BC |
| 25th Dynasty | 767–656 BC |
| **Saite Period** | |
| 26th Dynasty | 685–525 BC |
| **Late Period** | |
| 27th Dynasty | 525–404 BC |
| 28th Dynasty | 404–399 BC |
| 29th Dynasty | 399–380 BC |
| 30th Dynasty | 380–343 BC |
| **Persian Period** | 343–332 BC |
| **Ptolemaic Period** | 332-330 BC |
| **Roman Period** | 30 BC–AD 285 |

*Figure 3.1 Egyptian chronology (after Richards and Wilfong 1995).*

between the Fayum mouth and Memphis, and between Aswan and Qift (Butzer 1976: 100).

In reality, the necessary data – cemeteries, and more especially settlement sites – are rare in well-published form. These circumstances make it difficult to confirm or contradict the conclusions Baines and Yoffee reach about the larger society. Because settlement sites were typically on the flood plain and hence are difficult to locate and excavate, those for which we have some evidence tend to be peripheral and hence of doubtful significance for general trends (Hassan 1993). Buhen was an outpost in distant Nubia; its walled area occupied about 1.24 hectares, but only a tiny handful of structures survived erosion. At Elephantine, a border town, the outline of an expanding walled town ($1^{st}$–$3^{rd}$ Dynasties) had been traced, but its internal detail was lost or obscured by later remains. Far out in the western desert, in el-Dakhla Oasis, an impressive early town has been located and partially excavated, but its relevance to Nile valley urbanization remains unclear.

Within the "heart land" of southern Egypt two sites are of special significance. Walled Hierakonpolis has great potential in terms of a comprehensive overview of urban development over time, and significant discoveries have been made. These include a mound (possibly supporting a temple) and a monumental gateway, seemingly of an Early Dynastic palace. However, exposure of the town as a whole remains limited.

At Abydos, recent excavations have revealed the existence of a substantial (at least 8 hectares) stratified town, running back from the First Intermediate Period into Early Dynastic and even prehistoric times. So far, up to ten substantial households have been identified, varying in size and socioeconomic status, and their extraordinarily rich artifactual, botanical, and faunal remains are providing detailed insight into a complex First Intermediate Period community. But the overall significance of this site will develop slowly, as the necessarily painstaking excavations continue.

Beyond this, and allowing for significant work at the Delta sites of Kom el-Hisn and Mendes, there are no significant urban or even village sites under excavation for these early periods throughout the rest of Egypt. Thus Baines and Yoffee's suggestions about settlement sizes and re-locations, social structures, the absence of "city" development, and deteriorating living standards are impossible to verify by reference to settlement archaeology, the most comprehensive and sensitive data for these purposes.

Early provincial temples (referred to relatively often in textual sources) would be a special but valuable source of data. Such temples likely meant much to provincial communities, as they provided arenas for more modest displays of the world view, aestheticized artifacts and activities evident in mortuary contexts at

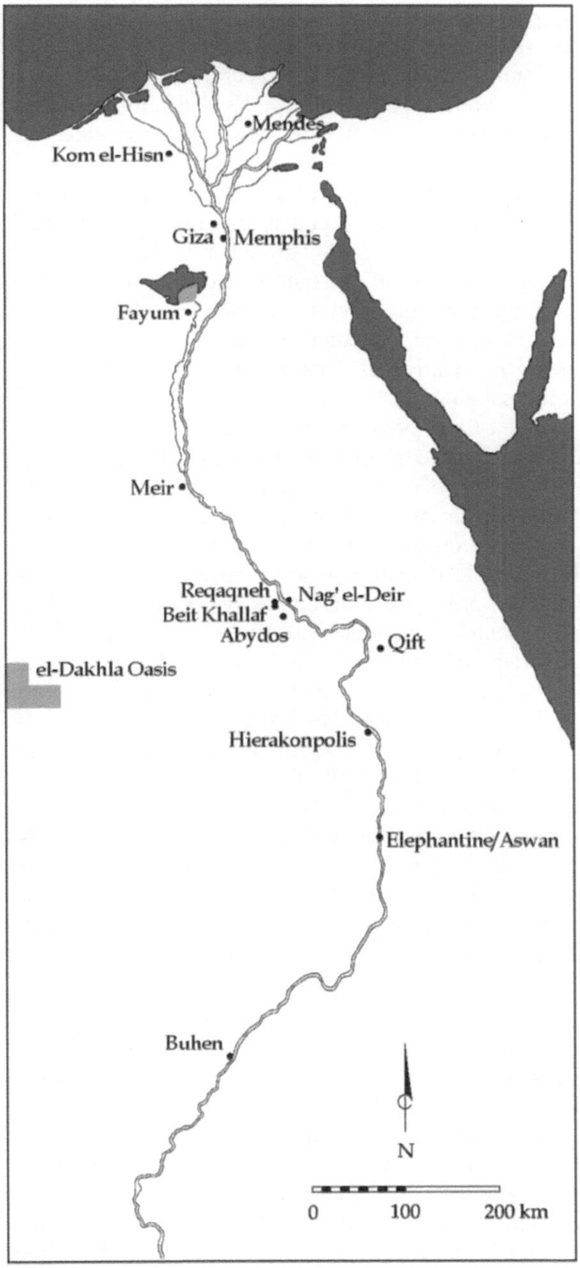


*Figure 3.2 Map of Egypt.*

the center, and might have been manipulated or even appropriated by royal representatives of the central elite.

Rarely excavated and poorly known, however, such temples are a matter of debate, not certainty (O'Connor 1993; Kemp 1994; Arnold 1996; Seidlmayer 1996). Some scholars suggest that they were modest centers of "local culture" before and during the Old Kingdom and largely ignored by the central elite. The norm would be small, irregularly built temples, like that of Satet at Elephantine, with its hundreds of votive objects but little trace in reliefs or wall paintings of the "formal theology which decorates tomb and temple in Egypt" (Kemp 1989: 72).

But the admittedly difficult issue of negative or absent evidence needs to be taken into account. At sites with supposedly identified early temples of simple type, there are typically larger temples nearby, and of later date. These may overlie the remains of the actual earlier temple of each site, and until this hypothesis is tested by excavation the size, regularity, and complexity of early temples remains uncertain.

Thus, cemeteries are our best available excavated data, even though they too are limited in number. Indeed, for earlier Old Kingdom provincial society only one set of cemeteries, centered on Thinis in southern Egypt, provides data adequate for our purposes. Thinis was a provincial capital, although the ancient town itself has never been located. A series of adjacent low desert cemeteries, however, were likely generated by the Thinis community, i.e. by the center and perhaps adjacent or related towns and villages. These cemeteries were located at Nag' el-Deir (eastern side of the valley; Brovarski 1982), with an initial series extending from prehistoric times (*c.* 3500 BC into the 3$^{rd}$ and 4$^{th}$ Dynasties), and forming in spatial terms a relatively tight cluster. In the 5$^{th}$ and 6$^{th}$ Dynasties the cemeteries expanded dramatically, and included many rock-cut tombs (some elite) which had been virtually unreported before. As reflected in these cemeteries, Thinite society was complex, since most cemeteries up to the 5$^{th}$ Dynasty included an evident, if "local," elite component, and the other graves can be graded along a hierarchy of size and comparative wealth.

Cemeteries at Beit Khallaf and Reqaqneh, on the west side of the valley, must also be taken into account (Garstang 1901; 1904). In the 3$^{rd}$ Dynasty, when Nag' el-Deir elite tombs were relatively modest, the mud brick superstructure of one Beit Khallaf tomb occupied 2,700 m$^2$ – enormous even by central standards – and another 1,155 m$^2$. Of three others, only one at 179.5 m$^2$ could be compared to the average size of the larger Nag' el-Deir tombs (average size 165.8 m$^2$). At Reqaqneh, larger 3$^{rd}$ Dynasty tomb superstructures averaged 339 m$^2$, far in excess of Nag' el-Deir sizes.

The larger regional picture is therefore, in social terms, complex. Not only were 3$^{rd}$ Dynasty tombs at

Beit Khallaf and Reqaqneh sometimes much larger than contemporary elite tombs at Nag' el-Deir, a pattern continuing into the 4th and 5th Dynasties; they also displayed aesthetic items such as decorated chapels (Beit Khallaf) and niche-stele or inscribed door jambs (Reqaqneh). Perhaps implanted royal officials were buried at both sites, while only a local elite was found at Nag' el-Deir. In any event, by the 3rd Dynasty the Thinite region had at least a four-tiered social structure, and later at least three. These circumstances are not easily reconcilable with the image of an increasingly depressed and impoverished provincial population, such as the model forwarded by Baines and Yoffee would imply.

"Impoverishment," another experience for the broader society postulated by Baines and Yoffee, is also a complex issue at Nag' el-Deir. In cemetery 500–900 the 3rd Dynasty graves were well supplied with expensive stone vessels and offering tables: these are rarer in 4th Dynasty graves, though the latter are similar in size and form to the earlier ones, i.e., socioeconomically equivalent. Ceramic vessels, common items, also displayed anomalies; in the 3rd Dynasty graves they are less frequent than stone vessels, yet the tomb owners could evidently have afforded more pottery vessels.

Reisner, noting that in cemetery 500–900 the numbers of both stone and pottery vessels decreased markedly in the 4th Dynasty graves with still some described as "very large" or "medium-sized," suggested that these phenomena reflected a change in burial customs. This was paralleled by similar changes in funerary customs at central elite sites such as Giza (Reisner 1932: 105), apparently disseminating outwards across the country.

This situation suggests two things. First, that elites and the broader society were not sharply differentiated from each other and instead shared important customs. And second, impoverishment may not have been the factor behind the apparent "poverty" of the relevant graves. Reisner (1932) thought that it was: "widespread national impoverishment" caused by the elite's grand plans which affected the archaeological record. Yet the actual archaeological record at Nag' el-Deir, as well as Reqaqneh, contradicts this conclusion. Thus the degree of interrelationship between elites and the broader society in the 3rd and 4th Dynasties may have been substantially greater than the arguments of Baines and Yoffee would suggest.

### An elite monument

Elite tombs and their attached chapels, like Pepyankh's, display great variety at all periods in both architecture and program, but I think they also shared basic ordering and functional principles over both space and time (O'Connor 1997). Pepyankh's complex therefore is a representative type which can be fruitfully examined from the perspective of Baines and Yoffee's model, i.e. as an artifact communicating order, legitimacy, and wealth, and the inextricable relationship or "intersection" of those three dimensions of "high culture." Yet the multidimensionality of such monuments requires that in reality several explanatory models must be called upon for their interpretation; and it is the interplay between these models that provides an opportunity to assess the relative explanatory power of Baines and Yoffee's model.

Here, I focus on a specific monument, an elite tomb and its attached chapel, in order to explore both the applicability of the interpretive model outlined by Baines in his introduction and the degree to which it necessarily co-exists with other explanatory models. For the later Old Kingdom, a wide range of monuments is available, primarily royal mortuary complexes and elite tombs, and my example here is a rock-cut example of the latter near modern Meir (in Middle Egypt), chosen for its generally representative character. Its owner Pepyankh – also called Heny the Dark – was governor of the 14th province of southern Egypt in the reign of Pepy II (*c.* 2350–2260 BC) of the 6th Dynasty (Blackman and Apted 1953).

Pepyankh's tomb and chapel – labeled Meir tomb-chapel A2 – were organized around a dendritic, axial structure (Figure 3.3). The main entrance opened on room A, around which were arranged a *serdab*, a sealed-off room originally containing statues; a burial chamber (E); and a large hall, B. The serdab was later partially cut away by an irregularly shaped hall (F), on the walls of which Pepyankh's embalming and funeral were depicted. Hall B was linked by a "portico" to the adjacent chapel of Pepyankh's father (Meir tomb-chapel A1); at B's rear was a small cult room, C, and Pepyankh's own burial chamber (D). The walls of A, B, C, and the serdab displayed a continuous series of scenes and texts, i.e. a "program," carved in relief and painted, while the two long side walls of F were, in part, covered with ink representations of the embalming and funeral. In all, the cutting out of the complex, as well as the impressive area occupied by the program (over 82.5 $m^2$ of wall space) represented a very substantial investment of labor, resources, and skill. In Baines and Yoffee's terms, Pepyankh's complex, and its complicated program, was unquestionably a "vastly expensive and . . . rarefied artefact" (Baines and Yoffee, chapter 2 in this volume, p. 15).

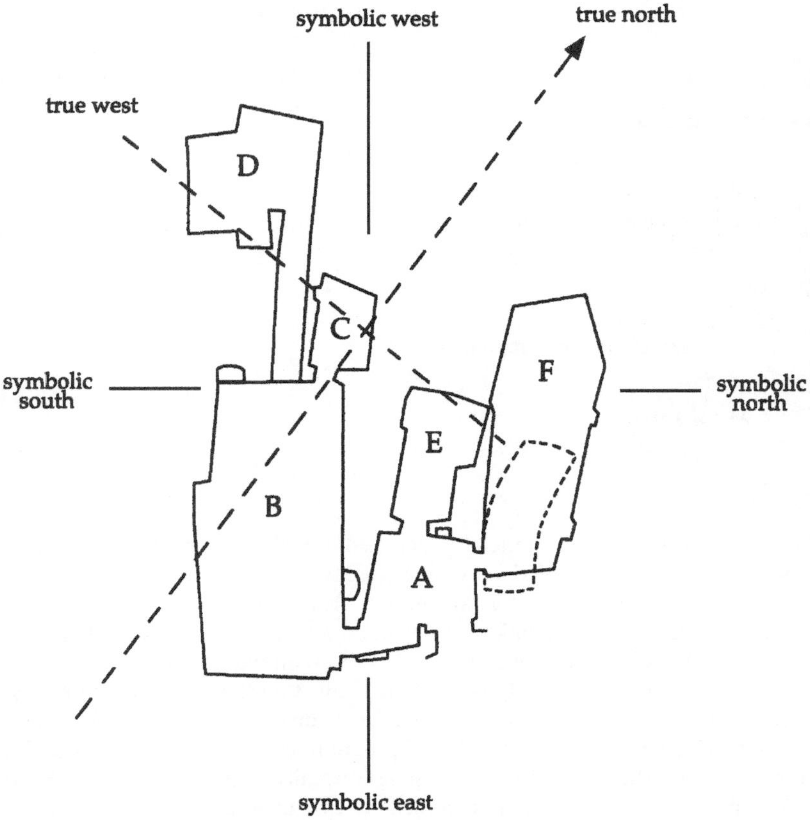


*Figure 3.3 Plan and orientations of Pepyankh's tomb and chapel (drawing by Deborah Vischak, Institute of Fine Arts, New York University).*

Monuments like Pepyankh's have several dimensions. These include a ritual dimension, for which a religious model is appropriate, and an artistic one, involving the formal and thematic aspects of its architecture and program combined. For interpreting these, an art-historical model is required. Beyond these, such monuments also have societal, cosmological, and individual dimensions, the study of which involves a complex interplay between the Baines and Yoffee model and another, which I shall call the individualistic.

The individualistic model requires further discussion. It focuses on the specific needs and concerns the tomb owner had about tomb and chapel, and how they affected the ritual, art, and architecture of the monument. This model underlies most art-historical discussions of elite mortuary complexes, albeit in a rather simple form which requires further development, as I shall show below. Robins, in an excellent history of Egyptian art, provides a typical example: "Tomb chapels," she states, were at all times "meeting places with the dead, and . . . provided a setting for the re-enactment of the funerary cult, during which the dead could manifest themselves in their statues and other images in the chapel. The decoration of the chapel was designed to ensure that the deceased was fully equipped for the next life and had a safe passage there" (Robins 1997: 252). Thus, such discussions focus primarily on the individual dimension, but give little attention to its intersection with the societal and the cosmological. Where the latter is noted, its significance is seen as essentially individualistic: "tombs . . . were microcosms that reflected the ordered universe" (1997), and in this way guaranteed the individual's "triumph over death and rebirth into the next world" (Robins 1997: 138, see also 69).

Initially, we need to study the ritual and artistic aspects of Pepyankh's complex, and their implications for the other three dimensions. Ritually, Pepyankh's tomb and chapel were designed to accommodate the conclusion of the all-important funeral, which ensured the deceased a successful transformation from a human into an "*akh*" being, a fully empowered inhabitant of the netherworld and celestial realms of the cosmos. The chapel was also a locale for a regularly repeated statue

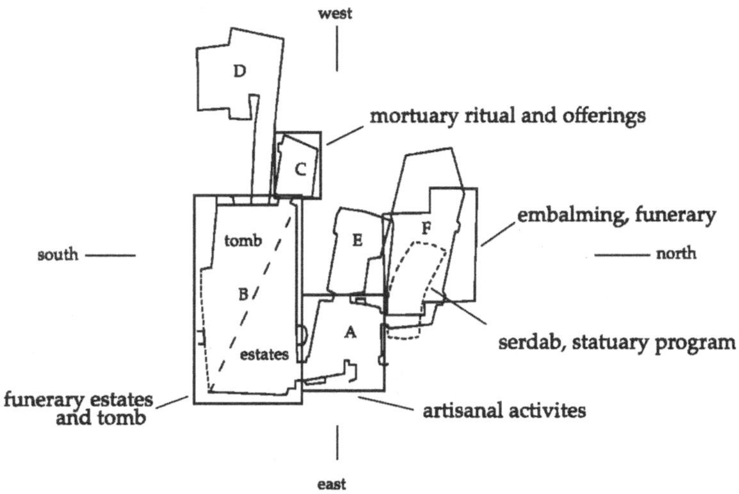


*Figure 3.4 Thematic analysis of the program of Pepyankh's chapel (drawing by Deborah Vischak, Institute of Fine Arts, New York University).*

and offering cult which, calling upon the deceased's "*ka*" and "*ba*," guaranteed him or her endlessly repeated renewals or rebirths based on the combined mythology of Osiris, ruler of the netherworld, and the sun-god, lord of the cosmos (Spencer 1982; D'Auria *et al.* 1988: 27–51).

The embalming and funeral rituals are relatively well documented, and those of the statue – and offering – cult less so, but it is clear that the latter pervaded the whole complex and provided it with a comprehensive ritual unity. Such rites were performed not only in cult room C, but presumably before the two engaged statues set in recesses in hall B, and perhaps another two in room A, as well as before the serdab or sealed statue house, which was probably linked to room A by slots (Blackman and Apted 1953: 45–46).

The art-historical analysis, on its part, reveals that the art and architecture of Pepyankh's complex, which seem quite diverse from one room to another, in actuality are also combined into a comprehensive and integrated whole. This is evident in two ways. All rooms shared an internal integrity in terms of architecture and program, albeit an integrity manifested differently in each room. Also, the internal artistic integrity of each room was linked into a unified totality through a complex network of spatial, compositional, and thematic relationships extending over the entire tomb and chapel (Figures 3.4 and 3.7).

In terms of individual rooms, Room C displays the strongest artistic integration, for its small size (*c.* 6m$^2$), and the programmatic content (statue and offering rituals) relates directly to its cultic function. Most of what is shown took place in C, but the massed offerings and butchery depicted on C/north more likely were located in B in actuality, and thus perhaps mark an implicit axial rotation, from the cardinally true orientation linking false door and coffin (Figure 3.3) to the symbolic cardinality of the complex as a whole.

The large (*c.* 48m$^2$) hall B on first examination seems to have a thematically diverse and compositionally loosely structured program, but in reality is thematically coherent and quite formally organized. The overall program is framed by two magically protective scenes (see below) of the tomb owner ceremonially fowling and fishing (Figure 3.5); placed adjacent to the southwest and southeast corners of B, they extend a protective aura over the hall and perhaps the entire chapel. Most of the rest of the program is structured around seemingly diverse episodes of Pepyankh "viewing" specific events, but again their placement is by no means random. Diagonally speaking, two episodes identify the west and south "half" of B with the locale of tomb and chapel; items and materials for both are presented on B/south, while offerings arriving at the chapel are shown on B/west. The north and south "half" of B is, programmatically speaking, the logical complement of the other "half." Its viewing episodes, and other scenes, evoke Egypt as a whole, as is emphasized by texts near the northwest and southeast corners which refer to "southern and northern Egypt."

Like that of hall B, room A's program refers to the world "outside" of tomb and chapel, but in a thematically more tightly integrated way. Viewing episodes provide the organizational structure, but here all relate to a single theme, the production of statuary, other objects, and materials needed for tomb and chapel. The

SCALE 1:6

*Figure 3.5 Pepyankh shown hunting birds in the marshes. Room B, west wall (Blackman and Apted 1953, Plate XXVIII; reproduced by permission of the Egypt Exploration Society, London).*

serdab's program, like that of room C, relates directly to its function and content as a statue house, for literally hundreds of statues of Pepyankh were once depicted on its walls.

Hall F also displays a high degree of compositional and thematic unity. F/east has a seemingly unrelated animal-count scene, but the opposing walls F/north and F/south depict in the form of a continuous narrative (from north wall to south wall) the elaborate ceremonies of embalming and the funeral procession. The last episode (F/south, upper right) seems to mark a striking transition from two to three dimensions, and from symbolic to true cardinality. It shows the coffin being carried towards the tomb, itself not shown and presumably represented by the actual tomb and chapel themselves.

The artistic integrity of each room is transformed into an overarching programmatic and architectural unity for the whole complex in two ways (Figure 3.4). First, each room programmatically evokes a different locale, either itself (burial chambers D and E, room C, the serdab) or different components of the outside world. However, the different rooms are so arranged that spatially and sequentially these different locales form a logically and appropriately laid out whole. Rooms A and B represent the world of the living and the flood plain, and are appropriately set "in front" of the others. Hall F is separate from A and B, and set further back than A and much of B; the appropriateness here is that programmatically F largely evokes the low desert (locale of mummification and funeral) between flood plain and tomb. Finally, the tomb chambers (D, E) and the core cult room C are themselves the essential components of the mortuary complex proper, and are set "behind" the

*Figure 3.6 Pepyankh being carried in his palanquin; B, East wall (Blackman and Apted 1953, Plate XXXI; reproduced by permission of the Egypt Exploration Society, London).*

representations of flood plain (A, B) and, for D at least, that of the low desert (F).

In addition to this overall linking procedure, an even stronger integrative mechanism is an extraordinarily complex pattern of programmatic and compositional cross-references which link together the different rooms of the tomb and chapel (Figure 3.4). To cite only the more important of many examples, I have already noted that C/north refers to occurrences in hall B, the west wall of which in turn depicts offerings being carried into room C, while much of the entire program of B is concerned with the production and administration of these same offerings. Room A's program relates to B's in that many of the items and materials shown being made on the walls of A are included, some with great specificity, among those presented to the tomb owner on B/south. Other important aspects of A's program relate to adjacent rooms, i.e. room E and the serdab (O'Connor 1996: 621–633). Moreover, the animal-count scene in hall F refers back to a related scene on B/north while, as noted above, the embalming and funeral episodes of F clearly relate to cult room C and burial chamber D.

Other cross linkages are more subtle. For example, a visually striking scene of Pepyankh carried in a palanquin, centrally placed on B/north, can legitimately be "read" in several ways. It shows Pepyankh moving from the episode of B/north, west end to that of B/north, east end, wherein he wears the same costume as in the palanquin. It may also show Pepyankh, as a deceased, empowered entity accompanied by symbols of sexually based rebirth such as small monkeys, moving into room A, which associates strongly with such a renewal (O'Connor 1996). This example of linkage between rooms is reinforced by yet another. On A/south Pepyankh, on foot, is escorted by two officials; on B/north, he is carried in a palanquin; on B/east he is implicitly carried in a ship along the Nile. Seemingly disjointed, these three episodes are presented as a more or less continuous sequence in an approximately contemporary tomb at Saqqara (Duell 1938: Plates 154, 158, 139–145) and may have been so understood in Pepyankh's complex, providing further cross-references between A and B.

Thus far we have seen that in its ritual and artistic dimensions Pepyankh's tomb and chapel display a pervasive unity and integrity. This suggests that the same may be true of its societal, cosmological, and individual dimensions, but analysis of these reveals that a single interpretive model is insufficient to explain the significance of and interrelationships between these three dimensions. Rather, these emerge from the interplay between two models, Baines and Yoffee's on the one hand and what I call the individualistic model on the other.

The importance of the interplay results from the complex ways in which the societal, cosmological, and individual dimensions of tomb and chapel interact. For example, the societal dimension of an elite monument has significant meaning for the elite in general, and perhaps others, with regard to the affirmation and reinforcement of the existing social structure, its supporting ideology, and its political and economic organization. However, societal and individual dimensions powerfully intersect, in that the tomb owner's activities and status within the social order demonstrates his or her individual concordance with the divine order (*ma'at*) as expressed through that order. On this depends successful entry into the afterlife, and subsequent reception of cult from the living.

Tomb and chapel also have a cosmological dimension, for via ritual, art, and architecture both are presented as a microcosmic version of the structure and processes of cosmos. But this dimension intersects significantly with both the societal and individual. On one hand, the cosmological dimension provides the ultimate justification for the inequitable social order depicted in the chapel, an order which, in human terms, mirrors a divinely ordained cosmic hierarchy. On the other, the cosmological dimension is vitally important to the deceased individual. The harmonization of ritual, art, and architecture with cosmos guarantees a successful afterlife, while the cosmological dimension also manifests and celebrates the empowerment whereby ritual and other processes ensure the repeated rebirths and renewals upon which that success is based.

Discussions of these issues will be found in Robins (1990b, 1994) and Kamrin (1992: 69–75). To these should be added Bolshakov's monographic treatment of Old Kingdom tomb programs as providing a "double world" meeting the essential needs of the individual deceased (1997). Kamrin's own study is a particularly important one for she is the first to provide a strong case that most elite mortuary chapels had a well-developed cosmological dimension. She argues that three coexistent and interpenetrative versions of cosmos are evoked via chapel programs: respectively "personal," "royal," and "macrocosmic," each providing the tomb owner with a specific persona important for successful transfer to the afterlife and subsequent continuity as a transformed being. She concludes: the "chapel can be considered a sort of temple . . . a private mortuary temple" (Kamrin 1992: 262; see also Lustig 1997).

The approaches discussed immediately above mostly focus on an individualistic interpretive model, i.e., the tomb chapel's role in assuring the deceased a successful burial ritual and then repeated mortuary cult. The societal dimension of such monuments, highlighted in Baines and Yoffee's model, is relatively neglected (but see Ruhlmann 1981; A. Roth 1988, 1993, 1995; Lustig 1997) and the cosmological – noted by Baines as societally significant, for the ruling elite together sustains the cosmos (Baines and Yoffee 1998: 206) – has not been explored in depth, except by Kamrin (1992). In any event, it is the interplay between the Baines and Yoffee model and the individualistic perspective that is perhaps the most important issue, and to examine this a more extended explanation of the individualistic model is necessary.

This statement draws on Kamrin's insights in particular, but differs somewhat in emphasis. It focuses first on the statue cult as the central event of mortuary ritual. The deceased had to be ritually empowered to embody himself or herself in the statues of the mortuary chapel and thus to benefit from the offerings presented, to reciprocate with benefits for the living and, above all, to experience a process of rebirth and regeneration that was essential for otherworldly survival. The empowerment required was achieved by calling upon the most powerful processes imagined by the Egyptians, namely the creation of cosmos, its daily renewal via the solar cycle, and its maintenance or rulership. Once the desired results had been achieved, they could be attested and celebrated, the purpose of much of a tomb's decorative program: but the program also had to address profound anxieties on the part of the deceased and the ritualist. Both feared the annihilating intrusion of destructive chaotic force, deadly to both and especially likely should any moral, legal or ritual deficiencies exist with regard to the mortuary monument and its owner.

Both issues – celebration of renewal, and the assuaging of anxiety – together provide a comprehensive explanation for the artistic and architectural unity that pervades Pepyankh's complex. Anxieties are addressed by first showing the deceased as worthy of cult through demonstrating that he, while living, had lived in accordance with *ma'at*, the divine order, through performance of his expected or assigned social functions; and now, deceased, has been transformed into an effective spirit (*akh*) via a proper funeral. As to the legitimacy and effectiveness of the cult, many features of the program attest to its capable ritualists, its legally endowed and properly administered estates, and even such details as the payment (implicit, in Pepyankh's case; A. Roth 1994) and ceremonial meals received by the cutters and decorators of the tomb and chapel. No flaw exists that would make the deceased fear embodiment in his statue, or the ritualist fear supernatural harm.

Nevertheless, anxiety was further assuaged by providing both deceased and ritual specialist with specific protection against chaotic force, an elemental or cosmic negative energy which, as part of its hostility to cosmos as a whole, sought to destroy mortuary cult and the effective spirits (*akhs*) it serviced. Such spirits were as essential to cosmic process as deities, or living or deceased rulers. Protection was provided by magically protective scenes, especially those of ceremonial fishing and fowling (B/south, B/east), but most powerfully through the cosmological integrity of the entire complex; *being* cosmos was the best protection for tomb and chapel against chaotic force.

But the cosmological dimension of Pepyankh's monument was much more than simply protective. It celebrated the tomb owner's achievement of repeated regeneration and rebirth by means of ritual identification with the creator, the sun-god and the cosmic ruler, and hence the empowering experience of the fundamental cosmological process associated with each deity. For this reason tomb and chapel, through its art and architecture, represent not only cosmic structure (sky, earth, and netherworld, and their divine, human, and other inhabitants) but also the process of structuration, growth, and vitalization cosmos experienced through the cosmogony, the daily solar renewal, and the manifestation of divine rulership. Interwoven with the multifaceted representation of cosmos and cosmological process are many references, primarily pictorial and architectural, to the actual means of regeneration, a series of analogous, parallel, and even interpenetrative experiences: transformation via the funeral; revitalization through the repeated statue and offering cult; and a sexually based mode of reproduction wherein the tomb owner impregnates a female partner, who gives birth to a renewed form of the deceased.

Now we turn to the question: to what extent does the interplay between this individualistic perspective and Baines and Yoffee's model provide understanding of an elite funerary monument such as Pepyankh's?

Certainly, their model – as outlined in their synthetic essay in this volume – provides a comprehensive explanation for much of the chapel's program. As an "artifactual embodiment of order", that program represents and conveys an ideology asserting "there should be a state, centralized leadership, powerful elites and their dependents," and also demonstrates that a variety of structures, groups, and social orientations are united under "one societal umbrella" (Baines and Yoffee, chapter 2 in this volume). The pictorial and textual means chosen to achieve these ends are sometimes subtle and implicit, sometimes explicit and definitive.

Thus, for an elite observer, the existence of the centralized state was conveyed not by depictions of Pepyankh's official duties (for the individual dimension of the complex required emphasis on other events) but by his official titles, which had meaning only by their relationship to a larger and centrally organized system of governance, and sometimes – honorifically – referred directly to the latter. Thus, Pepyankh held the titular rank of vizier, or prime minister. For Egyptians, the state was embodied by the king, but here too subtlety was called for: decorum allowed very limited reference to this august individual in a non-royal monument (Baines 1985: 277–305; 1991: 137 ff.). But the king, or royal institutions, are present in some titles of Pepyankh or others (e.g., "treasurer of the god [king]," "king's gentleman," "royal acquaintance," "king's companion," "royal scribe," officials of "the palace," etc.), while individual rulers (Pepy I and probably II) are present through their incorporation into the personal names of Pepyankh and others. The latter practice seems to relate to subtle hierarchization within the elite itself, for of 53 names only 6 refer to a king, and all are of Pepyankh, his close kin or especially important officials.

The differentiation between elite and others, and the subsuming of social variety into a societal unity, were themes unrestricted by decorum, and hence given full play pictorially: indeed, they dominate the overall pictorial structure of the program, via both thematic and compositional procedures. Visually, the chief component of the program is the human figure (over 800 individual forms were depicted), which is organized into socially significant units by means of scale, pose, dress, and grouping.

The elite – here represented by Pepyankh, his kin, officials, and attendants – are nearly always shown at a larger scale than artisans, agricultural laborers and the like (see Figures 3.5 and 3.6). Moreover, groups representative of the two classes are kept distinct from each other, with little compositional intermingling.

Despite this societal variety, unity is conveyed both textually and pictorially. Those depicted include kin-groups (Pepyankh's, and perhaps others), but also non-kin groups (the officials, and lower orders) incorporating different "economic groups," and "social orientations." The social unity binding these together is conveyed by the references to the centralized state system and its supporting ideology, already noted, and – in another way – by the artistic unity and integrity which pervades the entire program and its societally differentiated content.

Yet, despite the explanatory value of Baines and Yoffee's model, the individualistic model seems to have been more powerful in the shaping of Pepyankh's tomb and chapel, and in dictating the content of the messages or ideas thus conveyed. For example, the pictorial subject matter involves not Pepyankh's official duties, but his roles *vis à vis* his funerary estates, tomb, and mortuary cult – all items crucial to his individual survival after death, but not to his societal roles. Moreover, the central position and colossal scale assigned to Pepyankh in most scenes does not relate to a society-wide system of hierarchization. Officials of much lesser status and power than he are assigned to visually equivalent prominence in their chapel programs. Again, the influential factor is the individualistic model; each tomb owner is shown, within the context of mortuary cult and its effect, as having king-like and even god-like characteristics (Kamrin 1992; Bolshakov 1997).

Baines and Yoffee's model has been seen above as explaining the pictorial devices whereby elite and non-elite are distinguished from each other in the program, but even here the individualistic model has a perceptible impact. For example, both elite and non-elite differentiation in scale can relate not so much to the societal dimension as to the momentary importance some individuals acquire when they perform some significant individualized service for the tomb owner. Two examples of many illustrate this point.

On A/south (Blackman and Apted 1953: Plate XVI) Pepyankh is shown escorted by two named officials in an unusually intimate way (they hold his hands). To indicate the importance of this both are depicted on a much larger scale than any of the other elites present, although elsewhere one of the two – named Itjau – is shown on the same scale as the rest of the elite (Plates, XV.4, XXV.1, XXXII, XXXIV). An even more telling example is the central scene on B/north (Figure 3.6; Blackman and Apted 1953: XXXI). Pepyankh, in his palanquin, is escorted by a large number of elite individuals, but all of the latter are shown on a smaller scale than two anonymous, presumably lower-order individuals who provide Pepyankh the personal service of shading his palanquin from the sun!

In Baines and Yoffee's model legitimacy and wealth are, after order, the two other dominant themes. Like order, both find expression in Pepyankh's program. Programmatically and architecturally, Pepyankh's monument conveys or represents legitimacy in two ways. First, the highly hierarchized social structure (conveyed pictorially) and the political power of the elite (conveyed textually) is presented as an accepted given, its harmony mirrored in the unity and integrity of the complex's artistic dimension. Second, the strongly developed cosmological dimension provides the ultimate rationalization for the centralized power and social hierarchy depicted by the program: these mirror the divinely ordained rulership principles and structural hierarchization of all cosmos which, as Baines observes, is sustained by the ruling elite.

The securing and manifestation of wealth by the elite is seen by Baines and Yoffee as rendering wealth "an essential enabling factor whose potential is released, but also harnessed and contained, by societies and civilizations" (Baines and Yoffee, chapter 2 in this volume). This aspect of their model also has significant explanatory power for Pepyankh's monument. In itself, the complex and its erstwhile contents form a striking example of the "display and consumption of vastly expensive and generally rarefied artifacts dedicated to the gods, the dead, the ruler and the elite" (Baines and Yoffee, chapter 2 in this volume), while the chapel program conveys the notion that wealth, the product of morally worthy activity and status, is a characteristic of the elite. Exact figures are rarely provided, although in the animal-count scene on F/east a count of over 38,000 animals is cited, and specific amounts of linen are referred to on A/south. But, in pictorial terms, Pepyankh's abundant wealth is clearly represented, via his funerary estates, manufactories, lavish tomb goods, and massively heaped offerings.

Moreover, the issues of controlling wealth are also detectable. The program refers in a number of ways to the appropriate organization and disbursement of wealth, for example in setting up the funerary estates, and paying, supporting, and rewarding those responsible for the tomb and its cult. Comparatively, the similarity in approximate size between Pepyankh's tomb and chapel, and those of the other governors of the province in the later Old Kingdom is also suggestive of control; his complex (in its original form, excluding F) defines, very roughly, about 130 $m^2$, as does his older brother's (Blackman 1924), while their father's is larger, but not excessively, at about 158 $m^2$. These circumstances recall some important observations about a group of later Old Kingdom tombs at Saqqara. Here, mastaba dimensions tended to be uniform, reflective of both equivalent status and an externally controlled investment of resources, while decorative programs were more diverse in quality and extent, perhaps funded by other, less strictly controlled forms of wealth (A. Roth 1995: 58).

However, the individual dimension of the tomb and chapel also relates powerfully to the themes of wealth and legitimacy, more so perhaps than the Baines and Yoffee model. The wealth displayed programmatically and otherwise by Pepyankh's monument is societally significant in that it is emblematic of the wealth of the elite, and the power it provides them. But this wealth also has specific purposes vital to the deceased individual. When expressed in relationship to the luxurious and prestigious lifestyle many scenes imply, wealth attests to his *ma'at*-concordant life; while wealth also provides the items, services, and offerings required by the deceased Pepyankh.

As to legitimacy, I have noted that the monument's cosmological dimension provided the ultimate justification for the social and political system its program depicted; yet the elaborate development of that dimension in tomb and chapel is due largely to the individual needs of the deceased and is explained most powerfully by the individualistic, rather than the Baines and Yoffee model. This latter circumstance also shows why elaborately decorated monuments, royal and private, for deities or the deceased, were of very limited access and seemingly intended for small, even tiny "audiences," despite the thematic importance of their program's content, and their overall richness and elaboration.

Baines provides an explanation for this phenomenon in terms of the model he and Yoffee propose. He observes that ephemeral art forms were probably important and perhaps accessible to relatively large audiences and that relatively inaccessible monuments such as temples generated festival celebrations external to the temple that could "span all social groups." Nevertheless, he recognizes that "many high-cultural products . . . could not have been seen at all once they had been created or had the most restricted possible audiences," and that, in any case, the content and context of such products required "deep immersion in their genres to be comprehended." He thus concludes that, in terms of the model he is applying, "the principle focus of high culture was the very elites themselves," including non-corporeal ones such as deities and the dead (Baines and Yoffee, chapter 2 in this volume).

Insofar as this particular model is concerned, this analysis is reasonable, but co-exists I believe with the much more powerful impact of the individual dimension upon a monument's accessibility. The logic of the conceptual world which tomb and chapel represent requires that the monument be relatively inaccessible in order to fulfill a primary function, the celebration and attestation of the continuity, and repeated rebirths and regenerations, of the tomb owner.

Pepyankh's tomb and chapel are exemplary of the restricted access, and external modesty, of elite funerary monuments as a whole. Its facade was not elaborately decorated or architecturally embellished (Blackman and Apted 1953: 24 and Plate LI); it was visited, presumably, by a large group at the time of the funeral and perhaps rare festival occasions thereafter; and was regularly serviced by a "ka-priest" and a few attendants. Some Old Kingdom tombs inscriptionally invite visitors to a cemetery to enter and perform cult for the deceased, and A. Roth (1995: 25 ff., 54 ff.) and others have suggested the relative siting of tomb chapels and the arrangement and content of their programs were in part intended to encourage such visits. However, the potential audience involved was likely still relatively small and restricted, and even more so at places like Meir, where small clusters of elite tombs are set up high in the cliffs, remote from lower-lying general cemetery fields.

And visitors who did enter Pepyankh's multi-roomed chapel would find it quite difficult to see its program in any kind of comprehensive way (despite the evidently great thought given to its visual qualities), even with artificial light. Room A would have been relatively well-lit when the entrance door was opened, but the large halls B and F would have required artificial light, inevitably of limited effect, while cult room C must have been extraordinarily dark without it. It may well be that the inaccessibility and darkness or obscurity of Pepyankh's chapel are an ultimate expression of elite superiority and self-preoccupation, in terms of Baines and Yoffee's model, but they are also, and in my opinion more powerfully, explicable in terms of the individualistic model, especially insofar as it impacted on the cosmological dimension of the monument.

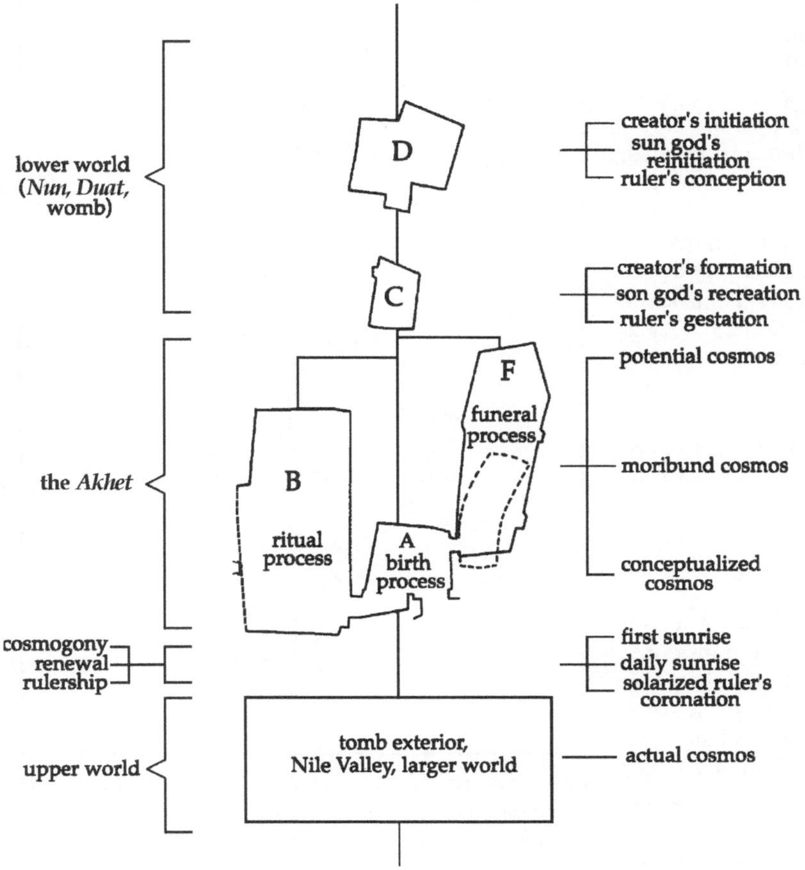


*Figure 3.7 Pepyankh's tomb and chapel analyzed in terms of cosmological and analogous processes (drawing by Deborah Vischak, Institute of Fine Arts, New York University).*

If, as suggested above, tomb and chapel represent cosmos in the three distinct but co-existent phases of cosmogony, cosmic renewal, and cosmic rulership, then extended analysis shows that their seclusion and darkness are a necessary part of this representation. Cosmogony, cosmic renewal, and the manifestation of rulership are each structured according to a sequence in which sun-rise is the culminating event, a sequence which provides our best understanding of the organization of the monument's architecture and program (Figure 3.7; on cosmic processes, see Allen 1988; on cosmology and architecture, O'Connor 1997).

In this interpretation, tomb chamber D and cult room C (the darkest and most remote parts of the complex) correspond to the creator's initiation and formation in *Nun*, the primeval liquidity; the sun-god's regeneration – after apparent death at sunset – in the *Duat* or netherworld; and the cosmic ruler's conception and gestation within a divine mother. Each of these beings has a vision, even "plan" (Allen 1988: 59) of a cosmos which each will fashion, then vitalize, and it is this vision which is presented via the carefully organized architecture and program of Pepyankh's monument.

In each case, the cosmos is presented from a terrestrial viewpoint, as is appropriate to the human, if transformed status of Pepyankh himself. With this limitation, the creator's potential cosmos, the sun-god's moribund one and the cosmic ruler's conceptualized cosmos are represented by halls B and F, and room A. The essential structure of cosmos is evoked primarily by the characteristics of the earth, such as the river (B/east) and flood plain, but the sky and subterranean world – the manifestations visible to humans of the celestial realm and the netherworld – are also subtly represented. For the former, the many open-air scenes imply the sky above, reinforced by the sun-shades displayed on B/north; and some Egyptian tomb-chapels (not Pepyankh's) actually had stars painted on their ceilings (Griffith and Newberry, n.d., 31). As to subterranean elements, tomb and chapel themselves are literally such, the former actually being also at a lower-lying level. The inhabitants of these three realms are also present in the program, humans, animals, and other creatures abundantly so, the deities and the dead more subtly. For the latter, Pepyankh (actually shown being embalmed and buried in hall F!) is the supreme example, although all humans depicted, in this context, may have been understood to have had both living and deceased personae. Decorum inhibited representations or references to deities, yet a representative selection in fact occurs: they include funerary deities such as Osiris (Blackman and Apted 1953: Plate XXIV and "the great god" of Plates XXXIII.2, XXV.2, XXIX), Anubis (Plate XXXIII.2), and also regional deities, some invoked directly (e.g., Horus of Hebnu, Plate XXXI), others evoked via personal names. The latter include Hapy (Plate XXX, XXXI), Ukh, a sacred entity associated with Hathor (Plates XV, XXXI, XXXIII.1), and Sobek (Plate XVIII).

By location (between D and C on the one hand, and the "outside" on the other) and in terms of the inner logic of the cosmological mythology involved, halls B and F, and room A, correspond cosmographically to the Akhet (on the Akhet, see Allen 1988: 6, 11–12, 25). This transitional and liminal zone linked lower and upper worlds, potential and actual cosmos, non-being and being. It was the venue for the coming-into-effective-being of creator, sun-god, and cosmic ruler and for the materialization of their respective visions of cosmos, as actually represented on the walls of these chambers. In Pepyankh's complex, these cosmic processes are strongly related to the individual dimension of the tomb and chapel, for they are equated with the means by which the deceased individual is empowered to regenerate and transform. Hall F corresponds to the initial funeral; hall B, the ante-hall to cult room C, corresponds to the statue and offering cult, while room A focuses on the (re)-birthing process. In A, there is allusive but recognizable reference to sexual intercourse and the subsequent rebirth of the tomb owner (O'Connor 1996); the many scenes of "creating" items, including statues, found only in room A, are clearly analogous to the birth process; and the serdab decoration (hundreds of statues) implies the endless "rebirth" of statues embodying a revitalized Pepyankh.

The Akhet, which enshrines the processes productive of cosmos and facilitating cosmos' vitalization, as well as Pepyankh's individual processes of rebirth and regeneration, were considered especially vulnerable to the attacks of chaotic force, hence the specifically protective scenes near the southwest and southeast corners of hall B, scenes which can be envisaged as extending protection over A and F as well.

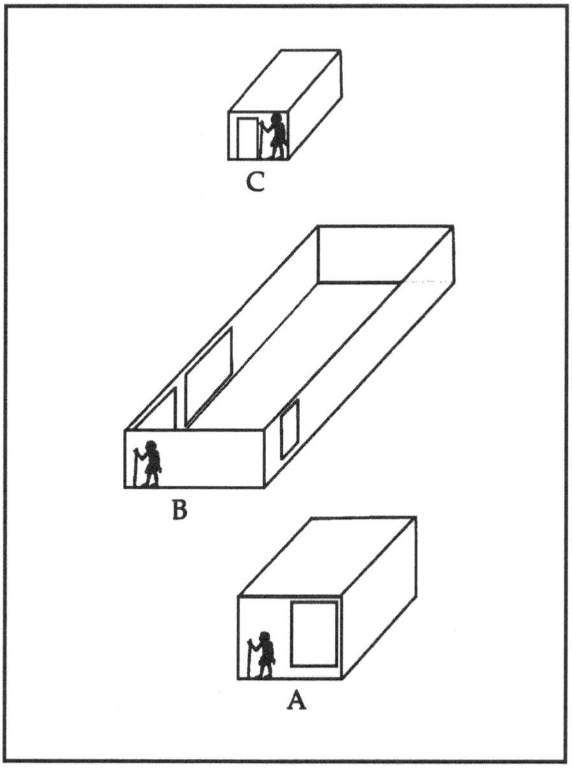


*Figure 3.8 Schematic of the relative sizes and proportions of the rooms of Pepyankh's chapel (original plan; excludes serdab and Hall F. Drawing by Deborah Vischak, Institute of Fine Arts, New York University.)*

The monument as a manifestation of cosmic structure and process provides the rationale for its relative inaccessibility, darkness, and internally changing form. That which takes place in the *Nun* (the primeval waters), *Duat* (the netherworld), and *Akhet* (the transitional zone between the upper and nether worlds) is by its nature, as well as the structure of the cosmography, hidden from human view, and needs to be so to be effective. The cosmos represented by tomb and chapel is not yet vitalized; rather, as potential, moribund, and conceptualized it is appropriately enshrined in darkness, another feature essential for its effectiveness. Finally, the gradual growth of this pre-vitalization cosmos, from small beginnings to cosmos-filling expanse, corresponds to the actual dimensions of the sequentially laid out chapel rooms: C is tiny, B is much larger, as well as higher and A, a kind of anteroom to B, while smaller, has an even higher ceiling (Figure 3.8).

In myth potential, moribund, and conceptualized

cosmos are all vitalized and made actual by being flooded with sunlight, the ultimate life-giving energy (Allen 1988: 10–12, 50, 53, 63). For the cosmogony, this is the first sunrise; for cosmic renewal, the daily sunrise; for rulership, the recognition and coronation of a solarized divine king, and all these must find expression in the cosmological dimension of tomb and chapel. Moreover, cosmological and individual dimensions intersect in that funerary texts make it clear that, as part of his or her renewal process, the deceased individual is envisaged as traversing the tomb and chapel and emerging into actual, vitalized cosmos – the "world outside" – via the chapel's entrance. In Pepyankh's case, this outward movement (often signaled by representations of the tomb owner on the entrance lintels, and even the tomb facade) is reinforced programmatically. Thus, Pepyankh moves "outwards" in his palanquin (B/north: on the ramifications of such scenes, see A. Roth 1994) or on foot (A/south). His implicit presence in the ships on B/east even carries him "north" and "south" along the valley as well. One might guess that ritual, as performed in the chapel and originating in cult room C, also reflected an "outward" progression given the diffusion of engaged statues and implied cult throughout B and A; in fact, the series culminates in a statue (A/west) facing outwards through the chapel's entrance, the "solar exit" from the complex.

The preceding therefore suggests that the owner's emergence from the chapel, or "viewing" of the world outside via the entrance, corresponds to the solar appearances that emerge from the Akhet and vitalize cosmos, transforming it from one of darkness-shrouded inertness to one of sun-drenched vitality. This in turn suggests that the program of Pepyankh's monument culminates in actual cosmos, i.e. the actual world of flood plain and river spread out before the tomb and chapel, and the entire territorial realm – and implicit celestial and netherworld realms – beyond it.

The preceding analysis of Pepyankh's tomb and chapel demonstrates that the interpretive model developed by Baines and Yoffee provides substantial insight into the functions and meanings of such monuments by relating them to the forces of order, legitimacy, and wealth which produce "high civilization." However, it is equally clear that this model interacts or interplays in each case with several others – religious, artistic, and individual – each of which provides access to a significant level of meaning embedded in the monument. Moreover, for elite mortuary monuments, at least, the individualistic model is the most powerful explanatory means of understanding what they meant to the Egyptians, for whom the societal issues emphasized by Baines and Yoffee here seem distinctly subordinate to others of special importance to the individual. It is of course quite likely that, in other kinds of monuments, the interplay between the different models and the relative explanatory power of each may well be somewhat different. In any case, even for elite mortuary monuments the individualistic model, despite its superior explanatory power, can reasonably be seen as the product of more generalized issues of order, legitimacy, and wealth and their operations in shaping a society and its culture.

Thus, the analysis of Pepyankh's monument demonstrates the complexities involved when one applies the productive analytical approaches suggested by Baines and Yoffee to individual elite monuments. Earlier in this chapter, I have also tried to show that the effects upon the larger society "beyond the elite" which their model predicts are difficult to confirm for early Egypt, because the necessary archaeological data are so insufficient. Here also, however, hints of a complex relationship between elite and other emerged, as in changing burial customs seemingly shared by many social levels, including the elite. Yet while Baines and Yoffee's model will necessarily be tempered by the realities of its application to specific cultural structures, I believe that it has substantial explanatory power that significantly shifts our perspectives on the development of early civilizations, a point I have also tried to demonstrate in this chapter.

# 4

# Modified order, responsive legitimacy, redistributed wealth: Egypt, 2260–1650 BC

JANET RICHARDS

## Introduction

Explicit ideologies of order, and the legitimation of hierarchy and authority within those ideologies, were materialized in the ancient world largely through ceremonies, monumental landscapes, precious symbolic objects, and written texts (De Marrais *et al.* 1996). Given the comparative silence of non-elite, non-literate groups in monumental and literary media, and their restricted access to the wealth underpinning systems of symbolic objects, their participation and role in these ideological systems is often obscured. Yet although elites may have been the primary actors in the construction of these ideologies of authority and hierarchy, the influence of bottom-up processes and of forces (such as environmental events) over which elites had limited or no control, can not be ignored in our attempt to understand the whole system within which elites operated (Kowalewski *et al.* 1992: 259).

Over the last ten years, there has been increasing concern with the consideration of non-elites in ancient complex societies. Scholars have sought to understand the points of articulation and interaction between elites and the rest of the population (Kowalewski *et al.* 1992; Brumfiel 1989; G. Marcus 1992: 293; Chase and Chase 1992: 16), and the arenas in which visual, oral, and written communication of dominant ideologies as well as resistance to these ideologies may have taken place (D. Miller *et al.* 1989a and b; Heyer 1988: 117). One avenue of tracking non-elite influence or agency in ideologies of power lies in patterns of materialization, or the transformation of ideologies into "concrete physical form," the process of which is "an ongoing arena for competition, control of meaning, and the negotiation of power relations" (De Marrais *et al.* 1996: 16). Never a simple correspondence, shifts in different aspects of materialization may, however, reflect processes of factionalism (Brumfiel 1996, 1989) and social and religious change, or responses by elites to the forces over which they have limited control.

In "Order, legitimacy, and wealth in ancient Egypt and Mesopotamia" (Baines and Yoffee 1998), John Baines described an early Egyptian state in which the ideology of order was the exclusive concern of an inner elite. Members of this extremely small group conceived and represented an ideal and cosmologically crucial order, and legitimized their position within it by emphasizing their unique role in its maintenance; only elites possessed the ability to vanquish the chaos which could undermine its unity. These concepts were materialized through the creation and consumption of "high culture," encompassing key symbols and art forms, built environments, literature, and the body. In Baines' model of Egyptian order, the communication and display effected by these high cultural forms was transmitted to a narrow audience only: they constituted a legitimizing dialogue within this elite (which included the Egyptian king) and between the elite and the gods (Baines and Yoffee 1998: 236, 244).

My intent in this discussion is to qualify the notion of such a limited band of communication and participation in a hegemonic ideology by examining diachronic change in and the renegotiation of notions of order, consequent elite legitimizing strategies, and the distribution of wealth supporting materializations of these ideologies. The inquiry will focus on a period of about 600 years, spanning two periods in Egyptian history: the First Intermediate Period, characterized by political decentralization and considerable social and symbolic transformation (2260–2040 BC); and the Middle Kingdom (2040–1650 BC) immediately following it, when Egyptian political authority was once again strongly centralized, the elite ideology of order was reformulated, and new legitimizing strategies were pursued by elites. If the Egyptian notion of order was the exclusive concern of an inner elite, how did it persist when political and cultural decentralization occurred, and how was it reconstituted in its quintessentially "Egyptian" form afterwards? If discourse legitimizing inequality took place within a limited circle only, how was the dominant social and political order justified to the wider population which must, to some extent, have subscribed to it? Was all below this circle chaos incarnate (*isfet*), the opposite of the Egyptian principal of

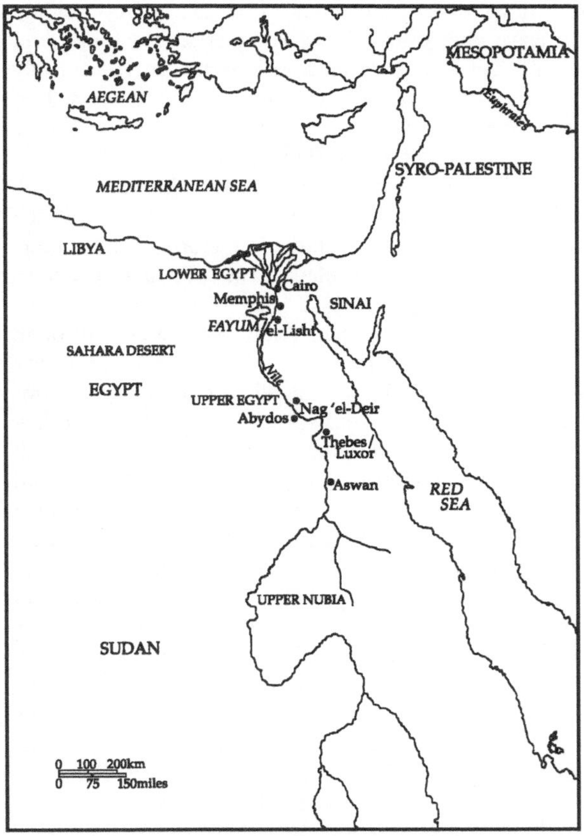


*Figure 4.1 Map of Egypt with key sites and places mentioned in the text (A. Sprochi).*

*ma'at* (translated as order, harmony, truth); or was it simply a second culture, with its own symbolic discourse and values, and a basic lack of concern regarding the activities and ideology of the governing elite?

At issue is the ultimate extent of the audience, over time, of "high culture," i.e., the materialized ideology of the Egyptian inner elite (Baines and Yoffee 1998; Baines and Yoffee, chapter 2 in this volume); the meaning it communicated to different social groups; and the degree of accountability felt or attention paid by the inner elite to the population over which they ruled. If high cultural forms remained completely exclusive, how do we explain the ongoing processes of emulation and innovation in Egyptian material culture? Can we completely discount the role played by individuals involved in or around the fringes of high cultural production and consumption, such as craftsmen, lower bureaucrats, and cult specialists, in disseminating information to the non-elite population? How do we account for shared ideological domains such as funerary practice? And finally, how can we comprehend a new style of kingship during the 12th Dynasty of the Middle Kingdom (*c.* 1950–1783 BC), with its seeming emphasis on humanity and responsibility?

I suggest that in the context of the inevitable and continuing development of a complex society such as ancient Egypt – with particular reference to the growth of a social group such as a semi-literate middle class (or "bourgeoisie") with the potential to formulate and materialize competing ideologies of moral order – the Egyptian inner elite could not and did not exist in static isolation from the mass of people it governed. The forms, styles, and meaning of Egyptian high culture were emulated down through the middle to lower levels of the socioeconomic range, sometimes immediately, sometimes with a time lag; its notions about such important matters as the afterlife were shared; and legitimizing strategies, including the representation of order in monumental art and literature, underwent deliberate adjustment and renegotiation over time as the Egyptian world changed. I will focus on select illustrations of the above, drawn mostly (and for these periods almost inevitably) from funerary contexts, but also from the divine realm of the actions and representation of the king and the gods, and the not-so-divine realm of speculation on the subject of archaeologically invisible "communication."

## Emulation, regional style and "democratized afterlife": the First Intermediate Period, *c.* 2260–2040 BC

Ancient Egyptian chronology from 2750 to 656 BC has traditionally been divided into "kingdoms" and "intermediate periods" (Figure 4.2),[1] each subsuming a number of dynasties (groups of rulers linked essentially by kinship). "Kingdoms" were eras of strongly centralized authority, and were territorially expansive to increasing degrees throughout the third and second millennia BC. Characterized by unified ideologies of kingship and hierarchy, and extensive display of royal and elite power through monumental building programs, each kingdom provided a potent and manipulable past for the inner elites of its successor kingdom (Baines 1989). Elites of the Middle Kingdom stressed ties with those of the Old, while New Kingdom elites revived select ideological strategies of the Middle. Intermediate periods, by contrast, were characterized by pronounced indigenous factionalism, invasion by non-Egyptian groups, or both; and evidenced little outward aggression or internal building on a monumental scale.

| | |
|---|---|
| **Predynastic Period** | |
| Badarian | 4800–4200 BC |
| Naqada I | 4200–3700 BC |
| Naqada II | 3700–3250 BC |
| Naqada III | 3250–3100 BC |
| **Early Dynastic Period** | |
| 1st Dynasty | 3100–2900 BC |
| 2nd Dynasty | 2900–2750 BC |
| **Old Kingdom** | |
| 3rd Dynasty | 2750–2680 BC |
| 4th Dynasty | 2680–2544 BC |
| 5th Dynasty | 2544–2407 BC |
| 6th Dynasty | 2407–2260 BC |
| **First Intermediate Period** | |
| 7th–10th Dynasties | 2260–2035 BC |
| 11th Dynasty (1st half) | 2035–2040 BC |
| **Middle Kingdom** | |
| 11th Dynasty (2nd half) | 2040–1991 BC |
| 12th Dynasty | 1991–1783 BC |
| 13th Dynasty | 1783–1650 BC |
| **Second Intermediate Period** | |
| 14th–17th Dynasties | 1720–1570 BC |
| **New Kingdom** | |
| 18th Dynasty | 1570–1293 BC |
| 19th Dynasty | 1293–1185 BC |
| 20th Dynasty | 1185–1070 BC |
| **Third Intermediate Period** | |
| 21st Dynasty | 1070–946 BC |
| 22nd Dynasty | 946–712 BC |
| 23rd Dynasty | 828–665 BC |
| 24th Dynasty | 718–685 BC |
| 25th Dynasty | 767–656 BC |
| **Saite Period** | |
| 26th Dynasty | 685–525 BC |
| **Late Period** | |
| 27th Dynasty | 525–404 BC |
| 28th Dynasty | 404–399 BC |
| 29th Dynasty | 399–380 BC |
| 30th Dynasty | 380–343 BC |
| **Persian Period** | 343–332 BC |
| **Ptolemaic Period** | 332-330 BC |
| **Roman Period** | 30 BC–AD 285 |

*Figure 4.2 Chronology of ancient Egypt (after Richards and Wilfong 1995).*

During these periods, actual authority devolved to powerful provincial kin groups.

From the unification forward and the emergence of a standard iconography of kingship, the ruler was presented as divine, the god Horus on earth, holding exclusive ability to liaise with supernatural forces and divine beings. His dominance was woven inextricably into the structure of the universe, and expressed in landscapes of power both cultic and mortuary. Until the end of the Old Kingdom (Dyn. 3–6, *c.* 2750–2260 BC), the ruler seems also to have held exclusive access to Osirian afterlife, attained through identification with the god of the dead Osiris, father of Horus. His subjects gained entrance to that blessed state through service to the state and king.

The First Intermediate Period, Dynasties 7 through the first half of Dynasty 11 (*c.* 2260–2040 BC), was traditionally classified by the elite-preoccupied Egyptological literature as "disastrous," "tumultuous" (Gardiner 1961), an "exceedingly dark time" (W. S. Smith 1981: 152) of confusion, social revolution, and general impoverishment. The art of the period was deemed "degenerate" and "wretched," and the overall material culture descended to a "shockingly low level"; "the deplorable state of Upper Egypt is clearly reflected in the clumsiness of its artistic efforts; evidently Egyptian civilization was at its lowest ebb" (Gardiner 1964: 111). These characterizations seem linked to two factors. The first lay in an early scholarly interpretation of the legitimizing, so-called "pessimistic literature," now dated to the Middle Kingdom, as true historical accounts from an earlier and utterly chaotic time. This traditional interpretation constituted in fact a naive acceptance of ancient ideological assertions as valid contemporary descriptions (see for example Gardiner 1964: 110). The second factor was art historical dismay at the complete absence of significant royal monuments, and the virtual disappearance of what were understood as "high cultural" forms.

In reality, however, the country did not plunge into a maelstrom of poverty and uncertainty. Central authority did break down, due perhaps in part to a decrease in agricultural prosperity caused by declining inundation levels. There continued to be kings of Egypt to whom nomarchs (or provincial governors) paid nominal allegiance; but order was maintained by these provincial elites who, as Baines comments, assumed the functional place of the inner elite during the First Intermediate Period (Baines and Yoffee 1998: 224), and emulated high cultural forms in their tombs and biographies. High cultural ideology did not therefore disappear, though the integrity of the inner elite must have eroded with decentralization; what did change was form, to a certain extent; style, in part due to level of access to diminished court workshops, but also in part to regional artistic choices; and dissemination, in that a much wider range of the Egyptian population, lower elite as well as non-elite, now gained access to key symbols and prestigious, envalued materials. Such shifts in the distribution of wealth may have subtly affected relations of power between elites and non-elites, if not exactly effecting significant changes in status.

In the mortuary environment of the First Intermediate Period there are increased signs of a "democratization" of beliefs and symbolism regarding the afterlife, a process which had become evident already during the Old Kingdom (see O'Connor this volume; see Bourriau 1991 for a dissenting view regarding this term). By the late Old Kingdom, and for the first time since the Predynastic period, there occurred large, lower order cemeteries located on the low desert (Garstang 1909; Peet and Loat 1914; Loat 1923); a phenomenon documented even more widely in the First Intermediate Period (Brunton 1927, 1937, 1948; Seidlmayer 1990). The inhabitants of these cemeteries were having themselves buried independently of elite or wealthier patrons, yet in a fashion which indicates a shared ideology about what constituted an afterlife, and what was necessary to ensure that afterlife. Cowgill (1992a: 207) has stressed the importance of tracking the manipulation of and access to symbols over time in both mortuary and habitation contexts, in attempting to understand communication between groups in society; and by the First Intermediate Period, non-elite Egyptians definitely had access to key symbols employed previously by only the elite, emulated in these lower order contexts in the form of amulets. These personal ornaments were placed with the body of the deceased, and endowed him or her with magical protection or capability (C. Andrews 1994; d'Auria *et al.* 1988; Hayes 1953).

Among these amulets were potent hieroglyphic signs such as the *wḏ3t*, representing the eye of the falcon Horus, a divinity previously associated only with royalty and the state solar religion. Also making an appearance is the *ḏd*, a pillar in the form of a stylized tree trunk, the hieroglyph meaning "enduring, stable," associated early in Egyptian history with divine rituals, and later as one of the important symbols associated with Osiris, the god of the Dead. Another key symbol is the scarab beetle, again, an expression in material form of a powerful hieroglyphic sign meaning "to come into being," having a close association with the solar religion so important to the king and the inner elite. Now, for the first time in any non-royal context, amulets in the form of royal insignia even appeared, such as crowns, the rearing cobra associated with kingship, and vultures, representing one of the tutelary goddesses of kingship (C. Andrews 1994; Hayes 1953).

Further, these amulets appeared in non-elite contexts in an extensive range of materials. Not only were these elite symbols imitated in cheaper materials such as faience, pottery, or mud, but also they were crafted in expensive materials such as gold and carnelian, indicating wider access to material resources, and therefore to the wealth which fuels inequality within an order. It is important to note that these symbols did not subsequently disappear from the high cultural repertoire even though they were no longer unique to it: depictions of royal regalia appeared subsequently on painted elite coffins of the Middle Kingdom (Willems 1988; Hayes 1953), and the other amulet forms entered into a symbolic complex associated with the growing industry of death, which both elites and non-elites continued to incorporate into their funerary display. Inequality within the mortuary order with reference to grave goods was henceforth expressed in terms of material, workmanship, and elaboration.

How do we account for the communication of these high cultural symbols to the lower levels of Egyptian society? Not an easily answered question. Could the inner elite have acted as interpreters of high cultural ideologies to the lower classes, as Marcus has suggested for certain Mesoamerican societies (J. Marcus 1992a), legitimizing their status by the measured revelation of secret knowledge? Or could information have trickled down *via* those middlemen cited earlier: craftsmen, priests, lower bureaucrats who had opportunities to observe the use of these symbols first hand (J. Marcus 1992a; see also Davis 1992; Assmann 1995)?

Another venue was perhaps the relaxation of restrictions on cemetery space over generations. The inclusion in decorated elite tomb chapels of "Appeals to the Living," beseeching passers-by to pronounce invocation offerings, suggests that these passers-by were anticipated:

> all people of Abydos, who shall pass by this monument in going downstream or in going upstream, as you love your king, as you praise your city gods, as your children shall remain in your place, as you love life and ignore death, you shall say: a thousand of bread and beer, oxen and fowl, ointment and clothing, incense unguent and all kinds of herbs, all kinds of offerings on which a god lives, for the ka of the revered prince . . . Sehetep-ib-re, the justified, son of Dedet-Nekhbet, the justified. (From the stela of Sehetep-ib-re, transl. Lichtheim 1973, I: 28–29).

It is clear that the elite counted on this eventual wider audience, as insurance against the inevitable time when neither priests nor descendants would visit their chapels to pronounce the necessary ritual formulae. Less clear is the point in time at which entry by the non-elite into high elite mortuary contexts became possible, given the limits on our knowledge of regulations concerning cemetery space. However, even if the communication implied by the "appeals to the living" was casual or unintended, it is important to note that it was not the symbols alone which were being transmitted in the mortuary environment, but also the meaning of these symbols, particularly given the absence of widespread literacy – indicating, again, a "common ground of symbolic communication within ranks of elites and between elites and lower-ranking levels of society" (De Marrais *et al.* 1996: 23), some level of shared ideology not limited to the dissemination of written documents.

During the First Intermediate Period, ideological inequality was also maintained and enforced in the mortuary realm through restriction of space, in that elite graves were typically cut into the rock cliffs lining the Nile River Valley, compared to the low desert context of the non-elite. These provincial elite graves too showed the emulation of earlier high cultural forms, in this case a reinterpretation of the crucial false door feature of the Old Kingdom inner elite tomb chapels. Signifying the focal point of offerings to the dead, the false door was transformed in a provincial context to a simple stela representing the grave owner and his wife receiving offerings, encapsulating in symbolic form the entire decorative scheme and intent of a large offering chapel. A principal source for these provincial stelae is a series of elite chapels at the complex of sites near Nag' el Deir (Dunham 1937; see Figure 4.1), which has yielded a large number of stelae evincing several different levels of workmanship, dedicated by a wide variety of classes of people. These chapels are small by elite standards, and were at first taken to signify the impoverishment and regional vulgarization of the Egyptian elite, due to the horrors of anarchy. However, most probably they do not represent a court-centered, inner elite which had gone home with the weakening of the central government. Rather, they should be understood to be, simply, lower level local elites – who were clearly sharing high cultural mortuary forms, but making style choices coherent with regional preferences, irrespective of access to high technical skill. Some of the best executed of these stelae display the most pronounced regional style markers, such as a lively and irregular use of color, pronounced noses and tiny heads, and high waists, at odds with the most correct canonical art of court or high cultural style (Figure 4.3).

*Figure 4.3 Mesheikh Tomb 101: First Intermediate Period chapel remains and stela (courtesy of Museum of Fine Arts, Boston).*

These stelae also provide evidence of the growing ethnic and economic diversity in Egyptian society: some were dedicated by Nubian mercenaries (Fischer 1961), others by individuals seemingly holding no government titles at all, yet able to commission a formally and symbolically correct work (cf. Renfrew 1985), and often by people who stressed a rise to power from meager beginnings – self-made men (Vernus 1970; cf. Lichtheim 1988: 66).

What is evident therefore during the First Intermediate Period is by no means a socioeconomic levelling process, but rather a change over time in the character and distribution of ancient Egyptian social groups, and in particular the emergence of what might be termed a middle class and some mitigation of the disparity of wealth between inner elites and the rest of the population (see Yoffee 1988b). This "middle class" was not an aberration in the Egyptian record that led nowhere, but a phenomenon that continued into the Middle Kingdom (Quirke 1991a) and seems to have become a significant force in society and economy. The growing power of this group was possibly one factor encouraging the development of a new high cultural complex surrounding elites and kingship, articulated through the media of literature and visual presentation. The overall impression promoted by this complex was far less remote than that of the Old Kingdom (Figure 4.4), whose kings personified the kind of serene and profound isolation proposed in the Baines model for the inner elite of all periods.

### The Middle Kingdom, 2040–1650 BC: a return to classical order, with a twist

During the second part of the 11th Dynasty (2040–1991 BC), the Egyptian state was reconsolidated; and the decentralized political situation of the First Intermediate Period ended as the Middle Kingdom began. Subsequently, the art and architecture of the early Middle Kingdom were characterized by the deliberate practice of archaizing – a revival of the high cultural complex of the Old Kingdom as a means of establishing and legitimizing the new political order. The iconography of royal statuary in the late 11th and early 12th Dynasties reproduced the serene, idealized vision of kingship as formulated in that earlier, "classical" period; relief work and decorative schemes in royal and elite funerary structures recalled or copied outright Old Kingdom models (compare, for instance, Figure 4.4 – a "classic" Old Kingdom royal statue – and Figure 4.5, an early 12th Dynasty representation more than five hundred years later). Once again pyramids were built: monumental structures that dominated the landscape, communicating to the population at large the king's link to the power of the past and his supremity in the cosmological order, and thereby legitimizing his authority over Egypt's productive resources – human, material, and agricultural.

But in contrast to that referenced past, elites of the 12th Dynasty stood at a pivotal point in the three-thousand-year trajectory of Pharaonic Egypt. Not only had non-elites diversified ethnically and gained enhanced access to material and symbolic resources during the previously decentralized period: the diversification of the Egyptian population continued throughout the Middle Kingdom, with an increase in migration of semi-nomadic peoples from both Syro-Palestine and Libya into Lower (northern) Egypt (Bietak 1996; Parkinson 1991: 11), alongside the continuing incorporation of Nubians into Egyptian society (Fischer 1961; Bourriau 1991). There existed as well further opportunity for resource accumulation through participation in the newly created standing army. The central government paid wages or granted land in lieu of wages to soldiers, thus providing additional avenues of income for non-elite families as well as the possibility of mobility within the political system (cf. Johnson and Earle 1987).

*Figure 4.4 Horus on earth, 4th Dynasty, Old Kingdom: King Khafre (copyright Hirmer Verlag München).*

Contrary to the relative insularity of their Old Kingdom predecessors, 12th Dynasty kings initiated aggressive military campaigns in the Nubian Nile Valley to the south and eventually also northwest into Syro-Palestine, foreshadowing the extensive empire building of the New Kingdom five hundred years distant. Concomitantly, and not surprisingly, a new faction arose within the Egyptian elite: that of career military officials, who from this time forward accumulated the wealth and political weapons necessary for periodic challenges to the authority of the reigning king (Peet 1914; Shulman 1964; Kemp 1989: 228). At the same time, non-royal cult specialists gained increasing political and ideological authority, as pronounced stress was laid on the pious deeds of the king (Quirke 1991b: 135). Royal building programs now emphasized the enrichment of existing gods' temples, or the endowment of new ones, alongside

*Figure 4.5 Invoking the power of the past: iconography of kingship in early 12th Dynasty, Middle Kingdom (Senwosret I) (copyright Hirmer Verlag München).*

the construction of royal mortuary complexes. It is notable that the great temple at Karnak, whose High Priests would ultimately maneuver for dominant political power in the New Kingdom and Third Intermediate Periods, was one of the temples founded at this time (Franke 1995: 739).

Baines and Yoffee have cautioned that change in the high cultural complex does not necessarily mirror change in power relations or the maneuvering of different interest groups (Baines and Yoffee 1998: 244). However, there were particular twists to the complex surrounding kingship and the inner elite of the 12th Dynasty which, when viewed as a whole, seem either to have reflected or encouraged a wider audience for what J. Marcus (1992a) has termed "vertical propaganda," communication from the elite levels of society aimed at lower levels of society; and to have catered to a "moral economy" (Scott 1985; Costin and Earle 1989; Baines 1995), which might have been attractive to non-elite levels of the Egyptian social order, thereby enhancing the legitimizing aspect of this complex (cf. Kus 1989).

Relevant to the widening of audience for high cultural display is the textually documented establishment of a new capital city called *It-tawy*, "[Amenemhat is the] seizer of the two lands," in the area of the Fayum, instead of a return to the long-lived capital city of Memphis. The design of new royal cities as built environments to showcase the ritual activities of the king, and to function as microcosms of the Egyptian universe where order is maintained and legitimized, is well known for the New Kingdom (O'Connor 1989), and has been assumed to date to that era. The exact whereabouts of *It-tawy* are still uncertain, although believed to lie in the neighborhood of modern el-Lisht (Bourriau 1991). Given that uncertainty, more than the fact that it existed can not be specified; but it is tempting to see the beginning of deliberately communicative, living (as opposed to mortuary) royal environments at least as early as the Middle Kingdom, especially since the entire Fayum was subjected to an intensive building and development program by the kings of the 12th Dynasty. In such a context the person of the king would be visible on selected occasions to a far wider audience than the inner elite alone, in staged events presenting and legitimizing the role of the state and the inner elite at its apex.

Given the new militarism of the Egyptian state, the acquisition of Nubian territories, and interconnections with (or minimally, awareness of) polities of the Aegean, the Levant, and the Near East (Ilan 1995; Kuhrt 1995), this ceremonial landscape played to an audience that had potentially widened beyond Egypt's inhabitants to include representatives of other social and political groups. The public monuments, ritual events, and controlled flows of movement throughout the royal city would communicate royal power and authority on several levels of discourse – among Egyptian elites, to the wider population, to the outside world (cf. Chase and Chase 1992: 10; De Marrais *et al.* 1996: 19; J. Marcus 1992a; Eigner 1996; see also Kuhrt 1995: 102 on competition in the display of royal palaces).

Additionally, in the 12th Dynasty there is evidence that wider access was now being granted to cult precincts, hitherto strictly reserved to priests (and ideologically to the king alone). Now, private individuals are allowed to erect votive monuments – stelae and statues – near the gates and in the outer courtyards of these temples (e.g., Simpson 1974; Bourriau 1991), where these individuals would no doubt see royal and perhaps divine statuary, experience firsthand the visual presentation of kingship and the face of the ideal, and emulate this ideal in their own statuary, as numerous private examples of the period attest. The individuals represented on these stelae include high officials, holders of different levels of titles in the bureaucracy or priesthood, farmers, and persons with no title or stated profession whatsoever; the size and quality of the stelae ranges from the finesse of workshop output all the way down to simple flakes of limestone with crudely scratched inscriptions (O'Connor 1985; Simpson 1997). This distribution suggests votive access by quite a wide sample of socioeconomic levels in Middle Kingdom Egypt.

At the same time, other previously sacrosanct zones were thrown open to private access. At the key ceremonial site of Abydos early in the 12th Dynasty, a zone associated with Early Dynastic kings which had been held inviolate for close to one thousand years seems to have been handed over to the local population for use as a burial ground (Leahy 1989; Richards 1999), while a local elite zone maintained its exclusivity – thereby signifying two levels of calculated concession or negotiation on the part of the inner elite. The royal family and the national elite may well have had no further use for the space (building instead much farther south at the site), but in symbolic terms this gesture must have communicated quite a significant concession.

### Accountability and the "moral economy"

Finally, I would like to examine briefly the notions of accountability and the "moral economy," and the role played by these notions in 12th Dynasty elite ideology. Costin and Earle have commented that "an elite can not maintain power efficiently if the bulk of its subjugated populace views their rulers as illegitimate" (Costin and Earle 1989: 692).

There is no question that force was employed by the ancient Egyptian government. Textual evidence in the form of actual administrative and private documents exists in greater quantity from the Middle Kingdom onwards (Griffith 1898; Kemp 1989; Parkinson 1991), as opposed to the bias towards monumental and religious texts in earlier periods; and the very real coercive mechanisms of the state can be glimpsed in papyrus fragments recording, for example, the punishment of persons fleeing compulsory labor, the operation of legal process and punishment, and the existence of police (e.g., Kemp 1989: 129; McDowell 1989; Parkinson 1991: 99–101).

However, it is equally clear that Egyptian inner elites did not rely predominantly on force for dominance of the population (cf. D. Miller *et al.* 1989b: 8). One common method of legitimation is the controlled dissemination of information to this wider group, which promotes and enhances the benefits derived from participation in the system (cf. Costin and Earle 1989; De Marrais *et al.* 1996). Perhaps relevant to such a strategy, there is a marked shift in the mood and subject matter of both private literature and royal monumental texts during the Egyptian Middle Kingdom.

In the literary realm, a series of texts ("teachings," "discourses," and "narratives") was produced, seemingly geared towards describing both a perfect order, often by contrasting it with chaos; and what constituted a person living in accordance with this order. These "poems of the high tradition" (Parkinson 1997: 13), while ultimately affirming loyalistic values and social solidarity, explored also the nature of society, individuals, and the cosmos, raising questions about the relationship between power and culture, and the realities of imperfection and of suffering (Parkinson 1997: 14–15). "Teachings," in particular, touched on the fallibility of kings (albeit decorously those of the past), emphasized the responsibility of elites towards non-elites (Parkinson 1997: 247), and signaled the existence of social mobility. Narratives such as the "Tale of the Eloquent Peasant" meditated on fundamental themes of truth and justice (Parkinson 1997: 55; Parkinson forthcoming).

Parkinson has recently argued that this potentially subversive body of literature allowed the articulation of elite dissent, and thereby effectively "accommodated, contained and constrained" it (Parkinson 1997: 16), mitigating incipient factionalism within the Egyptian elite. He does not, however, believe that these written texts were disseminated to other levels of society: "it seems likely that the written and oral forms were remote and separate from each other: the 'little' tradition of the peasants, as opposed to the 'great' tradition of the literate elite, is completely lost" (Parkinson 1997: 12).

Estimates on literacy rates in ancient Egypt vary from 10 percent downwards, with some recently posed figures at not much more than 1 percent of the population (Baines 1983). However, literacy was expanding in the Middle Kingdom; and Quirke (personal communication) has stressed the importance of allowing for the presence of differential "literacies" in Egyptian society.

Additionally, the probability of a thriving oral tradition sharing to some extent in the themes of this "great" tradition can not be dismissed, especially since it is likely many of these texts were written to be performed (Parkinson 1997: 11), and some also display colloquialisms suggestive of "more culturally peripheral or low traditions" (Parkinson 1997: 12). Such a tradition, along with the existence of those cultural middlemen cited previously (see above), might have facilitated the dissemination of the ideology presented in written literature (see Appadurai's notion of "bazaar-style information economies" [1984]).

In the realm of royal monumental and literary rhetoric, the themes expressed in private literature are echoed in a series of texts describing the role of the king within the Egyptian order, stressing the responsibilities, burdens, and disillusionment of kingship. In building inscriptions, boundary stelae, and hymns, the king was featured as "set . . . to be shepherd of this land" (trans. Parkinson 1991: 41); "a shelter, rescuing the fearful from his enemies . . . a warm corner, dry in the wintertime" (trans. Parkinson 1991: 47); and "one who takes thought for dependants, and stands by mercy" (trans. Parkinson 1991: 43). He was a warrior, "aggressive to capture . . . unmerciful to the enemy that attacks him" (trans. Parkinson 1991: 43); yet simultaneously worn and embittered by the cares of rule, as portrayed in a "Teaching" written in the voice of the assassinated Amenemhat I: "Trust no brother! Know no friend! Make for yourself no intimates – this is of no avail!" (trans. Parkinson 1997: 206).

The mood of this political discourse was mirrored visually in the iconography of kingship. Royal representation took a dramatic turn under king Senwosret III, though the beginnings of the new style were already visible in the statuary and relief of his grandfather Senwosret II (Bourriau 1988: 25; Petrie 1923: plate XVIII). The royal visage, in contrast to the serene and remote perfection of earlier kings (Figures 4.4, 4.5), conveyed an overall sense of grimness, fatigue, and age, to increasing degrees throughout the reign and life of the king – heavily lidded eyes, gaunt and furrowed cheeks, a sense of brooding; unusually large representations of ears (Figures 4.6, 4.7). The responsible, exhausted shepherd, displaying the burdens of his vigilance? The half-divine yet half-human being wielding supreme power, sensitive and attentive to the affairs of the world and the Egyptians under his care? The wise, mature symbol of rectitude? If, as seems evident, the audience for royal iconography had widened through the medium of private votive areas at or near temples, such a representation of the king would seem a vivid expression of his attention to a "moral economy," and a most effective legitimizing tool.

*Figure 4.6 Humanity, responsibility, disillusionment: Senwosret III (copyright The British Museum).*

One last note. It has been proposed that kings of the 12th Dynasty deliberately encouraged the proliferation of a bureaucracy, and thereby a middle class loyal to them alone (Hayes 1971; Bourriau 1988, 1991), possibly to provide a buffer of support against the now diverse array of factions within the Egyptian elite – provincial, military, and priestly. By increasing access to the high cultural complex, and promoting an impression of accountability and responsibility to a "moral economy," these kings would have been able to communicate the appearance of accessibility and enhance their legitimation, promoting the sense if not the reality that the lesser and non-elites fully participated in the "natural" order of Egyptian society, and themselves played a role in the maintenance of *ma'at* and the cosmos (Assmann 1989). In this modification of the ideology of order and the role of king and elites within it, accompanied by concessions in previously restricted mortuary and ritual space, it

*Figure 4.7 Senwosret III (photo courtesy of the Metropolitan Museum of Art. Purchase, Edward S. Harkness Gift, 1926. 26.7.1394.)*

may be possible to observe targeted *response* on the part of inner elites not only to accelerating factionalism within their own ranks, but to the growing agency of non-elites (and non-Egyptians) in a changing social, economic, and political landscape.

## Notes

I would like to thank the students and auditors in my course History of Art 437 at the University of Michigan (Winter 1994) "Egyptian Art and Archaeology," whose many thought-provoking questions and comments contributed to the ideas discussed in this paper. Thanks also to Joyce Marcus, John Baines, Terry Wilfong, Carla Sinopoli, Richard Parkinson, and Stephen Quirke, who read and commented upon earlier versions of this paper.

1 This long-held categorization begins some 300 years after the unification of Upper and Lower Egypt, *c*. 3100 BC, following what is called the Early Dynastic Period. As O'Connor demonstrates elsewhere in this volume, increasing data on that formative period have, however, reinforced its continuities with the Old Kingdom.

# 5
# Law courts and the mediation of social conflict in ancient Mesopotamia

NORMAN YOFFEE

### Law and order in social evolutionary theory: an introduction

In recent years social evolutionary theory, at least as it pertains to the rise of ancient states and civilizations, or more generally to the development and nature of profound degrees of inequality in wealth and power, has progressed substantially (Paynter 1989; Brumfiel 1992). Many specific studies fall into either of two categories, largely depending on the data upon which they are based. First there are those investigations that deal with the geographic transformation of a region in which a relatively dispersed settlement pattern becomes an urbanized/ruralized one (e.g., R. McC. Adams 1981; Wright and Johnson 1975; J. Marcus 1976). These studies focus on the creation of a new landscape for social and economic relations and are mainly derived from archaeological reconnaissance studies. Then there are studies that delineate the awesome power of the state and the creation of offices and which are based mainly on textual studies.[1] Although these offices reflect bureaucracies only in the weakest of Weberian senses and urban hierarchies are normally the scenes of intra-city-state competition, many authors have tended to consider the data for new forms of ranking as evidence for centralized political control. In fact, the new offices are important because they provide an arena in which powerful figures – including kin-group leaders – compete for power and superior access to wealth. Both types of studies often use the discourse of modern Western business schools to describe the control mechanisms of ancient states.

Less conspicuous in the literature is the realization that the aforementioned types of studies are inadequate in addressing significant aspects of state formation because they de-privilege much of the most visible archaeological materials. These are the monumental architecture and art which are usually associated in both the public mind and by professional archaeologists with the appearance of the first states. These grand materials are the symbols of the new ideologies of states, that is, the idea that there should be a state, centralized leadership, elites and dependents, powerful and powerless; kings are owed service because they are the guarantors of earthly law and order; since they communicate with the high gods to ensure the continuity of the cosmos, wealth must legitimately accrue to them and to an inner elite who create and preserve the overarching traditions that integrate a differentiated and stratified society. The symbols of these ideologies are everywhere – in decorative arts, architecture, monuments, and in the very construction of space in sites and in buildings (A. Smith 1996). These new ideologies are actively constituted in materials and in texts. They are not mystifications of the political and/or economic order but are the very stuff that allows us to talk about, for example, what makes Mesopotamia Mesopotamia.

Indeed, it is now a commonplace for Mesopotamianists to assert that there is no Mesopotamia in the political sense of the term at all (Yoffee 1995a, 1998). Mesopotamia was a land of city-states, regions, ethnic and linguistic groups. It was rarely the scene of territorial states and when these did occur – in the early Mesopotamian states of Akkade, Ur III, Hammurabi's Babylon (Figure 5.1) – they were unstable, evanescent, illegitimate. Nevertheless, there was a palpable idea that there should be *a* Mesopotamia. This is depicted, famously, in the Sumerian King List (Michalowski 1983), in the arrangement of city-names in Early Dynastic Period city-seals (Yoffee 1993a), and in the competition for control of strategic sites that were centers of holiness and venerability. Whereas kings could and did strive to attain this ideal, they were seldom successful. However, in the various independent city-states and regions, which jealously guarded their own autonomy, and through political vicissitudes of dynastic change of the most radical kind, elites maintained, commented upon, and reproduced a canon of Mesopotamian texts (and a commonality of writing system), iconography, and standards of material wealth. One might conclude, much as Childe did long ago, if for a different prehistoric context, that Mesopotamia created itself. First shaped as a meta-linguistic code through prehistoric regional interactions, Mesopotamia crystallized in the cauldron of state formation and then was remolded repeatedly for the next three thousand years.

| | |
|---|---|
| **Late Uruk–Jemdat Nasr** | *c.* 3300–2900 BC |
| **Early Dynastic** | *c.* 2900–2350 BC |
| **Old Akkadian (Akkade)** | *c.* 2350–2150 BC |
| **Ur III** | *c.* 2050–2000 BC |
| **Old Babylonian** | *c.* 2000–1600 BC |
| **Old Assyrian** | *c.* 1920–1780 BC |
| **Neo-Assyrian** | *c.* 1000–610 BC |
| **Neo-Babylonian** | *c.* 620–539 BC |
| **Achaemenid** | *c.* 539–333 BC |

*Figure 5.1 Chronological table of time periods mentioned in this chapter.*

In this chapter I present a case study of how the ideals of order and law in Mesopotamia were played out in a disorderly world. I discuss a legal case from the Old Babylonian period (*c.* 2000–1600 BC) that shows that newly wealthy elites negotiated their status within the same institutional structures that limited eliteness and restricted the transfer of wealth. Even in conditions of unprecedented economic and social mobility the interplay of order, legitimacy, and wealth followed traditional forms which were reaffirmed and strengthened in the process.

### Law courts and social conflict

No one has written a book about or has devoted an essay to "Mesopotamian law courts and the mediation of social conflict" so coupling these two subjects will seem puzzling to many of the philologists qualified to do so. Almost all studies of Mesopotamian law[2] have been investigations of social rules that are interpreted as legal categories (Schorr 1913; Driver and Miles 1952–1953): theft, homicide, treason, loans, or "harbouring married women" (Driver and Miles 1935). Documents concerning "adjectival law," that is, the mechanisms by which disputes are adjudicated, have been studied mainly according to the thing at issue (*Prozessgegenstand*) or by the description of the "place in the proceedings" (*Stellung im Verfahren*) depicted in the documents (Koschaker 1923: 134).

I have quoted German terms above because historically most scholars of Mesopotamian law have been Germans or were trained in Germany, and Mesopotamian law still flourishes as a subject in Germany. In the early years of this century German legal scholars, virtuously learned in Roman law, were attracted to the study of Mesopotamian law, treating it as an early stage in the development of Western law, and this is still the convention in many German law faculties. Some experts attempted to order Mesopotamian data into formal Western legal categories, in one example following the paragraphs of the German Civil Law Code (see Koschaker 1923: vii). Most of these studies considered Mesopotamian law in light of the Mesopotamian law codes, especially the Code of King Hammurabi of Babylon (Koschaker 1917).

A lively debate, which I can only briefly recapitulate here, concerns whether such formal "codes" had anything to do with law (see M. Roth 1995; Yoffee 1988c for references). On the affirmative side are the legal scholars who regard, for example, the "equitable rules which Hammurabi the able king has established"[3] on a two meter high diorite stela (and written sideways) as case-law for his country (Westbrook 1989). On the skeptical side are those who consider the code as a kind of juridical literature and part of a scholastic tradition, but having little or nothing to do with actual legal decision making. I take, of course, the Golden Mean in the dispute. That is, one can easily see that the so-called "code" of Hammurabi is not made of whole cloth, but has been composed on the basis of real Mesopotamian social behavior; it is hence useful in reconstructing rules and norms. However, it is equally clear that the various "codes" leave out a lot of rules. Even if they echo certain customs, the so-called codes embroider on them and, more importantly, do not speak to the regulation of disputes and conflicts.

A famous example of literary embroidery in the "code" of Hammurabi is "law" no. 21 which states that "If a man breaks into a house, they shall put him to death and hang him in front of that breach." The principle of "mirror punishment" illustrates how, under Hammurabi's putatively just rule – in fact he had just brutally conquered the cities he mentions in the prologue to the cases/laws – all thieves who make breaches in houses will be caught, the evidence of their crimes will be unambiguous, and the penalty will be executed swiftly and serve as a reminder for all to see. Wilcke (1992) has shown, however, that in instances of theft in the time of Hammurabi what robbed home owners want is not the death of the thief but the restitution of their property.

A recent German dissertation (Dombradi 1996) on legal decisions in Old Babylonian trials lists about 350 texts from the time 1900–1600 BC. (This corpus is also treated in an unpublished American dissertation [Fortner 1996].) The author, while not entirely in the German cuneiform law tradition, and in some cases seeking to differentiate herself from it, discusses all previous interpretations of case law (*Prozessrecht*) and refines opinion, with much new data, of the procedures in trials. She delineates (1) the introductory clauses in which one party sues another over an object, (2) the judges' formal acceptance of the case, (3) the examination of claims (through witnesses, documents, oaths), (4) the decision, and (5) the closing statements in which the parties agree not to return to court. The variations of the words used to describe these procedures are arranged chronologically and geographically (in typical dissertational completeness). Important for our purposes are the author's discussions of the *Richterkollegium*, that is, the people called "judges" and the *Körperschaften* ("corporate groups"), who decide cases. These other organizations are called, according to chronological and geographical distinctions, *ālum* ("city"), *kārum* ("port-authority", lit. "quai/harbor"), *puhrum* ("assembly"), *šībūtu* ("elders"), *šībūt ālim* ("elders of the city"), to cite the most common examples. There are also "mixed panels," of judges and port-authority, for example. It is not clear whether "judge" is a professional rank or whether "judges" were simply men of influence, who had shown themselves able to weigh evidence and make sensible decisions (as Dombradi puts it).

In the work of the legal anthropologist Hoebel (1954), who was strongly influenced by the legal realist Karl Llewellyn, trials or "trouble-cases" are the most important "road in the investigation of law-stuff." "Unless a dispute arises to test the principles of law in the crucible of litigation, there can be no certainty as to the precise rule of law for a particular situation, no matter what is said as to what will be or should be done" (Hoebel 1954: 37; see Yoffee 1988c). One could derive from a study of Old Babylonian trials, therefore, an overview of the sorts of cases that actually come to court. We are not interested in social pathologies, of course, but in the normal social tensions and grievances that occur in all societies and which lead to disputes and the need to deal with them. Who are the parties to disputes? How are disputes settled and by whom? How is a local conflict transformed into an arena with an accepted decision-maker and so that decisions do not further exacerbate social divisions and conflict?

## The dispute

I propose to illustrate how such an inquiry might proceed by means of an analysis of one text. Although no one can encapsulate the nature of the dispute and mediation on this basis, it is a particularly interesting document (Figulla 1967, no. 63) and leads to more questions than I can elucidate here. (When Mae West said "too much of a good thing is wonderful," she was probably not referring to this text. Several scholars have commented on the text [e.g. R. Harris [1969], with Charpin [1986] having edited much, but not all of it].) I begin with a translation (Figure 5.2) and append a transliteration.

The following summary is simply a *vade mecum* through the text.

First: Belessunu, whose status as a *nadītu* I shall explain anon, makes Amat-Mamu her heir, literally "the one who follows her estate." The property of Belessunu is then described. These fields are all in the same area, one in which a number of *nadītu*s owned land. Also described is the property in the *gagûm* section of the temple of Shamash in Sippar where Belessunu and other *nadītu*s lived. Belessunu's property in Sippar included a house and two plots of land, two slaves and household furnishings, of which two copper kettles are singled out as particularly valuable (see Reiter 1996 on the value of copper vessels and their commonness in dowries).

Second: "Her pin is set in the wall." This uncommon phrase (used only for a few years during the reign of Samsu-iluna in apposition to the absolutely normal line "from straw to gold" – I owe this interpretation to Claus Wilcke) expresses the transfer of the entire estate of Belessunu to Amat-Mamu, her heir. As long as Belessunu lives, however, she will continue to dwell in her own house and use her goods. As part of the inheritance agreement, Amat-Mamu agrees to support Belessunu

*Figure 5.2 Translation of* CT *47, 63 (including information on envelope [E]).*

On the 20th day of the 9th month, 1736 BC:

I. (1-22)

The inheritance of Belessunu, ***nadītu*** of Shamash, daughter of Manium: Amat-Mamu, ***nadītu*** of Shamash, is her legal successor.

a. (3-16)

5 iku (1 iku=.36 hectare, ca. 1 acre) field in the Puzur-Aba meadow adjoining the land of Sin-naṣir, son of Sin-magir and the field of Dummuqa, daughter of Nur-ilishu, and adjoining the field of Sin-ilishu, son of Uṣiyatum. The bottom side is the ditch of the meadow, the other side is its top. 20 iku field in the Puzur-Aba meadow, adjoining Nur-ilishu, one of the craftsmen (?), and adjoining the field of Belessunu, ***nadītu*** of Shamash, daughter of ... {E=Amat-Shamash and Nishi-inishu, the daughters of the brother of their father}; on the bottom side is the ditch of the meadow, on the other side is the field of Ur-Lugalbanda; 9 iku field, Akbarum meadow, adjoining the field of Munawirrum, son of Awil-ili, and adjoining the field of the ***nadītu*** of Shamash, which is adjoining the field of Sin-eriba, son of Mar-Sippar (E=...of Sin-iqisham, son of Utukam, and the field of Sin-eribam, son of Mar-Sippar). The bottom side is the Nuratum canal, at the top is the red feeder-ditch; 12 iku of field of the U/Pahuṣum meadow ..., adjoining ... At the top ... , at the bottom is the Z/Ṣabum canal. Altogether: 46 iku fields in the upper meadow.

b. (17-22)

1 1/3 sar (1 sar=36m², ca. 324 ft²) roofed property and undeveloped land in the *Gagûm* ("cloister"), adjoining the house of Amat-kallatum and adjoining the house of the daughter of Daqqum; 6 sar of undeveloped land in Great Sippar in Sibitti Street; 1 slave, Sin-mashmash and his brother; 1 slave, Ana-pani-Shamash-nadi, the singer (?); 2 copper kettles.

II. (23-35)

a. (23-26)

All this, her property, her estate, (even) her pin that is sticking in the wall, from straw to gold, everything which Belessunu, daughter of Manium, had or will have belongs to Amat-Mamu, her heir, the daughter of Sin-ili.

b. (26-27)

As long as Belessunu, ***nadītu*** of Shamash lives, Amat-Mamu will hold her property.

c. (28-30)

Amat-Mamu, ***nadītu*** of Shamash, will provide her per year 6 kur (1 kur=300 liters) barley, 12 mina (1 mina=.5 kg) wool allotment, 24 sila (1sila=1 liter) oil allotment; at each of 6 festivals 20 sila wheat, 2 pieces of meat.

d. (31-35)

Amat-Mamu, daughter of Sin-ili, has paid Belessunu's debt of 2/3 mina 5 shekels silver. Belessunu has got out of debt. None of her property will be liable for her debt. Whoever may give her grain or silver shall forfeit her property.

III. (36-40)

After Belessunu gave this inheritance to Amat-Mamu, daughter of Sin-ili, and she had supported her for 2 years, Amat-Shamash, daughter of Ili-iqisha, and Nishinishu, daughter of Anum-pi-Shamash, the daughters of the brothers of her (Belessunu's) father, sued (E=Belessunu) for the field(s) which are according to this tablet.

IV. (40-50)

a. (40-46)

At the gate of Shamash, Zimri-Erra, the *rabiānum* of Sippar and the *kārum* of Sippar examined the tablets concerning the dowry of Belessunu, which her father had given her, the tablets of the inheritance of Naramtum, sister of her father, whose inheritance she had given her, of her own free will (E=she had given her in writing, as it pleased her), and the tablets of the daughters of the brothers of her father, who had sued her.

b. (47-48)

According to her tablets they proved this was her estate, and they gave it to Belessunu.

c. (48-50)

Because Amat-Shamash and Nishinishu had made a baseless claim against her, they imposed the punishment (E=of Shamash) on them, and they gave them a tablet renouncing the claim.

V. (51-66)

a. (51-56)

After they gave them the tablet of renunciation and Belessunu died, Sin-ili deposited for safekeeping in the house of Ikun-pi-Sin, his brother, the inheritance tablet, the original documents of fields and house which Belessunu had given to Amat-Mamu, daughter of Sin-ili, and the tablet of renunciation which the daughters of the brothers of her father had made out.

b. (57)

From the house of Ikun-pi-Sin these tablets disappeared.

c. (58-60)

Sin-ili set the matter before Sin-ishmeanni and the *kārum* of Sippar, and Ikun-pi-Sin testified before Sin-Ishmeanni and the *kārum* of Sippar that these tablets are lost.

d. (61-62)

On the order of Sin-ishmeanni and the *kārum* of Sippar they gave this (very) tablet binding force (lit.

"made live").

e. (63-66)

The inheritance tablet, the original tablet, and/or the tablet of renunciation which Amat-Mamu, daughter of Sin-ili, received from Belessunu--in the house of Ikun-pi-Sin or wherever they may be seen--belong (alone) to Amat-Mamu, daughter of Sin-ili.

VI. (66-69)

In the future, by virtue of this (very) tablet, neither Ikun-pi-Sin, his children, nor the kin of Belessunu, male or female, as many as there may be, will bring claim against Amat-Mamu, daughter of Sin-ili.

VII. (70)

They swore by Shamash, Marduk, and King Samsu-iluna.

VIII. (71-78)

Witnesses:
Sin-Ishmeanni, *rabiānum* of Sippar
Nuratum, son of Ipqu-Annunitum
Ipiq-ilishu *wākil tamkārī*
Akshak-iddinam, son of Itti-Enlil-qinni
Sin-nasir and Warad-Sin, sons of Sin-iddinam
DINGIR-lu-lim, son of Lipit-Ishtar
Sin-iddinam, son of Shamash-illassu
Ikun-pi-Sin, son of Sin-tayyar
Ris-Shamash, son of Imgur-Akshak
Nuratum, son of Ibbi-Ilabrat
Shamash-bani, son of Ipiq-Adad
Ris-Shamash, son of Lushtamar-Sin
Pale-Shamash, son of Shamash-napsheram
Ipqu-Annunitum
Ibbi-Ilabrat, son of Nur-ilishu
Ishkur-mansum, son of Warad-ilishu, Gatekeeper of the *gagûm*
Amat-Shamash, daughter of Sin-iqisha
Nishinishu, daughter, of Anum-pi-sha
Ipiq-Aya, Scribe
IX. (89-90) Date
Month: Kislimu, 20th day
Year: (Samsu-iluna 14) The king [slew] the chief usurper

with grain, wool, and oil (the normal substances listed in such agreements of support). Additionally, at each of six religious festivals Amat-Mamu will provide special offerings. (The brothers of *nadītus* are supposed to provide such offerings, but often do not, as letters of *nadītus* complain.) Amat-Mamu further pays all of Belessunu's outstanding debts; no one can claim any of Belessunu's property as payment for the debts. Belessunu is declared incompetent; no one who loans her any money or goods can expect a return on the loan. (In fact we know from other documents that Amat-Mamu's family was inordinately rich. The father of Sin-ilum, Sin-tayyar [Amat-Mamu's great-grandfather], purchased much land and had four children. One of them, Ikun-pi-Sin, listed among the witnesses to this document, was an important official in the reign of Samsu-iluna, and his son, Muhaddum, was adopted by his sister, Beltani, a *kulmašītu* [another category of woman with certain religious obligations and rights]; another of Ikun-pi-Sin's sisters, Erishti-Shamash, was a *nadītu*.) The father of Sin-tayyar, the great-great grandfather of Amat-Mamu, is also attested. One of his daughters was a *nadītu*. (Rish-Shamash, son of Imgur-Akshak, listed among the witnesses, might be an aged relative of Amat-Mamu.) Amat-Mamu must have been quite young at the time of this document (see Figure 5.3).

Third: After two years in which Amat-Mamu had supported Belessunu according to the agreement they had made, two cousins of Belessunu's (the daughters of her father's brothers) claimed that they should be the legal heirs to Belessunu's fields. Note that they do not sue for the house and property of Belessunu which are in the *gagûm*.

Fourth: At the gate of the Shamash temple in Sippar, Zimri-Erra, the *rabiānum* and the *kārum* (port-authority) of Sippar examine relevant documents. These include (1) the tablets specifying the property that the father of Belessunu had given her; (2) the tablets that specify the property that the aunt (father's sister) of Belessunu had bequeathed to Belessunu; and (3) the tablets of the claimants. Zimri-Erra and the port-authority confirmed that Belessunu had full legal title to the property as described earlier. They further imposed a punishment on the false claimants and issued a document stating that the claimants would not sue over this matter again.

Fifth: After this case had been decided, the father of Amat-Mamu deposited in the house of his brother (i.e., Amat-Mamu's paternal uncle) the original documents which specified the property, certified the inheritance by Amat-Mamu of Belessunu's property, and the quitclaim deed from the first case. These tablets then went missing. The father of Amat-Mamu then went to Sin-ishmeanni, a subsequent *rabiānum* of Sippar, and the port-authority and testified that the tablets were nowhere to be found. At this point Sin-ishmeanni and the port-authority wrote this very tablet as a summary of the other transactions. If the other tablets turn up, they are the property of Amat-Mamu.

Sixth: This very tablet confirms that neither the affines of Amat-Mamu nor the kin-folk of Belessunu have any claim to the property of Belessunu which she had lawfully bequeathed to Amat-Mamu. Seventh: They swear by Shamash and Marduk, the chief gods of Sippar and Babylon, and King Samsu-iluna, son of King Hammurabi, that the aforesaid is true. Eighth is a list of witnesses, in the first position Sin-ishmeanni, *rabiānum* of Sippar and others, officials of the port-authority and *gagûm*. Ninth is the date: January 10th (as it were), 1735 BC.

## Social context of the text: nadītus in the Old Babylonian period

Two central questions require discussion: why did this dispute arise and who were the authorities who settled it? To begin to answer them we must review the history of this time. The Old Babylonian period, *c.* 2000–1600 BC, in which our document is written, follows that of the Third Dynasty of Ur (*c.* 2100–2000), one of the most centralized states in Mesopotamian history.[4] After the collapse of the hyper-bureaucratic state of the Ur III Dynasty, about 2000 BC, rival princes[5] constructed and dissolved alliances, seizing control of palaces, and proclaiming themselves legitimate successors to older royal houses. In the myriad of new contests for independence and dominion, social and economic life became transformed in unprecedented ways, as we may trace in one archive from the minor town of Dilbat (Koshurnikov 1984; Yoffee 1988a).

A stranger rides into town (a little Clint Eastwood music here, please), probably from neighboring Marad, perhaps not an arresting incident, but it is unusual to be able to document such movements in our texts. The stranger bought a house, actually only a room or two, judging from the size of the real estate, with a local Dilbatian; this may have been necessary since the stranger had no kin in Dilbat and thus was unable to secure property that was inalienable to outsiders. From this modest beginning, he bought adjoining structures, consolidating his holdings. He bought and sold real-estate, once being sued for part of a field he had

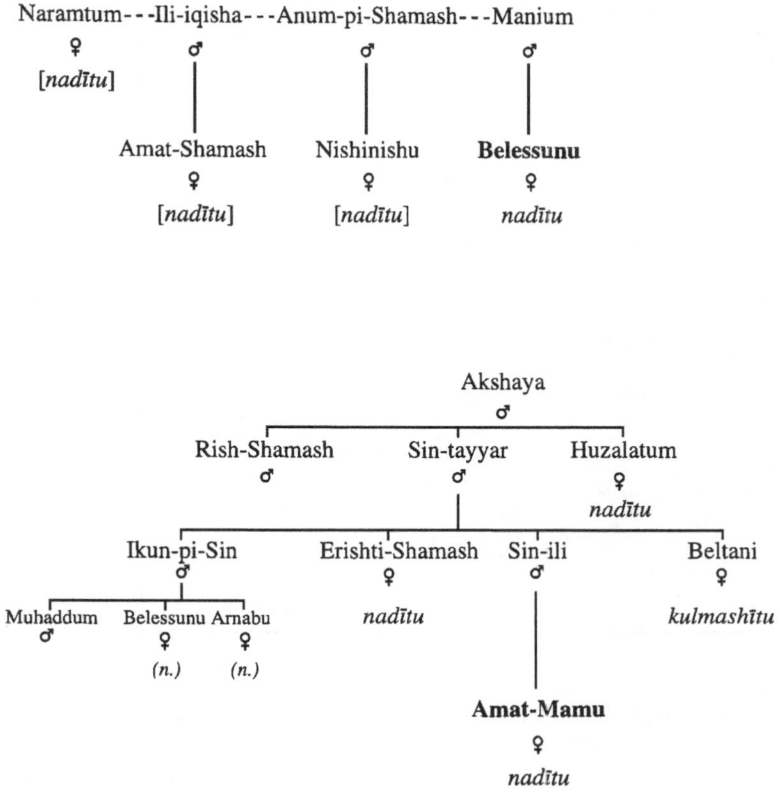


*Figure 5.3 The families of Belessunu and Amat-Mamu.*

mismeasured. When the stranger died, his property was divided among his post-mortem testators under Babylonian norms of partible inheritance. The cleverest of the inheritors succeeded in buying property from his brothers, and he eventually accumulated an enormous landholding in Dilbat, far more extensive than his father's. One sure indication of the status of this son of the stranger is that his daughter was assigned as a *nadītu* woman in the temple of Shamash in the town of Sippar, about 50 kilometers to the northeast (Figure 5.4). A brief discussion of the institution of *nadītu*s, modified but slightly from the extraordinary work of Rivkah Harris (e.g., 1964, 1975; see also Renger 1967), but with some new material, will bring us back to our text.

*Nadītu*s were for the most part elite women, daughters of kings, merchants, and community leaders. As females, they received their inheritance in the form of dowries, since they were inter-vivos testators. They did not marry, however, but were assigned to the *gagûm*-precinct of the temple of Shamash in Sippar – the situation differs in other cities (e.g., Stone 1982) – at an early age, receiving a distinctive name and dedicating their lives to Shamash and his divine spouse Aya. Their dowries consisted in two parts, immovable and movable property (cf. Dalley 1980). The immovable property was real estate – basically houses and fields – and a *nadītu* could not sell this, since it belonged to her brothers and passed at her death to those brothers or their heirs. *Nadītu*s, however, did enjoy usufruct rights on the fields.

With movable property, often described as "ring-money," they bought, sold, and leased land. Gains from these transactions they could bequeath to whom they chose, mainly other, younger *nadītu*s and/or their personal women servants, who were then manumitted upon taking care of the old lady and performing the funerary rites.

The institution of *nadītu*s was established in the early part of the Old Babylonian period and did not outlast that time. It was created precisely in the conditions of political and economic uncertainty that followed the collapse of the Ur III state, a time in which new properties were being accumulated and new problems were

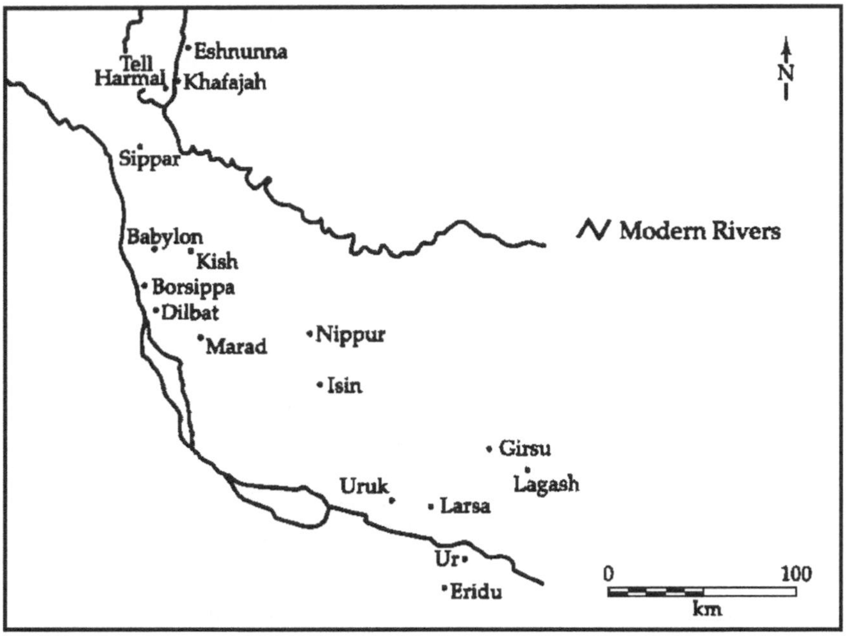


*Figure 5.4 Old Babylonian cities.*

arising of how to keep them together. One partial solution was found by assigning female inheritors to a temple, forbidding them to marry and thus to alienate the family property.

Since *nadītus* (of Shamash in Sippar) did not marry, it had been supposed that they had no children. One documented case, however, shows that sexual activity was not forbidden *nadītus*. When a *nadītu* bore a child, the baby was adopted, as the text says, "fresh from the womb," by the brother of the *nadītu* (Finkelstein 1970). The text further stipulates that the brother must pay the wet-nursing fee for three years (so that his sister may see her son grow to childhood). No father is mentioned in the text for the very good reason that this child will be acknowledged only in the family of the *nadītu* so that his mother's property can pass to him through his uncle's (adopted father's) estate. Legal children of *nadītus*, whose fathers and their kin could be new claimants on the *nadītu*'s family's property, were thus specifically prohibited.[6]

Since I'm telling this as a story, I shall now speculate a bit on the quality of the lives of *nadītus*. In their letters, they portray heartfelt devotion to the gods of the temples in which they lived. They also lived a long time, mostly freed from the rigors of childbirth of normal Mesopotamian women – unless an accident happened – co-residing with about fifty other *nadītus* in their *gagûm*. All of them had been initiated with ceremonial feasts, were given special names that indicated their religious affiliation, and were then ushered into the august presence of the gods.

In case anyone misses the point, let me draw the analogy to medieval English nuns and convents, precisely because this analogy has been criticized as an anachronism and failing to account for the wealth of Old Babylonian *nadītus*. In medieval English cloisters, however, there lived daughters of high-born men, especially well-educated daughters of the newly rich merchant class, who brought dowries with them, in spite of the church's injunction against the exaction of dowries. In practice, few girls' families could afford to send their daughters to a convent. In the latter Middle Ages, it was not uncommon for some nuns to have private incomes, private rooms with maids, and individual disposal of money and goods. Although the celibate ideal was fundamental and the nuns were called to do the work of the Lord, there was widespread evidence of human frailty. While the majority kept their vows, the image in fiction of the priest's mistress being a nun had a basis in reality. Since the church condemned apostasy more than unchastity, however, there was more dishonor in casting aside the veil than in bearing a child (Powers 1922).[7]

At this point in the story, I dare the following unanthropological, unhistorical thought: Old Babylonian *nadītus*, freed from the authority of fathers and husbands, enjoyed productive and interesting careers, interlacing their religious devotions with their business practices. Indeed, their lives may have been more interesting than other Mesopotamian women's, if such a value judgment may be hazarded by a male humanoid, who lives at a distance of 4,000 years and many cultural oceans apart from them. Such at least is the opinion of Eileen Powers, in her comparison of the lives of medieval English nuns to other medieval women, and she at least lived in the same country, shared more or less the same religion, and flourished only 500 or 600 years after the subjects of her inquiry. In Jo Ann McNamara's recent book on medieval nuns (1996), the retreat from the world clearly opened opportunities to women.[8] The most interesting facet of the comparison, in any case, is that both medieval English nuns and Old Babylonian *nadītu*s were often high-born and wealthy women, products of ages in which new wealth and status were being created, and in which new social and economic dislocations were mediated by the most venerable symbols and deeply felt traditions.

### Explication of the text

Why our dispute arose can be elucidated in light of the preceding sketch of the social context in which the dispute arose. First: Belessunu and Amat-Mamu were both *nadītu*s in Sippar, residents of the *gagûm*. Belessunu bequeathed to Amat-Mamu her property, which is presumably that which she accumulated as business transactions using her ring-money. This property was distinct from her inheritance share, which she could not bequeath as she chose and would pass back to her brothers upon her death. Second: the reason for such a bequest to a younger *nadītu* instead of a family member was because the *nadītu*'s brothers often failed to supply proper support for her and because the *nadītu* usually outlived her brothers and was estranged from their heirs. Whereas a *nadītu* also must have developed especially fond attachments to other *nadītu*s, it was clearly to the advantage of a younger *nadītu* to support an aged colleague. Amat-Mamu not only agreed to such support but also paid off the debts of Belessunu.

Third: the daughters of Belessunu's dead brothers laid claim to the fields of Belessunu. Their claim was presumably that these fields were those belonging to their family and upon which Belessunu only had usufruct rights. They did not sue for any of the household property of Belessunu, which she had either accumulated during her lifetime or which was part of the movable property in her dowry. Fourth: the authorities (to be discussed in the next section) verified that the bequest to Amat-Mamu was in order, and the claimants' case was thrown out of the moot. Fifth: All of the above transactions and the dispute had taken place well before this tablet was written. However, the previous documents, which had been deposited in the house of the powerful father's brother of Amat-Mamu, went missing, which fact is declared before the authorities. If the other tablets are found, they shall belong to Amat-Mamu. Presumably the implication is that members of Amat-Mamu's family, likely her own brothers, had stolen the tablets so that they might later establish their own claims to the property that Amat-Mamu had accumulated through this adoption by Belessunu.[9]

Sixth: this very tablet was then drawn up to confirm that none of the kin of Belessunu could claim the fields that had been bequeathed to Amat-Mamu. Furthermore, these fields were not part of the property of the *family* of Amat-Mamu, but were her property to dispose of as she pleases. The property will presumably be passed to a family member, as had occurred in this family for generations. In conclusion, all of this was duly sworn to and witnessed; the document was dated and sealed.

To summarize, we can see from this document, to which could be added numerous, similar if less complicated cases, that the unusual division of the property of *nadītu*s gave ample opportunity for litigation. We now turn to the question of who were the authorities that settled the dispute.

### The resolution of disputes

In our text the *rabiānum* and *kārum* of Sippar examined the evidence and decided the case against the family of Belessunu, and they confirmed that Amat-Mamu has been bequeathed the disputed land. The *rabiānum* was an Old Babylonian official (Stol 1976), literally "headman" of a city or a sub-section of city (e.g., *rabiān babtišu*). Whereas the title might well come from Amorite usage, *rabiānum*s were characteristically found in Old Babylonian cities. In the opinion of Stol (and others but with which I disagree) one sees a transition from the leadership ("sheikh") of Amorite nomads who later settle in cities at which point the *rabiānum* becomes a "burgomeister." In late Old Babylonian documents the *rabiānum* has been seen as a community leader, independent of the crown and sometimes carrying out actions in opposition to the crown's best interests (Yoffee 1977).

The *kārum* was an organization of urban self-government, as Kraus (1982) has described it in the Old

Babylonian period (repeating the opinion of Walther [1917]). In some cities, such as Sippar, the *kārum* often decides cases, while in other cities it was the *puhrum* (e.g., in Nippur), "elders," "elders of the city," or just the "city". In most of the cases in the Old Babylonian period, however, "judges," without any further specification, except as to city, i.e., "the judges of city-name," were the authorities who settle disputes. Sometimes royal officials along with some community organization decided cases in a "mixed" panel. Since some commentators (e.g., Klengel 1960) have regarded these community authorities who settle disputes as Amorite institutions that gradually lose their importance in urban cities and under powerful Mesopotamian kings, I shall briefly describe the history of "the community" and the "assembly" in Mesopotamia (see Liverani 1993b).

In one of the classic articles on early Mesopotamian history, Jacobsen (1943, see also 1957, 1959, 1978–9) argued that secular kingship arose not from sacral auspices, but from community assemblies. He contended that the incessant warfare in the Early Dynastic period resulted in the election or appointment of a war leader. His major source was the poem "Gilgamesh and Akka" (see Roemer 1980; Katz 1993; A. Shaffer 1983; Katz 1995) which refers to a "council of city-elders" (unken-gar-ra ab-ba uru$^{ki}$-na-ka) and a "council of guruš" (guruš being roughly male citizens [although the exact meaning is debated]). Gilgamesh, who wants to go to war against the king of Kish, is rejected by the council of elders, but with the assent of the council of guruš is able to proceed. Numerous commentators have questioned Jacobsen's use of this text and many other literary references to assemblies (e.g. Evans 1958), since it was likely written in the Ur III period, hundreds of years after the events it purports to portray. In fact the copies of the text all come from the Old Babylonian period, when we know that assemblies were significant parts of city-states (see Liverani 1993a: 61, and note 72). Since councils of elders are attested in the third millennium (Westenholz 1984; Wilcke 1970, 1974, 1975) but there is nowhere a "council of guruš," Dina Katz thinks that this second council in "Gilgamesh and Akka" is a literary parallelism, not part of the historical substance of the poem. In light of later evidence of "councils of great and small" in Old Assyrian texts (Larsen 1976) in which only the great meet for certain issues (Veenhof 1995) and of "councils of old and young" in the Neo-Babylonian period (Dandamaev 1981), the reference in "Gilgamesh and Akka" seems less likely to be only a literary parallelism. In fact, Jacobsen reasoned that the many references to assemblies of the gods in Ur III royal hymns and a variety of myths shows that what exists on Earth gets written into Heaven. References to assemblies of the gods, while literary constructs, were not simply inventions.

Diakonoff (1969, 1982) and Gelb (1969, 1979; Gelb, Steinkeller, and Whiting 1991) both pointed to the pre-Sargonic and Sargonic period land-sale documents as logically implying the existence of assemblies. In some of these documents leaders of extended family groups sold their land to elites. These lands were corporately owned, as argued by Diakonoff, since members of the selling lineage (?) witnessed the document and received gifts from the purchaser, usually clothes and other goods, but silver as well. I infer that the sellers never actually moved from their land but became clients of the powerful land purchaser. For Diakonoff the leaders of these social corporations were logically the "elders" of the "assemblies" mentioned in the literary texts.

This fragile evidence for assemblies in the third millennium BC (e.g., Pettinato 1977) is hardly buttressed by the putative words for assemblies (UNKEN) found in lexical texts. The earliest such texts are among the earliest Uruk IV texts we have (Nissen *et al.* 1990; Englund 1994; see Figure 5.5). They exist in many copies: writing was invented, one might think, so that there could be schools. In line 16 of the composite text are the signs GAL UNKEN, which, on the basis of their later readings, could mean "leader of the assembly." This title, however, is found in Uruk archaic administrative texts as well, always concerned with the administration of products in the (palace's?) bureaucracy. The sign UNKEN is in fact a pot, and Robert Englund considers the official title as something like "official in charge of animal fat" (personal communication). The text ED E (Civil 1969) also has the combination GAL UNKEN. In OB proto-LÚ, a continuation of the same lexical tradition, there is GAL-UNKEN-NA and GAL-ZU-UNKEN-NA. The latter title is found in royal correspondence of the Ur III period (Michalowski 1976) and has nothing to do with assemblies. GAL-UNKEN-NA is a royal official, which title is translated into Akkadian as *mu'errum*, and, again, has nothing to do with assemblies. The best third millennium evidence connecting the sign UNKEN to assemblies comes from Ebla (Durand 1989). There [KA] UNKEN = *da-da-mu* is interpreted as *tātamum*, which is practically a synonym for *puhrum* ("assembly") in Old Babylonian Mari texts.

From the Old Assyrian documents at Kanesh, Larsen has inferred not only the existence, but most important

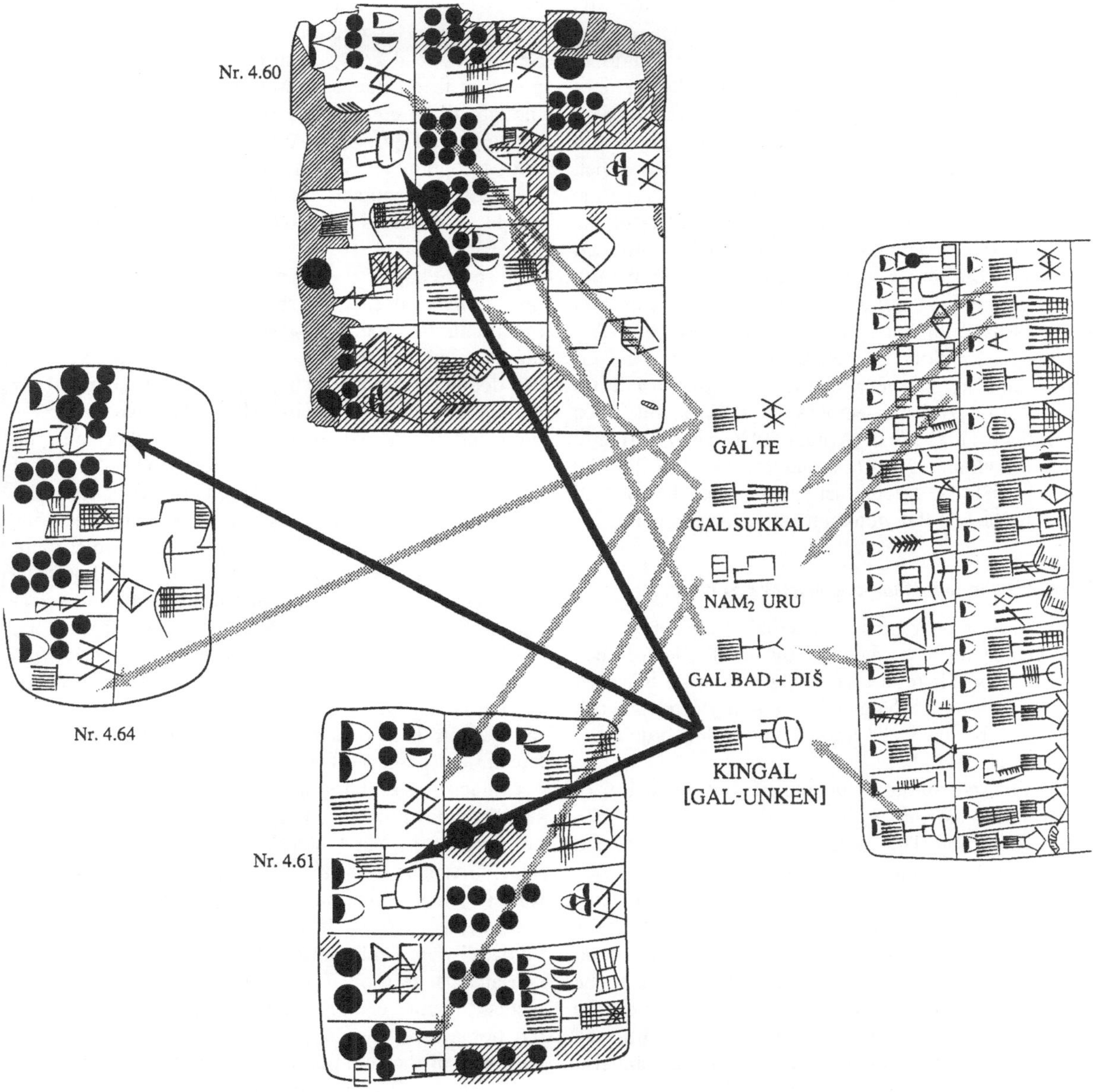


*Figure 5.5* *From the reconstructed "archaic list of professions" with titles also appearing in administrative texts (after Nissen, Damerow, and Englund 1990: 157).*

functions of the assembly at Kanesh and Assur. Its foremost duties were to serve as a court of law and to direct relations with the merchant colonies in Anatolia. The *bīt limmim*, or "house of the eponymy," sometimes called (or part of) the *bīt ālim*, "city-hall," was responsible for choosing from the assembly of "great and small" the nobleman who held the eponym (by which designation the year was named). In Larsen's view the assembly and eponymy consisted in the leaders of the wealthy merchant families and the landed elite. Although royal power certainly existed in the Old Assyrian period, the nobility shared political power with the king and court, at least until Shamshi-Adad's conquest.

I must pass rapidly over references to "elders" in Mari (and Ebla, Klengel 1989), in the realm of the Hittites (Klengel 1965; for "assemblies," see Beckman 1982; Imparati 1991), at Emar (Arnaud 1986, pp. 7–33), and in Neo-Babylonian times (Dandamaev 1981, 1982, 1988; M. Roth 1988, 1989; Kümmel 1979) – since these are all later than the Old Babylonian texts we have to hand.

## Community organizations and dispute resolution

This glance at references to assemblies and elders has not included an assessment of the legal roles of such organizations. There is much to do on this subject. A final word on the ontology of community organizations is therefore bound to be unsatisfactory and little more than a statement of belief.

Ethnologists routinely document the existence of councils and assemblies among the mechanisms for dispute resolution. This cannot be the place, however, to review pioneering and modern studies on the subject. (See, for example, Hoebel 1954; Gluckman 1973; Abel 1973; Moore 1978; Pospisil 1978; and Roberts 1979; for a recent example from classical Athens, see Cohen 1995.) *Arenas* exist in all societies for disputes to be played out; in them conflict can be pursued and the hierarchy of social power (Black 1976) can be affirmed and/or negotiated. Dispute-settlement arenas can also serve as instruments of social change. We may assume that pre-literate (prehistoric) Mesopotamian societies had elders, convened assemblies, and dealt with trouble-cases.

The documented existence of such councils and assemblies in historic Mesopotamia has been normally considered as a residue of these earlier institutions. The evolutionist program that is tacit in this conception finds that "primitive" corporate decision-making authority is progressively replaced by formal legal principles which are then embodied in codes of law and enforced by the professionalized, bureaucratized machinery of the central state. The state used law to reduce the competing power of social groups, especially the traditional legal power of these groups. In Mesopotamia the situation is thought to be complicated by the incessant process of fringe groups, primarily Amorite nomads, moving into the Mesopotamian urban environment, bringing their institutions of councils and assemblies, which over time would attenuate in significance in the civilizational process.

In this chapter I argue for a different, but not necessarily opposite, interpretation of the Mesopotamian data. References to assemblies in the third millennium are admittedly few – in part due to the nature of the documentation, which predominantly comes from temple and palace archives. Also, references to assemblies and the actual existence of assemblies must be related to the quantity of centralization in political establishments. Strongly centralized regimes, such as the Third Dynasty of Ur, do seek to monopolize decision-making, just as they seek to disembed and redistribute resources from local groups. In Mesopotamia, however, large regional states are rare and evanescent. One reference point to the power of Mesopotamian states is the work of Robert Adams who has shown how relatively little irrigation systems injuriously affected the Mesopotamian landscape, at least in comparison with the seriously centralized (Sasanian and early Islamic) states of late antiquity (see Yoffee 1997).

Councils, assemblies, and groups of elders are consistent features of Mesopotamian life and not simply to be reduced to "first steps" (Walther 1917; Lautner 1922; Greengus 1995) in a legal process that ended in a formal court setting with royal officials, or the king himself, as judges. In the Old Babylonian period "judges" were likely those elders who were empowered to render a decision in particular cases. In rare documents, the phrase *dīnam anniam ul ilqū* – occurs, "they did not accept this decision," implying less than iron authority of the community officials over the case. In a series of ten OB divorce cases (all I knew in 1984; Yoffee 1988c; Westbrook 1988), eight are decided by community authorities, the other two by royal officials and the king since royal officials were the major parties involved in the divorce. This example implies that some disputes, by their very nature, were properly resolved through community authorities. Mesopotamian councils, assemblies, and elders did not disappear over time. Indeed, under Achaemenid rulers we read of "councils of Egyptians" (Dandamaev 1982) and "elders of Jews" (Zadok 1979) living in Babylonia, each corporate group apparently empowered to decide cases pertaining to its members.

Whereas Mesopotamia has been classically labeled an example of "oriental despotism," we can see that there were constant tensions between local groups and their authorities and the alternately rising and waning power of centralized states. In considering principles of justice or legal rationality no straightforward evolutionist scenario of a progression from prehistoric assemblies and their traditional leaders as decision makers to the rule of law through written codes can be defended. Mesopotamians – in the example presented here living in the Old Babylonian period – were caught in the web of endemic social conflicts and organizational compromises that were both historically determined and culturally manipulable. If there were norms and rules of behavior in Mesopotamia, which there certainly were, Mesopotamians strove constantly to subvert them. *Nadītu*s, while a distinctive phenomenon of the Old Babylonian period, skillfully managed their new social arrangements within traditional Mesopotamian forms. While the economic *raison d'être* of the institution is clear, it must also be understood in cultural terms. There was no thought to challenge Mesopotamian order and certainly no questioning of the legitimate role of temples, which were enriched by the activities of *nadītu*s and kings alike. The wealth of *nadītu*s signalled the fulfillment, not the reversal, of tradition. Investigation of the arenas in which disputes and settlements occurred – such as this one about the property of a *nadītu* – yields insight into the ever-changing social and political structures of Mesopotamia and the cultural dynamics that shaped them and in turn were shaped by them.

## Notes

I wrote this paper for the University of Chicago Workshop on Ancient Societies' symposium law courts and the mediation of social conflict in the ancient Mediterranean world, March 30, 1996. I am grateful to Martha Roth for the invitation to participate in this symposium. I did the research and writing at the Altorientalisches Seminar/Institut für Vorderasiatiche Archaeologie, Freie Universität Berlin while on sabbatical leave in 1995–1996. I thank the University of Michigan and the Deutscher Akademischer Austauschdienst for their support of this leave and Johannes Renger and Hans Nissen for their hospitality in Berlin. While in Europe I lectured from working drafts of this paper. Mario Fales in Naples (where he was passing through) and especially Claus Wilcke in Leipzig, who thoroughly checked my textual apparatus, provided valuable insights to my understanding of the text. I am glad to acknowledge their friendly advice and criticism.

1 See Yoffee 1995c for a critique of this approach in Mesopotamia.

2 Sometimes called "cuneiform law" ("Keilschriftrecht" [Korošec 1964]) as if the script itself contained legal properties, or all people who wrote in cuneiform script shared common legal traditions that derive from the inventors of the script and hence of Mesopotamian culture in general.

3 Hammurabi *c.* 1755 BC; see M. Roth 1995 for full translation.

4 Subsequently I shall also refer to the foregoing Old Akkadian period, *c.* 2350–2150; the Early Dynastic period, *c.* 2900–2350; and the late Uruk and Jamdat Nasr periods, *c.* 3300–2900 (see Figure 1).

5 Especially Amorites; see Whiting 1987: e.g., texts 6, 7, 9, 11.

6 In a recent article, W. G. Lambert (1992) resumes the discussion of *nadītu*s as prostitutes (the normal term for which is *harimtu*). Certain lexical lists equate various categories of women with *harimtu* (especially *kezertu* and *ugbabtu*), including *nadītu* (in a roundabout way in which *šamuk/htu* = kar-kid (*harimtu*), *šamuktum* = *nadītu*). Lambert considers that *nadītu*s existed after the Old Babylonian period, adducing a solitary, unpublished reference (note 18) to a "late Babylonian ritual for Esagil in Babylon for the month Kislimu ($^{sal}$*na-di-tum*)." Although the Old Babylonian evidence leads Lambert to the conclusion that the *nadītu* is an "investment banker," he cites Finkelstein's discovery that a *nadītu* could have a child, and implies that this shows that *nadītu*s were prostitutes dedicated to the temple. In a recent article Klaas Veenhof (1994) studies new texts in which infant children of *nadītu*s are adopted. Veenhof translates the term *šilip rēmim* ("fresh out of the womb") as "child which had lost its mother prematurely, either in consequence of her death or because she was forced to give it away, to dispose of it since it was unwanted or illegal." In Finkelstein's text and in some of the new texts discussed by Veenhof it is clear that the newly born child of a *nadītu* is adopted by her brother. Finkelstein had argued that it was not sexual congress that was prohibited to *nadītu*s, but that legal children were, since they (or their fathers and other kin) could then claim the *nadītu*'s family's property. In one of Veenhof's texts, however, it is a man who sells the newly born child into adoption. This occurs presum-

ably because the *nadītu* mother had died in giving birth, and thus the sale of his son confirms the father's formal renunciation of any claim to the *nadītu*'s family's estate. It is difficult, but perhaps not impossible, to believe that the father of a prostitute's (or, a woman having sexual congress as part of a ritual) child could claim a share in her estate. For a recent, though idiosyncratic review of the evidence and literature on "cultic" prostitution in Mesopotamia, see Henshaw (1995).

7 This analogy to medieval nuns puts C. Janssen's discussion of "Samsu-iluna and the Hungry *nadītums*" (1991) in sociological context. The text she cites is one of a number of school copies (some dating to more than 100 years after the actual date of its composition) containing two directives from King Samsu-iluna to a variety of people, the *kārum* of Sippar and the judges of Sippar-Amnanum, *sanga* priests, overseer of the *nadītus*, the doorkeepers of the *gagûm*. The first directive relates that the people of Sippar had encloistered their daughters but then didn't give them sufficient food. The king orders that the fathers and brothers of *nadītus* must guarantee in writing that they will support their *nadītu* relatives. The second directive orders that if a man has a debt, the creditor shall not be able to seize property of the *nadītu* relative of the debtor. Whereas Janssen meditates on the possible reasons for the impoverishment of *nadītus* during the period of Samsu-iluna, Powers shows that it was quite normal for many medieval nuns to suffer want in the cloister. "In the history of the medieval nunneries of England there is nothing more striking than the constant financial straits to which they were reduced" (Powers 1922: 161). Janssen considers that the institution of *nadītus* was coming asunder in the period of Samsu-iluna and that the reference to the hungry *nadītus* being given food from the stores of "our lord" refers to Samsu-iluna himself. "Our lord," however, probably refers to Shamash, patron deity of the temple in which the *gagûm* is located, which storage house must bail out *nadītus* whose families were not providing them with the required support. There is no necessary or logical conclusion that "hungry *nadītus*" imply crisis conditions in the *gagûm*.

8 McNamara argues that stories of salacious nuns are constructions by others, not the nuns themselves. Nuns themselves speak convincingly in defense of chastity, and chastity indeed is empowering, allowing scholarly and artistic freedom but whose creative intensity could also make convents into emotionally risky places where hysteria and flagellation were far from uncommon.

9 I owe this observation to Mario Fales.

*Appendix: Transliteration of* CT *47, no. 63 (E=envelope; major differences from tablet are noted).*

1. ap-lu-ut Be-le-sú-nu LUKUR $^{d}$UTU DUMU.SAL Ma-ni-um

2. $^{I}$GEMÉ-$^{d}$Ma-mu LUKUR $^{d}$UTU DUMU.SAL Sin-DINGIR

(E= $^{I}$A-ma-a]t-$^{d}$Ma-mu)

3. re-di-it wa-ar-ka-ti-ša 5 GÁN A.ŠÀ A-GÀR Puzur$_{4}$-$^{d}$A-ba$_{4}$

4. i-ta A.ŠÀ $^{d}$EN+ZU-na-sir DUMU $^{d}$Sin-ma-gir ù A.ŠÀ Du-um-mu-qá

5. DUMU.SAL Nu-úr-ì-lí-šu ù i-ta A.ŠÀ Šu-ì-lí-šu DUMU Ú-ṣi-ia-tum

6. SAG.BI.1.KAM.MA a-tap A.GÀR SAG.BI.2.KAM.MA SAG.NI

7. 2 0 GÁN A.ŠÀ A.GÀR Puzur$_{4}$-$^{d}$A-ba$_{4}$ i-ta Nu-úr-ì-lí-šu ša KIN(?)$^{hi.a}$

8. ù i-ta A.ŠÀ Be-le-sú-nu LUKUR $^{d}$UTU DUMU.SAL (blank)

(E= ù i-ta GEMÉ-$^{d}$UTU ù Ni-ši-i-ni-šu DUMU.SAL ah-hi a[bi-ša])

9. SAG.BI.1.KAM a-tap A.GÀR SAG.BI.2.KAM A.ŠÀ Ur-$^{d}$LUGAL.BÀN.DA

10. 9 GÀN A.ŠÀ A.GÀR Ak-ba-rum(E=-ri) i-ta A.ŠÀ Mu-na-wi-rum DUMU LÚ-DINGIR

11. ù i-ta A.ŠÀ LUKUR $^{d}$UTU ša i-ta A.ŠÀ $^{d}$EN+ZU-eri-ba DUMU DUMU-ZIMBIR$^{ki}$

(E= [ù i-ta A.ŠA $^{d}$E]N+ZU-i-qí-ša-am DUMU $^{d}$UTU-KAM ù A.[ŠÀ

12. SAG.BI.1.KAM.MA $^{id}$Nu-ra-tum SAG.BI.2.KAM E Sa-mu-um

13. 12 GÁN A.ŠÀ A.GÀR Ú/PA(?)-hu-ṣum$^{ki}$

14. i-ta (blank)

15. SAG.BI.1.KAM (blank) SAG.BI.2.KAM ID Za-bu-um

16. ŠU.NIGIN 46 GÁN A.ŠÀ A.GÀR re-ša-am (E=URU x[ ])

17. 1 1/3 SAR É.DÙ.A ù KANKAL i-na GÁ.GI.A$^{ki}$ (E=gá-gi-im)

18. DA E GEME-kal(E=ka-al)-la-tim ù DA É DUMU.MUNUS Da-qum

19. 6 SAR É KANKAL i-na ZIMBIR$^{ki}$ GAL i-na SILA $^{d}$IMIN.BI

20. 1 SAG.ÌR $^{d}$EN+ZU-ma-aš-ma-aš ù ŠEŠ.NI

21. 1 SAG.ÌR A-na-pa-ni-$^{d}$UTU-na-di NAR(?)

22. 2 $^{urudu}$ŠEN$^{hi.a}$ mi-im-ma an-nu-um bu-šu-ša wa-ar-ka-sà

23. ṣú-(E=ul-)lu-ša ša i-na i-ga-ri-im za-aq-pa-at

24. is-tu pé-e a-di GUŠKIN ša Be-le-sú-nu DUMU.SAL Ma-ni-um

25. ir-šu-ú ù i-ra-aš-šu-ú ša GEMÉ-$^{d}$Ma-mu-ma a-pil-ti-ša

26. DUMU.SAL Sin-DINGIR a-di Be-le-sú-nu LUKUR $^{d}$UTU ba-al-ṭà<-at>

27. mi-im-ma (E=-mu) ša qá-ti GEMÉ-$^{d}$Ma-mu ú-ka-al-ma

28. i-na MU.1.KAM 6 ŠE GUR 12 MA.NA SÍG.BA

29. 2 BÁN 4 SILÀ Ì.BA 6 EZEN$^{hi.a}$ 2 BÁN ZÌ.DA$^{hi.a}$

30. 2 UZU.TA.A $^{1}$GEMÉ(E=A-ma-at)-$^{d}$Ma-mu LUKUR $^{d}$UTU DUMU.SAL Sin-DINGIR i-pa-aq-qí-sí

(E= a-na Be-le-sú-nu i-na-ad-di-[in])

31. 2/3 MA.NA 6 GÍN KÙ.BABBAR hu-bu-li $^{1}$Be-le-sú-nu

32. $^{1}$GEMÉ(E=A-ma-at)-$^{d}$Ma-mu DUMU.SAL Sin-DINGIR i-pu-ul

33. $^{1}$Be-le-sú-nu ú-ul uh-ta-ba-al

34. mi-im-mu-ša an-nu-um a-na hu-bu-lí-ša ú-ul iz-za-az

35. ša še-a-am ù KÙ.BABBAR i-qí-pu-ši i-na mi-im-mu-ša (E=-š[i?]) i-te-el-li

36. iš-tu Be-le-sú-nu ap-lu-sà an-ni-tam a-na GEMÉ(E=A-ma-at)-$^{d}$Ma-mu

37. DUMU.SAL Sin-DINGIR id-di-nu-ma MU.2.KAM i-pí-ru-ši

38. $^{1}$GEMÉ-$^{d}$UTU DUMU.SAL Ì-lí(E=$^{d}$EN+ZU)-i-qí-ša (E=ù) $^{1}$Ni-ši-i-ni-šu DUMU.SAL An-pí-$^{d}$UTU

39. DUMU.SAL$^{meš}$ a-ah-hi a-bi-ša a-na A.ŠÀ-am ša pí-i ṭup-pí

40. an-ni-im (E=a-na Be-le-sú-nu) ir-gu-ma-ma (E=$^{I}$Zi-im-ri-e-ra-ah ra-bi-a-an ZI[IMBIR$^{ki}$] ù kar ZIMBIR$^{ki}$ i-na KÁ $^{d}$UTU) ṭup-pa-at nu-du-ni $^{I}$Be-le-sú-nu (E=LUKUR $^{d}$UTU)

41. ša a-bu-ša id-di-nu-ši-im (E=ma-la ŠÀ-ša ú-ša-am-ṣú-ú-ši) ṭup-pa-at ap-lu-ut

42. $^{I}$Na-ra-am-tum a-ha-at a-bi-ša

43. ša ap-lu-sà id-di-nu-ši-im-ma ma-li ŠÀ-ša ma-ṣí-a-at (E=[a-šar] e-li ša ṭà-bu)

44. (E=ap-lu-sà na-da-nam iš-ṭú-ru-ši) ù ṭup-pa-at DUMU.SAL$^{meš}$ ah-hi a-bi-ša sa ir-gu-ma-ši-im

45. $^{I}$Zi-im-ri-E-ra-ah ra-bi-a-an ZIMBIR$^{ki}$

46. ù KAR ZIMBIR$^{ki}$ i-na KÁ $^{d}$UTU i-mu-ru-ma

47. a-na pí-i (E=KA) ṭup-pa-ti-ša mi-im-ma-ša an-ni-a-am ú-bi-ir-ru-ma

48. a-na Be-le-sú-nu id-di-nu (E=ú-bi-ir-ru) aš-šum GEMÉ-$^{d}$UTU ù Ni-ši-i-ni-šu

49. i-na la i-di-im ir-gu-ma-ši-im ṣe-er-tam (E=ṣe-re-et $^{d}$UTU) i-mi-du-ši-na-ti

50. ù ṭup-pí la ra-ga-mi-im ú-še-zi-bu-ši-na-ti

51. iš-tu ṭup-pí la ra-ga-mi-im ú-še-zi-bu-ši-na-ti

52. ù Be-le-sú-nu a-na ši-ma-ti-ša il-li-ku

53. ṭup-pí ap-lu-tim ṭup-pa-at um-ma-tim ša A.ŠÀ-im ù É

54. ša Be-le-sú-nu a-na GEMÉ-$^{d}$Ma-mu DUMU.SAL Sin-DINGIR id-di-nu

55. ù ṭup-pí la ra-ga-mi-im ša DUMU.SAL$^{meš}$ ah-hi a-bi-ša šu-zu-ba

56. $^{Id}$Sin-DINGIR [a-na] ma-ṣa-ar-tim i-na É I-ku-un-KA-Sin a-hi-su i-zi-ba

57. ṭup-pa-tum ši-na i-na É I-ku-un-KA-Sin ih-li-qá-ma

58. $^{I}$Sin-DINGIR ma-har Sin-iš-me-a-ni u KAR ZIMBIR$^{ki}$ iš-ku-<un>-ma

59. $^{I}$I-ku-un-KA-Sin ki-ma ṭup-pa-tum ši-na hal-qá-a

60. [a-na] Sin-iš-me-a-ni u KAR ZIMBIR$^{ki}$ iq-bi

61. [a-na] qá-bé-e Sin-iš-me-a-ni u KAR ZIMBIR$^{ki}$

62. ṭup-pa-am (E=ṭup-pa-šu) an-ni-a-am ú-ba-al-li-ṭú-ma

63. ṭup-pí ap-lu-tim ṭup-pi um-ma-tim ù ṭup-pí la ra-ga-mi-im

64. ša GEMÉ-$^{d}$Ma-mu-ma DUMU.SAL $^{d}$EN+ZU-DINGIR it-ti Be-le-sú-nu la-qí-a-at

65. i-na É I-ku-un-KA-Sin ù e-ma in-na-ma-ra

66. ša GEMÉ-$^{d}$Ma-mu-ma DUMU.SAL Sin-DINGIR U$_{4}$.KÙR.ŠÈ ša pí-i ṭup-pí an-ni-im

67. $^{I}$I-ku-un-KA-Sin DUMU$^{meš}$-su ù ni-šu-ut Be-le-sú-nu

68. NITA ù SAL ma-li i-ba-aš-šu-ú a-na GEME-$^{d}$Ma-mu DUMU.SAL Sin-DINGIR
69. ú-ul i-ra-gu-um
70. MU $^{d}$UTU $^{d}$AMAR.UTU ù Sa-am-su-i-lu-na LUGAL it-mu-ú
71. IGI Sin-iš-me-a-ni ra-bi-a-an ZIMBIR$^{ki}$
72. IGI Nu-ra-tum DUMU SIG-An-nu-ni-tum
73. IGI SIG-ì-lí-šu UGULA DAM.GÀR$^{meš}$
74. IGI Akšak$^{ki}$-i-di-nam DUMU KI-$^{d}$EN.LÍL-qí-in-ni
75. IGI Sin-na-ṣir ù ÌR-Sin DUMU$^{meš}$ Sin-i-di-nam
76. IGI DINGIR-lu-lim DUMU Li-pí-it-Ištar
77. IGI Sin-i-di-nam DUMU $^{d}$UTU-KASKAL.KUR-su
78. IGI I-ku-un-KA-Sin DUMU Sin-ta-ia-ar
79. IGI Ri-iš-$^{d}$UTU DUMU Im-gur-Akšak$^{ki}$
80. IGI Nu-ra-tum DUMU I-bi-$^{d}$NIN.ŠUBUR
81. IGI $^{d}$UTU-ba-ni DUMU SIG-$^{d}$IŠKUR
82. IGI Ri-iš-$^{d}$UTU DUMU Lu-uš-ta-mar-Sin
83. IGI Pa-le-e-$^{d}$UTU DUMU $^{d}$UTU-na-ap-še-ra-am
84. IGI SIG-An-nu-ni-tum
85. IGI I-bi-$^{d}$NIN.ŠUBUR DUMU Nu-ur-ì-lí-šu
86. IGI $^{d}$IŠKUR-MA.AN.SUM DUMU ÌR-ì-lí-šu
87. IGI GEMÉ-$^{d}$UTU DUMU.SAL Sin-i-qí-ša IGI Ni-ši-i-ni-šu DUMU.SAL AN-pí-ša
88. IGI SIG-$^{d}$A-a DUB.SAR
89. ITI GAN.GAN.È U.20.KAM
90. MU LUGAL IM.GI$_{4}$ GÚ.BAR.RA.NA

# 6
# High culture, Mesoamerican civilization, and the classic Maya tradition

ROSEMARY A. JOYCE

## Introduction

John Baines and Norman Yoffee (1998; chapter 2 in this volume) have proposed a model with interesting analytical possibilities for exploring sociopolitical complexity cross-culturally, and they use that model to specifically examine the contrasts and similarities in the Egyptian and Mesopotamian cases. My goal is to consider implications of the general model for the case of Mesoamerica. Having suggested some of the ways that the model can fruitfully redirect research on the initial development of Mesoamerican civilization, I will turn briefly to the comparative dimension, using the Maya subtradition as my example.

## Aspects of the model: order, legitimacy, and wealth

At the risk of radically simplifying an elegant and densely detailed argument, I would like to identify a few key concepts that suggest significant dimensions of variation that are implicit in the model proposed by Baines and Yoffee (Figure 6.1). Their model fundamentally relates the establishment of order to the creation of ideological arguments for political legitimacy, and to the definition of standards of economic value, resulting in the possibility of recognizing certain possessions as wealth. Wealth and legitimacy, Baines and Yoffee argue, facilitate the imposition of order on the phenomenal world, an order that is commonly presented as an instantiation of cosmic order uniquely perceived by an elite. Order is materially embodied in high culture, and high culture is justified as required to maintain cosmic order.

Cosmic order needs to be maintained through the actions of humans due to its inherent fragility. Because of the close relationship between cosmic order and political and economic order, fragility is also typical of these orders, which are underwritten by the establishment of standards of wealth and legitimacy. Fragility of order, presented as a feature of the cosmos, requires the constant support and expansion of order, achieved through the material re-expression of order in high culture.

Order, legitimacy, and wealth are defined by elites, who use their legitimate standing to authorize definitions of high culture and their special access to wealth to directly support the material forms of high culture. The relations between these three concepts imply that order results from control of wealth and control of the definition of legitimacy. But to an observer within the system, this directionality is reversed: order authorizes legitimacy which results in wealth.

While Baines and Yoffee do not make the point explicit, high culture embodies in distinct ways two separate spheres, the economic and the ideological, wealth and legitimacy. The elite definition of high culture requires identification of features that are expensive (requiring wealth for their creation) and others that are exclusive (requiring legitimacy for their use). It is these dual dimensions that frame the creation of high culture by elites.

As a pragmatic matter, then, under this model the emergence of civilization involves the creation and promotion of enduring categories of value, covering both what may be regarded as expensive and what may be regarded as exclusive. The potential utility of a model that places the creation of standards of value at the center of the emergence of civilizations for understanding the three millennia of continuity covered by the term Mesoamerica is immediately apparent. Mesoamerican societies, politically independent, organizationally diverse, and changing through time, are nonetheless differentiated from others by continuity in the use of particular materials as wealth and in the assertion of particular grounds for legitimacy. I turn now to these topics.

## Mesoamerican civilization

Mesoamerica (Figure 6.2) was never politically unified. Like Mesopotamia in this regard, it encompassed a set of what political scientists call anarchic states-systems engaging in "band-wagon" and balancing behaviors that created shifting political alliances through time

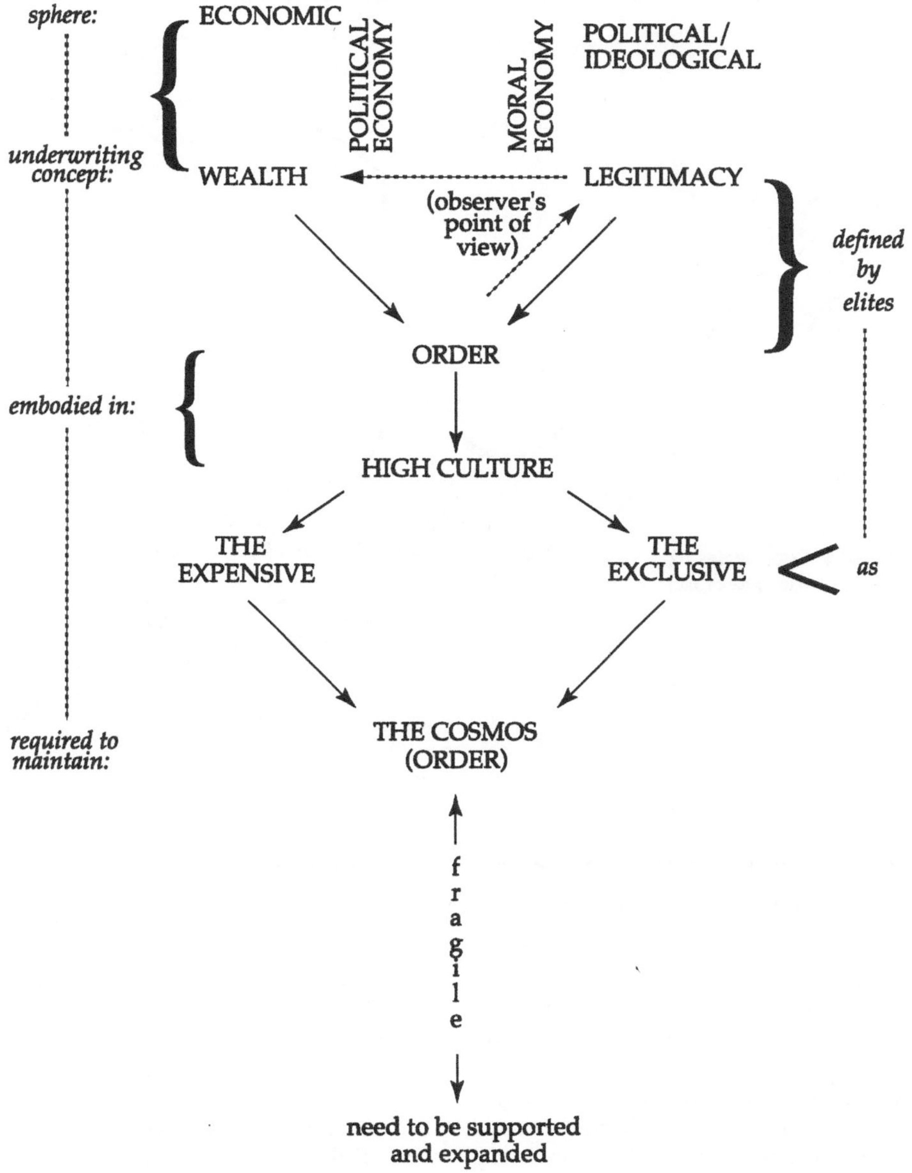


*Figure 6.1 Schematic outline of Baines and Yoffee model.*

(Almazan 1994). Mesoamerica was originally defined as a "culture area" by Paul Kirchhoff in 1943 on the basis of a trait list derived from descriptions of polities encountered in the area of modern Mexico and Guatemala by Europeans in the sixteenth century (Kirchhoff 1968). The trait-list approach has serious limitations, due to its implicit assumptions of long-term stability that archaeological research clearly falsifies. However, archaeologists found Mesoamerica to be a useful concept, envisaging it as an "area co-tradition" (Willey and Phillips 1958), made up of cultural traditions with time-depth within a bounded area. Similarly, linguists have been able to treat Mesoamerica as a linguistic area in which, as a result of intensive contact between

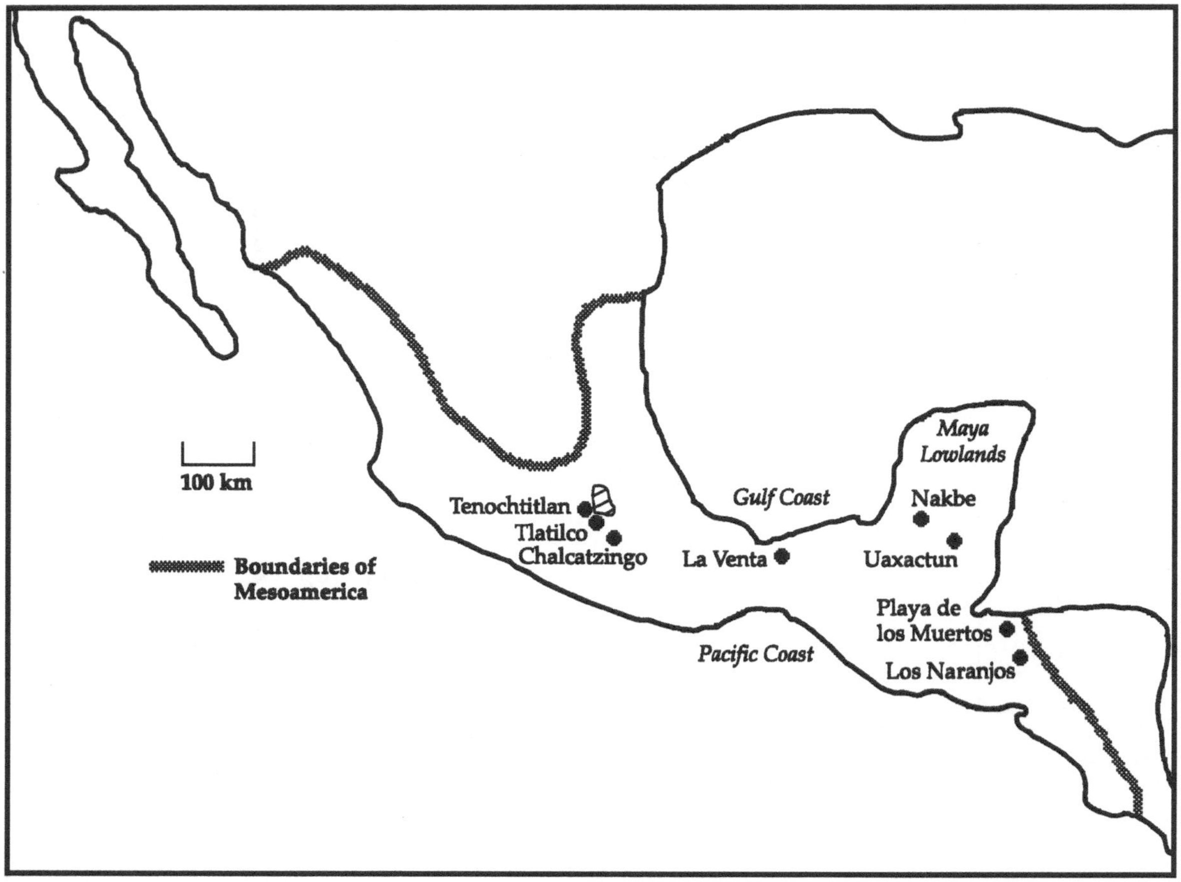


*Figure 6.2 Map of Mesoamerica with places mentioned in the text.*

speakers of distinct languages, convergence can be seen in phonetic, grammatical, and semantic features (Campbell 1976; Campbell, Kaufman, and Smith-Stark 1986).

The traits Kirchhoff selected ranged from basic religious concepts to details of body ornament and costume. They covered economic, political, social, and religious domains and crossed political and linguistic boundaries. But the vast majority of traits diagnostic of Mesoamerican civilization can be seen as expressions of a common high culture propagated by social elites (Figure 6.3): exclusive practices in cuisine, costume, and building; exclusive and expensive ceremonies; and the creation of historical documents.

Sophie Coe (1994) has provided an outstanding overview of the importance of specific preparations of key foods in creating and maintaining Mesoamerican high culture. Chia, cacao, corn, and meat hunted with blow guns – the principal foods whose production characterizes Mesoamerica, according to Kirchhoff's trait list – were among the raw materials transformed by specific preparations into markers of difference between elites and others. Similarly, Patricia Anawalt (1981) has demonstrated the crucial significance of the marking of social distinctions through costume, the focus of a large number of other traits singled out by Kirchhoff. This account omits only two of his core Mesoamerican features, periodic markets and the use of weapons made of wooden clubs with embedded obsidian blades. I would argue that the latter trait is essentially a form of elaborate costuming, not (as it is typically considered) a technological response to the requirements of warfare. The conduct of markets in sixteenth-century Mesoamerica, while clearly serving economic functions, was also thoroughly embedded in and conditioned by the prior existence of a shared set of values, explored in

| GENERAL PRACTICE | SPECIFIC TRAITS |
|---|---|
| Cuisine | Blow guns with clay pellets<br>Cacao, chocolate<br>Chia cultivation<br>*Chinampa* agriculture<br>Corn processed with lime and ground<br>Digging stick |
| Exclusive costumes | Labrets<br>One-piece warrior costumes<br>Polished obsidian ornaments<br>Pyrite mirrors<br>Rabbit hair used in weaving<br>Sandals with heels<br>Turbans |
| Ceremonies | 13 used as ritual number<br>(ballgame) ball courts with rings<br>Human sacrifice<br>Paper and rubber used in ritual<br>(burial and sacrifice) stepped pyramids<br>*Volador* ritual (participants suspended from central pole) |
| Exclusive buildings | Ball courts with rings<br>Stepped pyramids<br>Stucco floors |
| Writing history | Books of bark paper and deerskin<br>Mathematics with place notation<br>Writing<br>Year of 18 months of 20 days plus 5 extra days |

*Figure 6.3 High cultural practices implied by Mesoamerican traits (after Kirchhoff 1968).*

detail below, which are part of a Mesoamerican civilizational order. Even the features that characterize Mesoamerica as a linguistic area may be attributable to the development of specific forms of the verbal arts that were part of Mesoamerican high culture, both as oral traditions and written literature (compare Baines and Yoffee, chapter 2 in this volume).

As a civilization, Mesoamerica must be conceptualized in Baines and Yoffee's terms as an order negotiated by elites, legitimated by the wealth of an inner elite. Mesoamerican civilization thus should have a beginning point close to coincident with the earliest polities of recognizably Mesoamerican form. Willey (1966: 78) expresses what is perhaps the consensus of specialists in Mesoamerica, identifying its coalescence with the time period, around 2000 BC, when village life dependent on corn agriculture took form in the area of Central America that extends from Central Mexico to Guatemala. This argument draws on Kirchhoff's identification of Mesoamerica as the locus of a specific agricultural system centered on maize, privileging one part of the economic domain in giving specific character to the civilization. Certainly, Mesoamerica could not exist as a separate civilization prior to these developments, but maize agriculture, shared with culture areas both north and south, is not one of the more distinctive parts of the Mesoamerican cultural complex. In contrast, what is made of maize agriculture, both in terms of the elaboration of a unique cuisine, and of mythologies in which the survival of maize gods was attributed to the actions of elites and their predecessors, *is* part of a Mesoamerican civilizational order (e.g., S. D. Coe 1994; Taube 1985, 1989; Monaghan 1990).

As Baines and Yoffee (this volume) note, many aspects of high culture are not regularly preserved in archaeological assemblages, and among these would be the first traces of the ideology and cuisine that made maize agriculture specifically Mesoamerican in character. Distinctive, visible, material features of the Mesoamerican civilizational order include certain kinds of public architecture, notably monumental platforms; the employment of relief carving as a medium for public and semi-public political imagery; and the use of a restricted range of materials (especially jade) to produce costume ornaments and sumptuary goods. These features crystallized between about 1500 BC and 500 BC as unprecedented, radical innovations, a punctuated shift like those identified by Baines and Yoffee (1998) in Egypt and Mesopotamia. While innovations were made in each, no later polity recognizable as Mesoamerican lacked its own variants of these features.

I have elsewhere suggested that these developments constituted a Formative revolution which partially circumscribed the choices open to later Mesoamerican elites that attempted to forge their own civilizations (Joyce and Grove 1999). Following the arguments proposed by Baines and Yoffee, this implication stems not merely from the limiting force that initial steps toward political complexity had on polities claiming legitimacy through successorship, but more significantly from the possibilities in the original definition of order that were embodied in the material media we recover archaeologically. The creation of particular *kinds* of wealth and legitimacy itself gave order to Mesoamerican civilization. Later successor polities worked within a history framed by these initial developments, a history in which the difference between ideal order and its realization in the present was a reminder of the fragility of order (compare Baines and Yoffee, this volume).

| Dates in years | Period |
|---|---|
| 1200–900 BC | Late Early Formative |
| 900–400 BC | Middle Formative |
| 400 BC–AD 250 | Late Formative |
| AD 250–930 | Classic |
| AD 930–1521 | Postclassic |

Note: There is no single archaeological chronology that is employed by all archaeologists for all of Mesoamerica, but a broad division into Formative (or Preclassic), Classic, and Postclassic periods is generally recognized. Transition dates will vary depending on the region referenced and on specific criteria employed by different authors. This chart employs the terminology and approximate dates for the Formative period Olmec societies of the Gulf Coast of Mexico for the early part of the chronology, and the terminology and dates for Maya societies for the Late Formative through Postclassic. Maya archaeology often uses "Preclassic" in place of Formative. The beginning and ending dates for the Maya Classic period are based on the calendar used by Maya Classic polities. The ending date for the Postclassic corresponds to the conquest of Aztec Tenochtitlan by Spanish forces.

*Figure 6.4 Chronology of Mesoamerica.*

## The expensive and the exclusive in Mesoamerican civilization

Of the three concepts central to the model, wealth is most palpable, and I thus begin my discussion with it. Baines and Yoffee (1998: 213) describe wealth as a product of the "division and administration of society," and they see the possibility of exploiting great distances to generate wealth as a byproduct of "the organizational capacities of the new social forms" in early stratified societies. These statements could be taken to imply that wealth is used here simply as an alternative for economic "surplus," leaving aside the issue of formalization of value. That this is an unintended implication is suggested by later statements that "the acceptance of agreed *measures* of wealth and the creation of storable and to some extent convertible forms of it transform its social potential" (Baines and Yoffee 1998: 253; my italics). Indeed, the idea of evaluation is basic to classic definitions of wealth in economic anthropology, as the "total of desirable (i.e. valuable) goods, both social and material . . . In real life it is highly variable from time to time and person to person. That which is scarce and desirable and hence wealth to one person is not wealth to another" (Schneider 1974: 256). We can begin an examination of the formation of Mesoamerican civilization, then, with the question of how and in what forms economic surplus was embodied in hierarchies of value that allowed the definition of "the expensive" and the measurement of relative wealth.

In the sixteenth century, Spanish sources recorded three kinds of materials as widely used standards of value and exchange in Mesoamerica, equating them with European currencies. These were finely woven cotton cloth, cacao beans, and jade beads (Durand-Forest 1967, 1971, 1980: 23–24). Sixteenth-century vocabularies of the Nahuatl language reveal the moral value of the Aztec exchange system in which these goods circulated (compare Parry and Bloch 1989; Toren 1989: 144–154; Sallnow 1989: 221–228). The dictionary compiled by Fray Alonso de Molina (1970), originally published in 1555 and 1571, includes one set of terms for trading, goods, the trader, and the marketplace itself, with no related word for currency. The definitions of these terms center on the exchange of one thing for another with which it is equivalent, following moral guidance offered by proverbial knowledge. The same root serves as the basis for the verb for "to marry." The marketplace itself is described as a scene of social activity, the site of "*ferias*," a place through which to walk. The moral nature of marketplace exchange is emphasized by terms for the violation of expectations, with selling for more than a fair price described with a term which also means to envy or be angry at someone. Selling something for less than its worth is described with the same term used for taking away a privilege or office, or reducing the tribute offered. The moral nature of the marketplace in Aztec society is amply illustrated in longer Nahuatl texts recorded in the sixteenth century by Bernardino de Sahagún (1954, 1961), which make the role of the nobility in ensuring the morality of exchange explicit. In market exchange, two items, cloth and cacao, represented the fundamental standards of value whose legitimacy was ensured by nobles.

Cloth was particularly important as a tribute good (Brumfiel 1996, 1997; Hicks 1991, 1994), cacao was employed as a ceremonial drink, and jade beads formed costume ornaments worn by nobles. Regardless of their status as actual currencies, the use of these goods as standards of value raises interesting issues about the nature of wealth in Mesoamerica. The consumption of perishable forms of wealth, cloth, and cacao, reiterated both their expensive nature and the legitimate privilege of unlimited access to wealth on the part of elites (compare Baines and Yoffee, this volume). Cloth, jade, and cacao all saw use in costume and ceremonial practices in which non-elite participation was limited and carefully controlled. At the same time, these materials did form part of non-elite life at certain marked points, and thus they did not, of themselves, embody the complete exclusivity that ideally would separate elite high culture. For example, jade, cloth, and cacao were required for marriage exchanges among the Postclassic Maya (Gillespie and Joyce 1997; compare J. Marcus 1992b). The exclusivity of high culture must be sought elsewhere.

While jade, cloth, and cacao are the most easily specifiable wealth items recorded for Mesoamerica, they represent only a small part of the goods that were products of high culture preferentially appropriated by sixteenth-century elites. Nonetheless, they are paradigmatic, as costume items and paraphernalia used in ceremony, of other goods that can be considered wealth in Mesoamerica. Feathers from tropical birds, and minerals such as turquoise, metals, and obsidian, employed in ornaments that were restricted to elite use, also formed part of the category of wealth. Turning to the origins of scales of value in Formative Mesoamerica, the same practices – costume ornamentation and ritual performance – were fundamental in the definition of an inner elite.

**Formative Mesoamerica: creating value**

The earliest recognizable products of "high culture" in Mesoamerica include well-made and decorated pottery vessels; hand-modeled individualistic human figurines; and elaborate costume ornaments, especially those made of jade, marine shell, and iron ore, produced in a florescence of contemporary Early Formative activity. I argue that this creative explosion in Formative Mesoamerica reflects the high social significance of comparative evaluation of the appearance of people and their possessions, judgments that would have influenced the success of individuals and their social groups in contracting alliances with others (Joyce 1992a, 1996, 1999).

For example, individual hand-modeled figurines from the Middle Formative (800–300 BC) Playa de los Muertos complex of northern Honduras (Figure 6.5) combine a few simple garments, or sometimes no clothing, with a great diversity of treatments of hair and of ornaments worn on the forehead, ears, neck, and wrists. These figurines are both a reflection of the now-inaccessible practices of bodily adornment of the living people of these settlements, and a permanent, material objectification of adornment, itself subject to further comment in society. I suggest that these figurines, and the practices of ornamentation they document, were part of a discourse about "beautification," the social marking of the body as desirable and the person as "persuasive" to others (Munn 1986: 96–97, 101–102), achieved by increasing the sensory attraction of the body by the addition of materials, worked with skill, that set the specific person off from others.

At the same sites where Playa de los Muertos figurines were made and used, a great deal of effort was expended on the elaboration of even the most functional of ceramic forms (Kennedy 1981; Strong, Kidder, and Paul 1938; Popenoe 1934; Joyce 1992a, 1992b, 1996). Unslipped jars and bowls are well polished, often marked with red-painted motifs or grooved or incised designs, regardless of the effect that use-wear would have on decoration. Kennedy (1981) notes that brazier plates, clearly exposed to fire, were nonetheless decorated in red and white paint on their interior surface. The degree of elaboration rises sharply for the everted-rim bowls, spout-and-bridge bottles, and stirrup-spout bottles that are particularly common in burials. These combine red and white paint, grooving, incising, modeling, and in some cases, achieve polychrome through the use of post-fire orange, white, and red paints. The adornment of pots, like the adornment of the body, is a means of marking these vessels as special by beautification. The distinctiveness of the appearance of beautiful pottery is an appeal for a response, making ornamented vessels the subjects of comment, evaluation, and ranking, and creating reputations for the vessels and their makers/users. Particular kinds of relations are created between the makers/users of these vessels and others in their community through these comments, relations which encompass the recognition of shared standards for adornment and for execution and the measurement of each attempt at beautification against those standards.

Rather than reflecting a natural criterion, I argue that beauty was a social construct whose validation came in the form of greater social success. And this success, in turn, laid the groundwork for certain individuals and their social groups to have greater access both to more labor and to additional resources through their social connections. In a detailed analysis of over 200 burials from the Central Mexican Formative Period site of Tlatilco, I demonstrated that certain clusters of burials (likely placed in and around house compounds) shared a series of significant features (Joyce 1999). These burials incorporated the widest range of exotic materials; were the resting place of the only individuals buried wearing imperishable costume ornaments; contained evidence of

*Figure 6.5 Playa de los Muertos figurines, Ulua Valley, Honduras, Middle Formative Period (courtesy of the Peabody Museum, Harvard University. Photograph by Hillel Burger.).*

specialization in ritual practice; and included the tools and raw materials for specialized obsidian industries. I argue that the inhabitants of these clusters were engaging in a form of conspicuous display of wealth, consumption that was made less risky by their apparent monopolization of certain religious and technical skills and of procurement of exotic raw materials.

My argument here accords with suggestions made by John Clark (Clark 1987; Clark and Blake 1994; Clark and Parry 1990) concerning the likely importance of patronage of the development of specialized craft skills in Formative Mesoamerica. Examining obsidian blade production, Clark demonstrates that the skill necessary to excel in the craft requires constant practice to maintain virtuosity. He suggests that patronage of craft workers was one of the ways that would-be elites of the Mesoamerican Formative distinguished themselves. He draws analogies with ethnographically described "hypertrophic" craft production, situations where craft specialists are underwritten and develop their skills to the point that they are capable of extreme degrees of elaboration, testing the boundaries of a technology.

While stone tool production is the technology for which we have the most abundant evidence in Formative Mesoamerica (due both to its status as a reduction process that creates waste materials, and to the resistance of stone to decay under tropical conditions), other kinds of craft production may have developed under similar patronage. Hendon (1999) describes evidence for specialization in textile and shell bead production from the Formative Period Maya site of Uaxactun. A small number of burials at Tlatilco contained bone needles and picks typical of the tools of textile production (Joyce 1999). The specialized expertise necessary to produce other products, such as Formative Period iron ore mirrors (Carlson 1981; Pires-Ferreira 1976), also suggests the possibility that craft specialists were underwritten by elites.

The scale of production of these specialized craft items would have been limited to the output from the individual artists who could be supported by only a few social groups in Formative Mesoamerica. To the extent that products of these craft workers perpetuated success in display by their patrons, the same social groups would continue to set the standards of beauty, one of the scales of value by which wealth could have been assessed. The pre-eminent products of Formative Period craft specialization, prototypic examples of "high culture," were, like the standards of economic value in sixteenth-century Mesoamerica, costume ornaments used by a restricted number of people, and regalia likely used in ritual. Hirth (1992), noting that such items have traditionally been labeled "status badges," calls for attempts to explain how they became symbols of authority in Formative Mesoamerica. I argue that specific craft products gained this second kind of value through their use by a small number of individuals whose legitimacy was given material expression in the exclusivity of high culture.

**Formative Mesoamerica: exclusion in practice**

Claims to exclusivity were likely made long before their inscription on the Formative landscape, but it was in the creation of permanent monumental architecture and art that these claims gained irrefutable force. Typically, the first monumental architecture across Mesoamerica took the form of single, massive earthen platforms rising up to 25 meters above ground level. I have suggested that the initial implementation of programs of building on this scale (taking place before we have any evidence of institutionalized social classes) must have had an appeal sufficient to enlist the labor they required (Joyce 1992b). I speculate that these monumental works could have been forms of community-wide beautification, analogous to the ornamentation of the individual person and of household possessions that was a preoccupation in the same sites at the same time. Michael Love (1992, 1999) has explored the effects that the creation of these built mountains would have had on the daily lives of people in Formative Mesoamerica. He argues that they would have functioned as structures of discipline (following Foucault 1977) affecting the habitual patterns of movement of people through space, and confronting them constantly with the reality of external forces beyond their individual power to resist. By creating different kinds of space within sites, the continuing elaboration of monumental architecture served to create spatial arenas with restricted access, a constantly visible form of exclusivity.

It is especially significant that in many Mesoamerican sites these platforms became the location of privileged burial of individuals wearing costumes incorporating the most elaborate ornaments made of marine shell, iron ore, and jade beads. Such burials define the extreme of consumption of exotic materials, and manifest hypertrophic craft specialization. Some of the largest jade ear ornaments ever made in Mesoamerica were included in a burial of this kind at the site of Los Naranjos, Honduras (Baudez and Becquelin 1973: 49, 91–93). The only individuals buried wearing costume ornaments at Chalcatzingo, Morelos, Mexico were placed in the major earthen platform at the site (Grove and Gillespie 1992). Abstracted from the communal burial setting under the house compound floor, a setting that continued to be used by others throughout the period, these are the first individuals who can convincingly be described as likely representatives of an elite in Mesoamerica.

The placement of burials in these exclusive settings itself demonstrates acceptance of the legitimacy of claims to exclusive access to some of the products of high culture by at least those segments of society which supported their mortuary rites. It does not simplify the issue of how, and on what grounds, these individuals (and the social groups from which they came) managed to successfully advance those claims. Most analyses of Formative Mesoamerica suggest that early elites claimed special access to knowledge of the supernatural, and enjoyed special status as religious practitioners (e.g., Reilly 1994; J. Marcus 1989; Gillespie 1993; Grove 1981). This argument, while in keeping with the propositions advanced by Baines and Yoffee, is not always formally supported with data from the nascent phases of Formative life, but more generally draws on interpretations of later monumental art (but see Drennan 1976; Flannery 1976). It is suggestive that a cluster of burials at Tlatilco contained musical instruments, masks, and tokens that may have been used in divination. The members of the social group responsible for these burials may have claimed special status as ritualists, and the group was among those with the highest levels of consumption of exotic resources (Joyce 1999; compare Ochoa 1996, who identifies one of these buried individuals as a probable shaman). Iron ore mirrors, a costume item worn by a number of these individuals, likely served in divination (Carlson 1981). Iron ore mirrors are among the costume items that are part of the stereotypical regalia of the individuals buried in monumental architecture at slightly later sites such as Chalcatzingo and La Venta. They are also an item of personal adornment regularly depicted in Mesoamerica's earliest Formative Period monumental art.

Monumental art was a second medium through which exclusion was given permanent material form. The thematic content of Formative monumental art is varied, but in general presents adult male human subjects with elaborate, individualized headdresses and stereotypical ear ornaments, pendants, and other items of costume.

These individuals are generally interpreted as political elites. Compositions place these figures in direct contact with supernatural locations and beings, with special emphasis on the imagery of agricultural fertility (de la Fuente 1992; Gillespie 1993; Benson and de la Fuente 1996). The monuments themselves form parts of spatial settings that further the division of sites into more and less exclusive zones (compare Grove 1999). One category of monument, the monumental thrones originally called altars (Grove 1973), is in effect an exclusive space itself, with an elevated platform offering highly visible seating for a privileged individual. At many sites, such as La Venta, earthen platforms surround the plazas in which monuments were set, restricting their visibility (Grove 1999). In other cases monuments are set away from the occupied area of sites. At Chalcatzingo, some of the monuments are carved directly on the natural cliff side, requiring potential viewers to climb up to view the reliefs. The setting of monumental art in exclusive spaces reaches its extreme with the placement of paintings in caves far from the centers of habitation (Grove 1970).

Monumental architecture and monumental art, both products of high culture, were particularly effective material expressions of the exclusivity that stemmed from the limitation of legitimacy to an elite. They formally imposed order on the three-dimensional space within which social life took place. They transformed spatial order utterly from what had gone before, changing the patterns of habitual movement of all the inhabitants of the site, stratifying space and hence the people who were allowed access to different space, creating and marking centers and peripheries. Within the space so defined, monumental art permanently inscribed a small number of figures as actors linking the natural and supernatural world. Those actors – all adult, almost all male – shared a common repertoire of gestures and common costuming. Living elites wearing the same regalia and carrying out the actions embodied in the gestures represented in art, occupied an exclusive place within the new Formative Mesoamerican polities. As patrons of attached craft specialists, they preferentially consumed the products of shell, jade, and iron ore workshops for their distinctive costume, and fostered the development of art and architecture to elaborate the settings for their action.

### The legacy of Mesoamerican civilization: making a classic Maya tradition

Different local variants of the general Formative pattern emerged across Mesoamerica, from Honduras and El Salvador to Guerrero (Sharer and Grove 1989; Clark 1994). Politically independent, the new polities had in common a vocabulary of ritual performances, a suite of iconographic motifs relating to a shared conceptualization of the cosmic order, and the use of certain valued materials. These commonalities set parameters within which all later Mesoamerican elites operated. The initial practice of constructing monumental platforms produced the effects of marking specific places on the landscape as sites of memory, and breaking the space within settlements into qualitatively different types, according to patterns of circulation and access. These effects of the initial forms of monumental construction provided a history for the later construction of monumental architecture that gave members of new polities a ready-made store of understandings about the meaning of such architecture. Even innovation in later monumental architecture was framed against the background of prior practices of construction, marked as an innovation by its divergence from the visible and remembered forms of earlier monumental constructions. Short of introducing radical inversions of prior forms, there was effectively no way to free monumental architecture from the history that it invoked. Yet even radical inversions, had such been attempted, would have been intelligible first as negations of the traditional forms, and hence completely caught within the webs of meaning that traditional architectural practices set up, once they were institutionalized.

In the same way, the iconographic motifs and selection of valuable materials that were transmitted to successor societies constrained reinterpretation. New meanings could, of course, become attached to these practices, but always with a residual weight derived from the histories of their prior use. The knowledge that these forms of value originated earlier in some degree naturalized them as givens, traditional knowledge and action that non-discursively framed everyday practice (Bourdieu 1973, 1977). The extreme conservatism over long periods of time of many material practices that began in the Formative Period is evidence of the inertia exerted by such material goods. These include costume ornaments and ritual regalia first featured as high culture in the Formative Period, made of materials described as standards of value in the sixteenth century.

Ear plugs, ornaments placed in pierced openings in the ear lobes, are one example (Figure 6.6). Jade was employed beginning in the Middle Formative period to create ear ornaments with a cylindrical stem and expanding flare or perpendicular flanges forming a wide

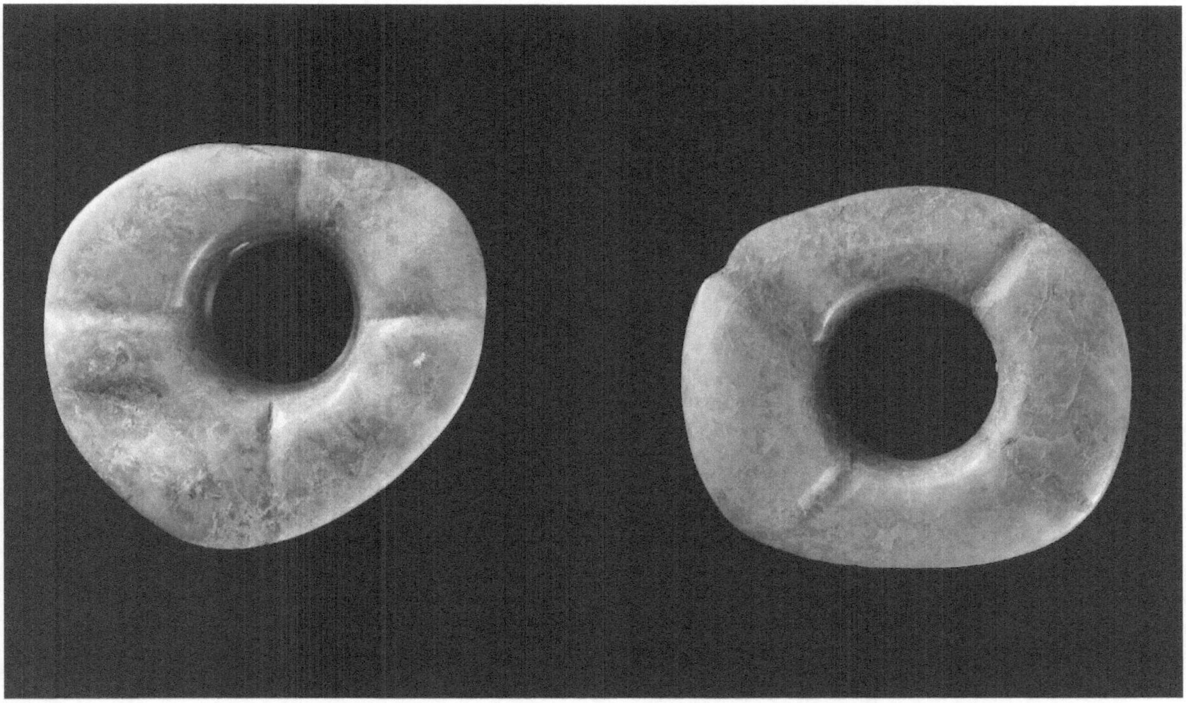

*Figure 6.6 Pair of Late Classic Maya jade ear flares of standard size excavated at Copan (courtesy of the Peabody Museum, Harvard University. Photograph by Hillel Burger.).*

front surface, or face. The diameters of the stems of such flanged ear ornaments fall within a narrow range of measurements throughout their history, implying very long-term continuity in the manner of piercing the ears and expanding the pierced hole (compare Kidder, Jennings, and Shook 1946: 106–111, 124–125, 215; Piña Chan 1971: 173–174; Rands 1965: 563–565; Caso 1965: 897–909; Woodbury 1965: 175–176). While different decorative motifs for ear flares came in and out of style, they did so literally against a background of continuity in the valued material and desired form of these ornaments, which remained linked through form and material over the entire history of the Mesoamerican civilizational order.

The maintenance of such practices was not facilitated by political continuity, as Mesoamerican societies experienced a pattern of alternating centralization and destabilization throughout the three millennia from the Formative Period through the end of the Postclassic Period. By about 400 BC, structural transformations had affected all the early complex societies of Mesoamerica. These Late Formative structural transformations remain poorly understood and their elucidation is outside the scope of this paper. Among the visible symptoms of major change during this period, however, are abandonment of sites, or a drop in new construction, at what had earlier been important centers on the Gulf Coast. Settlement in the Gulf Coast region was apparently less centralized between the decline of the Middle Formative Olmec centers, such as La Venta, and the emergence of early Classic centers centuries later. In the precocious polities of the Pacific coast and southern highlands of Guatemala, Honduras, and El Salvador, typified by Los Naranjos, the construction of monumental architecture also declined. At the same time that intensive building programs ended at sites that had previously flourished, the use of monumental architecture and art began at other places that had not previously been focal points for centralization, notably in the Maya lowlands (Ringle 1999; Hammond 1999; Love 1999).

Successor polities in the Late Formative period were faced with very different problems in defining a new Mesoamerican order than those that had challenged the first centralizing elites. The most visible innovation across many Mesoamerican polities at this point was the incorporation of writing and calendrical notation in

(Silverblatt 1988). Second, they continued to use rituals associated with kin-based reciprocity in their relationships with provincial groups. Tribute was phrased in terms of the provision of labor, rather than the production of goods, and ritual feasts as well as the exchange of gifts remained important components of almost all transactions with the state (Costin and Earle 1989; C. Morris 1982; C. Morris and Thompson 1985; Murra 1980). Gold and silver were integral components of the gift-giving cycles. As Berthelot (1986) has shown, the Inkas owned all sources of precious metal, but they allowed some mines to be worked by provincial rulers. These mines provided them with metals that were then used to fashion gifts for the king; gold and silver, of course, also flowed in the opposite direction, with the Inka bestowing gifts on provincial leaders, local huacas, and state temples in conquered territories (Figure 7.4).

The Inkas employed the language of kinship in their interaction with provincial populations, not because the state was organized along kin lines, but to facilitate imperial integration during a period of explosive growth. In fact, the discrepancy between form and practice may have only fueled conflict in some provinces. While a number of conquered groups appear to have incorporated Inka ideology into their own systems of belief (Silverblatt 1988), others resisted and rebelled against the state (Patterson 1991). In the absence of ideological control over their hinterlands, the Inkas employed force, a strategy with particularly high costs in a rugged land with few means of transportation, and one which ultimately cost them the empire.

Patterson (1986, 1991) suggests that the Inkas' inability to dominate subordinate cultures was due, in part, to the existence of traditional religious leaders in conquered territories. Provincial intellectuals were tied to shrines dedicated to sacred places and local ancestors, often associated with specific ethnic groups. These individuals, not priests working under state auspices, were the primary interpreters of imperial ideology in rural areas, and could easily either subvert or ignore Inka doctrine.

*Figure 7.4 Silver Inka figurine, probably used as an offering. Provenience unknown (courtesy of the Museo Contisuyu, Peru. Photograph by Bruce Owen.).*

### Historical and ethnographic evidence for continuity without inner elites

The foregoing discussion has highlighted the Inka's reliance on notions of order that were widespread in the Andes, and their attempts to legitimate imperial rule by casting novel relations in familiar terms. Historical data about Andean populations after the Spanish conquest shed some light on the persistence, modification, and monumental art. In the sixteenth century, Mesoamerica's multiple polities were participants in a single system marked most obviously by the use of calendars that combined a solar/agricultural year of 365 days with a ritual-divinatory cycle of 260 days (Broda de Casas 1969: 13–19, 73–93; compare Drucker 1987). These calendars, and a variety of related astronomical observational cycles, were recorded using a common mathematical notation system in base 20 that in its most developed form employed three characters (signs for zero, one, and five). During the Late Formative Period, the shared system of mathematical and calendrical recording was combined with other varied notational systems to create both ritual and political-historical texts (Justeson 1986, 1988; compare Broda de Casas 1969: 77–80).

Seen against the background of previous elite craft patronage, this development extends the range of specializations sponsored as part of high culture to a new intellectual domain. It is quite likely that the appearance of calendrical notations in imperishable form does not mark the first use of calendars. Nor does the implied ritual-political subject matter of the texts change the general nature of the messages conveyed previously through imagery alone. What is new about these Late Formative monuments is the explicit claims they make to history, and indeed, to a deep history, for the political elites they commemorated. The first dated monuments of the Late Formative period place contemporary events in cycle 7 of the Mesoamerican Long Count calendar (M. Coe 1957, 1976; Sharer and Sedat 1973), effectively positioning them over 3,000 years after the posited beginning of linear history represented by the use of this calendar. The actual displacement in time of the polities of the Late Formative from even the earliest simple sedentary villages of Mesoamerica, occupied 1,000 to 1,500 years earlier, was far less than the deep history claimed in the newly prominent dates carved on monuments.

Claims to historical precedent were also created by the continuation of forms of high culture first created in the Early and Middle Formative. Items of costume regalia were executed in new materials but traditional forms: the iron ore mirrors of the Formative period gave way to composite mosaic mirrors of iron pyrites, for example, noted by Kirchhoff (1968) as one of the defining traits of Mesoamerica in the sixteenth century (compare Figure 6.3). In the Late Formative and early Classic periods, writing was used to inscribe texts on some jade objects produced in earlier times noting specific names of actors who took part in ritual and political celebrations and even the dates on which these events took place (e.g., M. Coe 1966). Such ancient items, heirloomed and recycled, continued to circulate among elites of the succeeding Classic and Postclassic Periods, as the presence in the fifteenth-century Great Temple in the Aztec capital, Tenochtitlan, of a Middle Formative Olmec mask most dramatically illustrates (Matos 1996).

The Classic Maya tradition took its distinctive form in the Late Formative reformulation of Mesoamerican civilization. David Freidel and Linda Schele (1988a, 1988b), noting that the villages of the Maya Lowlands in general did not take part in developments of initial Early and Middle Formative civilization, offered a model for the abrupt appearance of Maya states in the Late Formative that stressed the active role of elites in creating ideologies that supported exclusive access to and display of wealth. They argued that Maya societies systematically suppressed the expression of real distinctions in social status until the Late Formative. They noted that across the Maya Lowlands of the Peten and Belize, over a very short period of time during the Late Formative, monumental architecture bearing representational imagery referring to supernatural themes was built at a number of sites. Richard Hansen (1992), working at the site of Nakbe, claims a slightly earlier date for the phenomenon at this northern Peten site. As long as the initial argument for a tightly integrated set of developments is not taken too literally, his findings do not seem to invalidate the general model; they simply place Nakbe as a precocious attempt at the same achievement.

Freidel and Schele (1988a, 1988b) argued that the new buildings at Late Formative Maya sites provided stages for performances by an emergent elite, who claimed a special relationship with the supernatural and gave it material form in ceremonies enacted in these settings. They noted that slightly later monumental platforms were ornamented with human portraits in the positions previously occupied by supernatural beings. They suggested that the medium of standing relief sculpture, in the form of stelae, was adopted at the beginning of the Classic Period for the depiction of human actors dressed in regalia that connected them to the same supernatural beings in order to associate them with historical dates. These monuments incorporated texts that used Mesoamerican calendrical notation to specify dates in the lives of the elites depicted as actors, and that elaborated on their specific claims to legitimacy.

Freidel and Schele (1988a, 1988b) suggested that emergent Maya elites advanced the idea that they were uniquely able to maintain the order of the cosmos through the practice of shamanic ceremonies. They identified jade items newly important in Late Formative Maya society as paraphernalia for divination. Because divination in Mesoamerican societies involved counting out numerical positions in the calendars, jade objects – costume ornaments that were the products of high culture – became identified with the general process of calculating value (Freidel 1993). Among the jade costume ornaments used by these emergent elite ritualists were a number of earlier Olmec jade items, retained as heirlooms and sometimes inscribed with specific calendrical information or texts (e.g., E. W. Andrews 1986; Proskouriakoff 1974; Freidel and Sabloff 1984).

The model for changes in Late Formative Lowland Maya societies proposed by Freidel and Schele has been elaborated greatly by them and others. For my purposes, the crucial point is the lag in the Maya Lowlands in the emergence of patterns of social complexity seen elsewhere in Mesoamerica centuries earlier. When complex social relations do develop, they do so within not only the intellectual boundaries established by previous polities, but literally within an already defined vocabulary of material products of high culture. The recycling of earlier costume ornaments is only one of the signs of the structuring of later Maya civilization by a pre-existing Mesoamerican civilizational order. The use of monumental platforms as settings for exclusive performances, and even the stela and altar as a format for freestanding sculpture, were already long-established in Formative Period Mesoamerica (for example, at Middle Formative Chalcatzingo; Grove 1987).

Seen against a background of the prior emergence of Mesoamerican civilization, the Late Formative Maya compress the creation of exclusivity into construction of monumental architectural settings that are simultaneously iconographically rich monuments expressing connections between elites and cosmic order. By adopting these traditional Mesoamerican media of state formation, Maya elites opted into Mesoamerica. Their subsequent use of the common Mesoamerican calendric system, and their elaboration of it to its greatest degree, created an almost paradigmatic example of classic Mesoamerican civilization.

What is notable here is that the Late Formative Maya developments began with the given notion of order that had been developed across Mesoamerica centuries earlier. The material actions undertaken by these Maya elites in building monumental architectural settings marked through imagery as stages for elite action presupposed the existence of exclusivity, and of legitimate claims by a few to impose order based on an ideology of special connection to gods and ancestors. Remarkably absent from these early formulations is the open expression of wealth. Freidel and Schele argued that differentials of wealth were already accumulating in Formative Maya villages, but without any means for their recognition as legitimate. The Late Formative Lowland Maya assertion of exclusivity in effect allowed the expression of wealth for the first time, and of the scale of value that defined the expensive as part of high culture. The lavish use of items of high culture by later Classic Maya elites (Figure 6.7) was extremely traditional in the selection of valued materials, particularly jade and shell, and in the forms created using these materials (Schele and Miller 1986; compare Fields 1991; Reilly 1991).

Returning to my schematic outline of Baines and Yoffee's model (Figure 6.1), the development of Late Formative Maya states took place within an already existing civilizational order. The position that both elites and non-elites occupied was that of the observer internal to that order. For those observers, legitimacy flowed from order, and the free expression of wealth followed legitimacy.

The Late Formative Maya situation contrasts with that faced by the persons who originated the Mesoamerican civilizational order. For them, the contention that order gave rise to legitimacy and wealth was not a given. It had to be proposed in ways that made it effective, that conveyed concepts about cosmic order in compelling fashion. The explosion of imagery in villages of the later Early Formative should be viewed as a visual product of the formation and promotion of concepts of cosmic order. In these societies zoomorphic creatures that are surely ancestral to later Mesoamerican representations of personified natural forces are repeatedly represented (Joyce, Edging, Lorenz, and Gillespie 1991; Quirarte 1977; Reilly 1991). But unlike later representations, in the initial Formative Period imagery depictions of human figures are rare. By the end of the Early Formative, personifications of natural forces were represented as settings for the actions of select human beings. Not coincidentally, at the same time the most common media for these representational images shifted from the more widely distributed pottery vessels of the Early Formative to incised jade ornaments of much more restricted circulation.

This transformation, the punctuated emergence of Mesoamerica's civilizational order, entailed a number of separate developments implied in the terms order, legitimacy, and wealth. Agreement on shared standards that I

*Figure 6.7 Late Classic Maya stela showing noble woman dressed in jade beaded skirt and jade belt with shell pendant. Naranjo Stela 24 (Graham 1975: 63). (Used with permission of Ian Graham, Director,* Corpus of Maya Hieroglyphic Writing. *Drawing by Ian Graham.).*

suggest may be usefully conceived of as beauty, rather than value, underlies the spread not only of the incised jades but also of the earlier carved pottery vessels. The shared aesthetic domain within which these vessels were made and evaluated facilitated the comparison of cosmological concepts which were the subject matter of these vessels, making concepts supported by beautiful representations more persuasive both sensuously and intellectually. For Mesoamerica, I would suggest, order originally flowed from persuasion and persuasiveness from beauty.

The constraint that earlier precedent exercised on the course of newly emerging Lowland Maya society in the Late Formative is interesting not only intrinsically, but for what it suggests about the momentum created by the successful establishment of a civilizational order. Once the difficult work of constructing convincing claims of legitimacy and the definition of wealth is accomplished, the order that is expressed in the high-cultural manifestations of these claims becomes naturalized. The preferential consumption of high art becomes a moral act that evinces cosmic order. Elites become exemplary participants in that cosmic order. As Baines and Yoffee (1998; chapter 2 in this volume) argue, there is little incentive for non-elites to question the order in which they now live. And perhaps even the strongest claim Baines and Yoffee make – that most high culture is essentially self-referential and unconcerned with non-elites – can be sustained, with Classic Maya art directed primarily at a narrow audience of elites, motivated primarily to satisfy their felt need for luxuries that were their unquestioned right within the Mesoamerican civilizational order.

# 7 Political fragmentation and ideological continuity in the Andean highlands

MARY VAN BUREN

Current scholarship on Andean civilization can be traced to the 1960s when historians attempted to push beyond Inka-centered models of Andean achievements in order to uncover the cultural foundations of the empire. This was accomplished, in part, by turning their attention from the classic histories composed by Europeans who based their accounts largely on interviews with Inka elites, to documents produced by Spanish bureaucrats who were attempting to consolidate control over rural groups. Close study of the latter, in conjunction with archaeological research on provincial populations, has revealed the fragility of the Inka state and the degree to which it depended on and was structured by the polities it absorbed. Cultural and organizational continuity has thus emerged as an important theme in the investigation of social complexity in the Andes, but it has often been attributed to peasants and provincial leaders, rather than the inner elites identified by Baines and Yoffee (1998) as the sole carriers of high culture. An examination of the Inka state in terms of Baines and Yoffee's model provides an opportunity to test the general applicability of their ideas and also encourages a more precise conceptualization of continuity in the Andes.

Briefly put, Baines and Yoffee (1998) maintain that the development of complexity is coincident with the emergence of new understandings of social and cosmic order that justify disparities in wealth and power. The maintenance of order, in part through the deployment of wealth, becomes the responsibility and privilege of the elites, and is a task that also legitimizes their position in society. Elites thus play a key role in the elaboration and persistence of a high cultural complex that forms the underpinning of civilization.

This scenario conforms well to what is known about many of the complex societies in the Andes, including the Inkas. However, the authors then go on to argue for the almost complete separation of elite high culture from the rest of society. They emphasize the novelty of elite notions of order, discount the role played by non-elites as an audience for state ideology, and suggest that alternative value systems did not exist in archaic states. It is here that the model's fit with the Andean material breaks down, and this lack of congruence is the point of departure for an examination of the Inka case. This paper will first consider notions of order in the Inka state and their connection to the beliefs and practices of rural groups incorporated into the empire, which will be illustrated with an examination of the production and use of precious metals. This will be followed by a brief look at the period after the fall of the Inka empire in order to consider the mechanisms that are responsible for continuity despite the absence of inner elites.

## Order and the Inka state

A sustained episode of political fragmentation occurred during the three hundred years preceding the emergence of the Inka state in the south-central highlands of Peru (Figure 7.1). This period was marked by a high level of competition among relatively small polities that developed after the collapse of the Wari empire in approximately 900 AD, and the Tiwanaku state 100 years later. No predecessor state has been documented in the highlands during this period, and thus inner elites could not have directly transmitted Wari or Tiwanaku high culture to emergent Inka rulers. Nonetheless, similarities between these societies are pronounced, so continuity must have occurred through some other mechanism. The proposition that the Inkas drew on notions of order found in their own as well as many other Andean societies, rather than adopting high culture transmitted by inner elites, provides the most reasonable explanation of this phenomenon.

Conrad and Demarest (1984) have offered the most thorough analysis of the emergence of the Inka state and the relationship of ideology to imperial expansion. Their study reveals a clear link between the rapid growth of the empire and the development of a new view of social and cosmic order. The Inkas were one of many relatively small, competitive polities in the central Andes during the fourteenth century. Their emergence as a regional power coincided with the development of a new state cult that emphasized the solar god, Inti, and identified the Inka leaders as divine children of the sun. The living

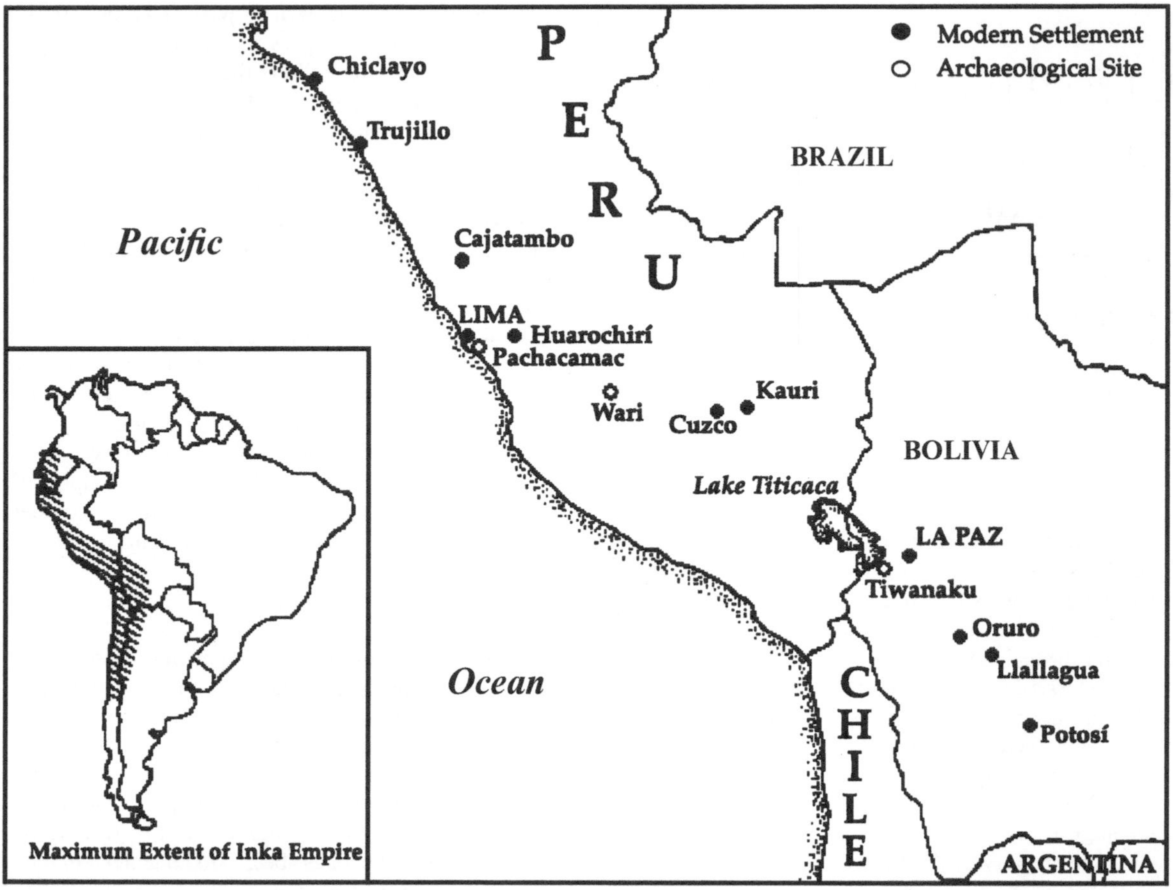


*Figure 7.1 Map of the Andes indicating locations mentioned in the text.*

as well as the dead, mummified Inka rulers were the earthly incarnations of the sun as well as other forces related to fertility, and had to be properly attended in order to ensure the well-being of the population. Inka rulers retained their possessions after death, and were cared for by descendants who managed their estates. New rulers were thus required to conquer additional territory in order to increase their own holdings, fueling imperial expansion in the process.

The relationship between order, wealth, and legitimacy in this instance is parallel to the Egyptian and Mesopotamian cases examined by Baines and Yoffee. However, the development of Inka ideology and its role in the expanding state cannot be understood without reference to the majority of the people who resided in the empire, most of whom were either commoners or provincial elites. The relationship between sun worship and the belief systems of the subject population was analyzed in the seventeenth century by Father Bernabé Cobo, a Jesuit priest whose insights – and cynicism – owed much to his critical attitude towards Inka rule. Following a discussion of the broad array of sacred phenomena, or *huacas*, worshiped by Andeans, Cobo (1990: 25) commented that:

> Sun worship grew much because of the Incas' diligence. Since they boasted of being children of the Sun, the Incas made every effort to legitimize and enhance Sun worship with more brilliant services, a larger number of priests, and more frequent offerings and sacrifices. Little effort was necessary to establish the Sun's reputation among these people. They were highly respectful of these secondary causes because of the good they received from them. In the case of the

| | |
|---|---|
| Spanish Colonial Period | AD 1532–1824 |
| Late Horizon (coincident with Inka empire) | AD 1438–1532 |
| Late Intermediate Period | AD 1000–1438 |
| Middle Horizon (includes periods of Wari and Tiwanaku expansion) | AD 600–1000 |
| Early Intermediate Period | 200 BC–AD 600 |
| Early Horizon | *c*. 800–200 BC |
| Initial Period | 1800–*c*. 800 BC |
| Preceramic Period | 3000–1800 BC |

*Figure 7.2 Andean chronology.*

> Sun, the effects that this planet produces are so obviously beneficial for mankind that the people themselves already held it in high esteem. The authority and example of the Incas only served to make the exterior demonstrations of veneration more costly and elaborate.

This quote clearly shows the way in which wealth was used to promote notions of order that legitimized elites and suggests how the populace might also come to depend on such displays to maintain the social and cosmic order necessary for their well-being. However, in Cobo's opinion the success of sun worship was rooted in the fact that conquered groups already viewed the physical world as highly sacralized and worshipped a wide variety of natural forces and objects including the sun. The sun, though, transcends local geography, and the Inkas no doubt promoted its worship not only to enhance their own status, but to foster pan-Andean ritual activities that superseded those of groups incorporated into the empire.

The complicated relationship between the beliefs and experiences of rural populations and the expensive displays of elite control over the cosmos can be illustrated through an examination of the role of precious metals in the Inka empire. Gold and silver are almost universally associated with high culture and were used in archaic states for the fabrication of objects that marked the distinctive status of both elites and gods. This was certainly true in the case of the Inkas who restricted the use of these substances to elite and sacred environments where it was lavishly employed in the adornment of temples, ritual paraphernalia, and high status individuals. However, in addition to their aesthetic qualities and social functions, gold and silver were also imbued with specific meanings; both were associated with agricultural fertility, but gold was linked more tightly to the sun, maleness, and maize, while silver was tied to the moon and femaleness.

Analyses of the relationship between metallurgical techniques and Andean culture by Heather Lechtman and Mary Helms have provided a great deal of insight into the way in which precious metals were deployed in the communication of state ideology. A characteristic of Andean metal-working that clearly distinguishes it from the metallurgy of neighboring groups to the north as well as that of Mesoamerica, is its emphasis on the use of flat sheets of metal to cover or create three-dimensional objects. Lechtman (1996) was the first to note this and to explore it in terms of technological style – the way in which meaning inheres in the physical production of material culture. Sheet metal used to create large objects must be sufficiently rigid to hold the desired shape, a technical problem that was solved by Andean smiths through the addition of copper to gold or silver in order to produce stronger alloys. These alloys, however, do not appear golden or silvery – a need that was met by the development of sophisticated enrichment and depletion gilding processes that drew silver and gold to the surface of the alloyed metal. Lechtman believes that this particular solution was shaped by Andean beliefs regarding the relationship between underlying structure and the visible manifestation of its essence. In the case of metal alloys, golden and silvery colors had to be derived from within the metal itself. These techniques were employed by many different Andean societies, although the most spectacular metal work of this type comes from the Moche on the north coast of Peru, and its successor state, Chimor. Chimor was the largest and most powerful state in the Andes at the time that the Inka empire was emerging and supported a variety of specialized craftspeople. After it was conquered by the Inka, many of the metalsmiths were taken to Cuzco where they continued to practice their craft (Cieza de León 1959: ch. 113) and probably transferred their technical knowledge to the new state in the process. Stylistically, though, they appear to have had little impact; some hybrid Inka-Chimú objects have been found on the north coast, but most of the extant Inka metalwork is distinct.

Drawing on Lechtman's work, Helms (1981) has argued that the difference between the sheet metal tradition of the Andes and the metallurgy practiced in northern South America and Central America, which emphasized the casting of small, personal objects, can be understood in terms of political organization in the two regions. In the latter case, gold was worn by people of all statuses, although the leaders of these ranked societies often had more elaborate ornaments or a larger quantity of them. In contrast, upper-class members of the Inka state expressed their inherent celestial qualities by covering parts of themselves and their environment in sheets of gold and silver, underscoring their essential difference from the rest of the populace. As Sallnow (1989) has pointed out, though, the Inka appear to have used both kinds of objects, since precious metals were also worn as personal adornments and given to provincial leaders.

Among the Inkas the use of gold and silver was a monopoly that clearly distanced elites from their subjects, but the meaning of these metals and the ways in which they were produced had important parallels with the everyday activities common to all peasant households, and were probably structured by them. Lechtman (1996) has pointed out similarities in the production process of precious metals and textiles, an older and highly esteemed form of material culture in the Andes. Both involve the manufacture of pliable, two-dimensional sheets that are joined to create or cover three-dimensional bodies. The visible characteristics of precious metals and textiles are generated by the underlying structure; in the case of metal alloys this is accomplished by enriching the surface of the object with the gold or silver that lies within, while the designs on textiles were created by the manipulation of warp and weft threads rather than surface embellishment. Parallels in the production process are echoed by equivalences of use; both textiles and precious metals were offered in sacrifices, redistributed to lower-level elites, worn to display status, and used to represent deities. For example, the most sacred shrine on the Island of the Sun, the place where the sun first emerged, was a naturally occurring rock outcrop half of which was covered in beaten gold and half in *cumbi*, a fine cloth woven by specialists working for the state (Cobo 1990: 97).

While manufacturing objects of precious metals was structurally akin to weaving, the extraction and processing of ores were comparable to another common peasant task, agriculture. That native Andeans conceived of mining and farming in similar ways is indicated by their use of the same words to denote comparable phenomena in these two different spheres of action (Berthelot 1986). In Aymara, for example, *illa* and *mama* referred to distinctively shaped agricultural products that were saved and worshiped by peasant households for their generative powers and assistance in producing an abundant harvest. These terms were also used for particularly large or fine pieces of ore that were regarded as the mothers of mines and sometimes became the foci of regionally important pilgrimage centers (Abercrombie 1998: 266). Other parallels include the perceived relationship between rain, storms, and lightning and the productivity of both fields and mines, the use of the word *ccoya* to mean a furrow in an agricultural field as well as a mine shaft and the term *papas* to refer to both potatoes and lumps of silver (Berthelot 1986; Pizarro 1921: 391). The technology and division of labor employed in the two activities was also similar. In colonial times, as today, Andean men plowed the earth, while women planted and participated in the harvest. They were also responsible, like women everywhere, for preparing food. Few data are available about the gender division of mining activities in prehistory, but sixteenth-century documents indicate that men extracted ore and women were often the ones who sorted and processed it. The grinding equipment found at prehistoric mining sites that was used in this procedure is identical to that employed in households for processing food. Indigenous women also sometimes smelted ore during the Colonial Period (Ocaña 1969: 202–203), an activity that is very rarely done by females in the rest of the world, but which is explicable in light of the parallels between mining and farming; they also bartered it in open markets where today their female descendants sell vegetables. These similarities in meaning, technology, and the division of labor are at least partially explicable in terms of two organizational features of the Inka empire: the maintenance of the household as the fundamental unit of production and the use of a rotating labor tax and part-time specialists to produce goods for the state (Berthelot 1986). As a result of these practices, families that worked in the mines and probably even many of those who produced metal objects were also engaged in routine agricultural activities to sustain their households.

While most members of the rural populace did not own precious metal, the metaphors and experiences associated with it would have allowed them to understand its use in state-sponsored rituals such as the spectacular Inti Raimi, or Festival of the Sun, that took place at the end of the maize harvest in Cuzco. As Bauer (1996) has shown, one part of this ceremony was based on an origin myth specific to the Inkas and demonstrated their divine ability to control nature. For eight days the royal mummies in Cuzco were assembled at the edge of the city just before sunrise. Over 600 Inka lords

*Figure 7.3 Illustration by Guaman Poma showing Inka nobility breaking the earth to inaugurate the new agricultural year (courtesy of the Royal Library, Copenhagen).*

dressed in cloth adorned with silver and wearing gold disks on their foreheads and in their ears faced the rising sun and began to chant, increasing the intensity of their hymn as the sun climbed towards noon, and decreasing it again until it set, after which they and their ancestors retired for the evening. At the end of this period, the Inka, followed by the nobility, used gold digging sticks to break the earth (Figure 7.3), inaugurating the new agricultural year and ensuring its success (MacCormick 1991: 75–77). Inti Raimi clearly identified the Inkas with the sun's movement and its role in producing an abundant crop, a metaphor that was communicated, in part, by sheathing the nobility and their implements in gold. Commoners and provincial elites most likely understood the use of gold in state rituals that asserted the Inkas' responsibility for the well-being of the empire, and, from a historical perspective, their beliefs probably played a constitutive role in the formation of these elite notions of order.

**Legitimacy and Inka provincial organization**

While the cult of the sun was a novel construction of the celestial and earthly order, it was, as Cobo noted, anchored in systems of belief that were common to many Andean communities of the time. Conrad (1992) identifies ancestor worship, the cult of the dead, and a generalized sky god, all of which were widespread in the Andes, as key elements in the Inka state religion. Inti, in fact, can be traced to a manifold celestial god who was worshiped at the site of Tiwanaku and perhaps even earlier. This generalized sky deity did not, however, disappear as a result of the promulgation of Inka state religion, but remained important to many conquered groups as well as to the lower-ranking Inka moiety in Cuzco itself (Demarest 1981: 46). The presence of alternative belief systems throughout the empire that entailed not only a generalized sky god, but distinct bodies of myth and the worship of local ancestors and sacred places, indicates that state ideology was not all-encompassing.

Diversity in the belief systems of conquered groups is closely related to the Inkas' reliance on indirect rule to govern most of the provinces. Over the last few decades archaeologists and historians have demonstrated that Inka control of conquered groups was highly variable and often mediated through local elites. Sacred huacas and their associated ritual specialists were also frequently allowed to function unimpeded, and were sometimes even supported by the state (Patterson 1991: 104). The most famous example of the co-existence of a regional shrine and imperial religion is Pachacamac, an ancient coastal oracle next to which the Inkas constructed an imposing temple for the Sun.

While in many respects the Inkas attempted to impose a new world view and novel forms of organization (cf. Julien 1982; Silverblatt 1988), one of the most interesting findings to emerge from recent scholarship is the degree to which they relied on local notions of social order to legitimate their control of conquered populations. The Inkas incorporated two important aspects of the belief systems characteristic of small-scale polities into state ideology. First, they attempted to cast themselves and their gods as the ancestors of conquered peoples, promoting the notion of an inclusive social order based on kinship as well as their privileged place within it loss of Inka notions of order in the absence of an indigenous inner elite. Of course, the Spanish colonial world differed substantially from periods of political fragmentation in precolombian times. Most importantly, the population was incorporated into a hostile and completely foreign empire that actively attempted to destroy native religious practices (Wachtel 1977). Of less consequence, perhaps, is the fact that while most rural villages were illiterate, many Spaniards and some indigenous leaders knew how to read and write, and thus may have constituted a source of knowledge about the past that would have been differently maintained in prehistoric times when *khipus*, knotted string devices, were the primary means of record keeping (but see Urton 1998). However, while the situations are not entirely analogous, a look at the fate of Inka ideas regarding the relationship of precious metals, the sun, and political hierarchy after the empire's collapse does suggest some of the processes by which elite notions of order are maintained and transformed.

Colonial descriptions of Inka religious practices were based on observations of state rituals that continued in Cuzco until 1535 when the Inkas established a government-in-exile in Vilcabamba, or on interviews with elites who had witnessed or been told of such events. As Spaniards gained firmer control of the Andes, indigenous religion at all levels was specifically prohibited. However, while the dominant trend throughout the colonial period was the active eradication of native practice, clerical opinion on the incorporation of indigenous iconography into Christian representations was divided (Gisbert 1994: 29–35). Philosophical differences regarding the use of native symbols to facilitate conversion to Christianity appear to have characterized different religious orders. The Dominicans, for instance, explicitly rejected the representation of the sun, moon, or stars in religious art in order to prevent the continuation of native practices in Christian guise. Augustinians, on the other hand, quite conspicuously adorned their churches with these images, and the sun, in particular, is a common feature in colonial religious art. Gisbert contends that the sun was often equated with God the Father, an argument that is supported by the use of sun symbolism in depictions of the Trinity as well as the placement of ocular openings in scenes of the Annunciation within churches. While some Europeans chose to equate the Christian god with Andean deities such as Pachamama or Viracocha, the Sun took precedence in Christian art, and like the Quechua language of the Inkas, was promoted by clerics as a means for conversion. However, the salience of such representations for native people and their understandings of them are not known.

Most of the extant information about native beliefs after the late sixteenth century was recorded during campaigns conducted by Spanish priests in order to eliminate idolatry in the rural villages under their control, which were, of course, the places where Inka ideology was least likely to have been influential. The data are temporally and geographically scattered and reflect neither the full complexity and diversity of colonial belief systems, nor the development of specific communities over time. However, the testimony given by indigenous witnesses often provides remarkably detailed information about aspects of rural religion.

The most extensive body of mythic history, and the one that most closely approximates a truly native literature, was collected in the province of Huarochirí, probably in the first decade of the seventeenth century. This compendium of oral tradition was apparently intended, at least in part, to provide a guide to native religion that would enable Spaniards to more effectively destroy it. The majority of these stories relate the historical and mythical relationships among local peoples, but a number deal with regional cult centers, and a few explicitly mention the Inka. While the people of Huarochirí apparently did not practice Inka sun worship at this time, they clearly recalled its importance (Salomon and Urioste 1991: 276). However, their perception of imperial beliefs was strongly shaped by their own position in the empire, which suggests, as Patterson (1986) has argued, that state ideology was contested by provincial subjects. So, for example, the narrator, in his description of the Inka's relationship with the powerful coastal oracle of Pachacamac stated that "We don't in fact know much about the Incas' great reverence for Pacha Camac. But we do know a few things. In the highlands, they say, the Incas worshiped the sun as the object of their adoration from Titi Caca, saying 'It is he who made us Inca!' From the lowlands, they worshiped Pacha Camac, saying 'It is he who made us Inca!'" (Salomon and Urioste 1991: 111) and then offered his own interpretation as to why the Inka thought this way, concluding: "It was no doubt with such thoughts in mind that the Incas worshiped these two huacas more than the other huacas, and even placed the sun next to the lowland huaca Pacha Camac. The place where they set it is called Punchau Cancha, the Sun Court, to this very day" (Salomon and Urioste 1991: 112).

The notion that the Inkas had dual origins in both the Sun and Pachacamac was not part of imperial dogma, although Patterson (1985) suggests that the ruler Topa

Inka's decision to build a Sun temple at Pachacamac may have been part of a strategy for countering the influence of competing kin groups in Cuzco. Such a conception of Inka origins may have been espoused by a specific royal faction, and would have found a receptive audience among the residents of Huarochirí who were themselves linked to Pachacamac through a branch oracle.

The Huarochirí manuscript, then, suggests that the imperial cult of the Sun was no longer maintained, but that the memory of Inka domination was still clear and continued to shape local notions of order. Testimony obtained from the people of Huarochirí and nearby provinces during the following decade provides a somewhat different perspective on indigenous conceptions of the sun. Rather than being asked to recount local myths, residents were interrogated by Spanish clergymen in order to identify individuals who continued to worship huacas and practice other forbidden rituals. In 1621, Father Arriaga, one of the clerics involved in this campaign, published a manual describing their findings in order to aid others in the extirpation of idolatry. Arriaga's work revealed that native religion was flourishing in the mountainous regions surrounding Lima; in many areas a loose hierarchy of priests continued to organize public worship of local huacas, including ancestral mummies, stone figures, geographic features, and natural forces such as the sun. Such rituals often entailed confession, song, dance, music, and the sacrifice of maize, feathers, mineral powders, and other materials to the huaca. Gold and, especially, silver still played a role on such occasions; some huacas retained the gifts of precious metals and fine cloth that had been bestowed on them by the Inka, and Arriaga (1968: 69) complained that idolatry was encouraged by the natives' continued use of ritual ornaments and vessels of silver, gold, and copper that should have been destroyed during earlier campaigns. Duviols (1977: 374) suggests that the precious metals sacrificed to huacas were an important motivation for finding and destroying idols. Certainly by the end of the seventeenth century gold disappeared from native ceremonies, although silver, particularly in the form of coins, became more accessible to rural populations, who continue to use it for ritual purposes.

Despite continuity with prehispanic practices, many of the indigenous aspects of colonial religion were clearly distinct from those of Inka times. As Spalding (1984) points out in her analysis of Huarochirí, the worship of huacas associated with the integration of large-scale political units eventually disappeared as a result of the reorganization of such groups by the Spaniards and the general prohibition against native religion. Rituals that ensured the well-being of specific kin groups, households, and individuals, often performed in secret, predominated. The sun, while still worshiped as a sacred force critical to agricultural success, appears to have been no more highly regarded than other celestial phenomena in Huarochirí.

An interesting contrast to this situation comes from the highlands to the north where an extensive campaign to identify and destroy idolatry was mounted in the seventeenth century. Cock and Doyle's study of the sun cult in the Archbishopric of Lima revealed evidence of solar worship in fifteen villages during the period from 1615 to 1677. Testimony from different individuals indicates somewhat contradictory attitudes towards the sun. One person stated quite explicitly that the most important cult was that of the mummified ancestors, followed by the worship of stone huacas, and finally the veneration of the sun, moon, stars, and meteorological forces, while another confessed to having worshiped the sun as the creator of all people and having offered it sacrifices to ensure the success of his harvest (Cock and Doyle 1979; Huertas Vallejos 1981: 71, 73). Such statements accord with the testimony made by individuals in Huarochirí half a century earlier that the sun was merely one of many huacas that influenced human affairs, most especially agriculture. However, witnesses interrogated in the village of Cajatambo in 1656 had a less egalitarian understanding of sun worship. They believed that the sun had been born in Lake Titicaca and had created the ancestors of the people who originally populated their province. They venerated the sun because it had given rise to these local elites, and the cult of the sun as well as its ministers was held in especially high regard (Huertas Vallejos 1981: 28, 70). Such a view clearly echoes Inka ideology and was used to support hierarchical organization after the Spanish conquest. While the origin of such beliefs is difficult to determine, Cock and Doyle argue that organized solar worship represents the maintenance of pre-Inka religious forms that facilitated imperial expansion, rather than the persistence of Inka ideology.

The link between the sun and indigenous elites is not, of course, unexpected, and was most pronounced at the highest levels of the native hierarchy. The Spaniards respected nobility, native or European, and from the start elites asserted their noble status by demonstrating descent from the Inkas. Such claims were bolstered by the production of European portraits showing nobility in Inka garb, much of which is in clear imperial style even two hundred years after the Spanish conquest

*Figure 7.5 Portraits of four Inka rulers: Tupa Iupangui, Huayna Capac, Uascar Inga, and Ataguallpa. Unknown (probably eighteenth-century Peruvian; accession number 47.119. Courtesy of the Brooklyn Museum of Art.).*

(Rowe 1967). In the seventeenth and eighteenth centuries Inka rulers as well as many male members of the current nobility were shown wearing a personified golden sun on their chests (Figure 7.5) – a Europeanized version of the gold disks worn in the past (Gisbert 1994: Figs. 96, 100, 109, 164). Portraits such as these may have been visible primarily to those who visited wealthy households, but elaborate Inka costumes were also worn by individuals in processions conducted in the streets of Lima, Cuzco, and Potosí (Gisbert 1994: 141–142), and the famous seventeenth-century paintings of the Corpus Christi procession in Cuzco were displayed in a local church (Dean 1990).

Outside Cuzco, most people in the sixteenth century remembered the Inkas with some distaste, emphasizing imperial control and the demands made upon them for labor, resources, and occasional human sacrifice. However, as native groups were subjected to increasingly tight control by Spanish authorities and indigenous elites experienced mounting discrimination in their attempts to participate in colonial society, views of the Inka shifted. Rather than an oppressive government, the Inka empire came to be regarded by many as a utopian order characterized by justice, abundance, and health to which all could return after the Spaniards had been expelled from Peru (Flores Galindo 1987), and the sun emerged as a more inclusive symbol of native ethnic identity.

This utopian movement culminated in the Tupac Amaru uprising of 1780, during which hundreds of people, led by an indigenous trader from the native elite, attempted to eliminate the Spaniards in their midst. The revolt failed, but had far-reaching consequences. The colonial government prohibited representations of the Inkas, including portraits, dress, and texts such as the account of the Inka empire written by Garcilaso de la Vega and used by Tupac Amaru as the basis for his utopian vision (Flores Galindo 1987; Gisbert 1994). The privileges previously enjoyed by the native nobility were withdrawn by the state, and elites disappeared into the impoverished Indian population, fully rupturing their attenuated connection to the Inka empire in the process.

Little information regarding indigenous beliefs and practices exists for the nineteenth century, but ethnographic studies made during this century suggest that reverence for the sun, agricultural rituals, and the conceptual linkage between precious metals and both fertility and social order do exist in some Andean communities. One example of the former comes from the village of Kauri in the Department of Cuzco where Mishkin conducted research in the 1930s (Mishkin 1963). A number of people interviewed by him equated god, Christ, and the sun – which they called Inti Huayna Capac, the name of the last precolombian Inka. However, while the sun was regarded as a source of agricultural productivity and human health, it played little role in either the daily concerns or rituals of the villagers. O. Harris (1980: 84) notes that the Laymi of central Bolivia also identify Inti and the Spanish god as the same entity, and like the people of Kauri view him as a relatively remote deity.

Tschopik (1963) found a similar situation among the Aymara of Lake Titicaca, although in that area fragments of myths that are almost identical to those recorded in the sixteenth century are still current. One such myth, which probably predates the Inkas (Salles-Reese 1997), relates that, after an initial act of creation, the deity Viracocha rose from the lake and led people to Tiwanaku where he turned the disobedient ones to stone and then made the sun, moon, and stars, while others state that the sun rose directly from the lake and became the husband of the moon. The ancestry of the villagers themselves, though, was traced to a variety of local features that gave rise to different kin groups, and not to distant celestial bodies.

While Tschopik represented these myths as isolated remnants of the Inka past, Michael Sallnow and Olivia Harris, two scholars who have provided insightful and sustained analyses of the meaning of precious metals in Andean communities, show how such beliefs cohere to produce understandings of the contemporary world that are rooted in presumably ancient systems of thought. Sallnow (1989) reports that in many parts of the central Andes a hierarchy of nature spirits who reside in local mountains and other geographical features are believed to be subordinate to the Peruvian state. They have rich stores of gold and silver which, according to some accounts, are obtained by transmuting the offerings of food and other substances made to them by villagers in return for fertility and protection. Every August these spirits offer their treasure as tribute to regionally important mountains, and in this way it travels up the hierarchy until it reaches the Peruvian treasury. Such a conception expresses both the community's position in the republic as well as the role it plays in sustaining the state apparatus.

The close association between precious metals and political order is also apparent in stories that reverse the relationships expressed above. So, for instance, the utopian vision of Tupac Amaru lives on in Inkarrí myths that describe the period prior to the Spanish conquest as one in which both gold and crops were abundant; when Inkarrí (a fusion of the Inka Atahualpa and Tupac Amaru) was killed, the gold disappeared and agricultural yields dwindled. Sallnow (1989: 219) also relates a myth reported to June Nash in Oruro, Bolivia, in which social and economic chaos ensued when the spirit of the mountain in which a mine is located gave gold and silver to the people rather than offering it to the Sun. Order was restored only with the intervention of the daughter of the Sun and the replacement of the local language with Quechua.

The relationship between precious metals, agricultural fertility, and political order was also identified by Harris (1989) among the Laymis of northern Potosí. According to Harris the Laymis do not think of mining and agropastoralism as separate economic spheres and conduct similar rituals to enhance the production of metals, animals, and crops. As in the fifteenth century, metal is thought to grow in the mountains like potatoes, and the same term, *llallawa*, is used for unusual lumps of ore as well as for distinctive agricultural products, and is also the name of a nearby mining center (O. Harris 1989: 263). Money, in this case coins, is also clearly associated with fertility. Libations, for example, are poured for three types of abundance: livestock, crops, and *phaxsima*, a word that refers to money but which literally means "like the moon." However, the Laymis also recognize that money is manufactured by the state. Its dual and somewhat antithetical sources thus create a conceptual (and perhaps practical) conflict that is played out and integrated in ritual behavior and thought.

## Conclusion

Contemporary beliefs surrounding precious metals, the sun, and agricultural fertility obviously do not constitute evidence for the persistence of Inka high culture over the last five centuries. The residents of Andean villages have not retained state ideologies, nor do they produce the kind of aesthetic items that embody elite culture. Instead, general notions of order as well as some specific beliefs and practices have endured outside the context of an indigenous state. The persistence of such beliefs in largely illiterate villages suggests how continuity in certain aspects of civilization could occur despite political fragmentation and the loss of inner elites over time.

As this brief consideration of the periods both before and after the Inka empire indicates, a variety of actors played a role in this process. Under the Inka, provincial elites were a key audience for state-sponsored rituals, as they could either use imperial ideology to bolster their own positions or lead their people in rebellions against the empire; after the collapse of imperial control the appropriation of Inka ideology, usually in attenuated form, was one strategy for maintaining their status. While unlikely to understand the esoteric details of elite high culture, commoners also constituted an audience for state ideology, if not directly, then as it was mediated through their leaders. Perhaps more importantly, however, folk traditions appear to have been historically constitutive of the notions of order that shaped civilizations. The fundamental metaphors and mythic structures surrounding the productive forces that make life possible are the most enduring aspects of high culture, and most likely predate its development. Finally, artisans and religious specialists, about whom we know relatively little, also seem to have had a part in this process, particularly with regard to maintaining (and transforming) the distinctive style of material culture and the belief systems associated with specific cults.

While the groups involved in the creation and maintenance of high culture are much more varied than Baines and Yoffee suggest, inner elites do play a critical role in these processes. Inner elites appear to sustain the constellation of myth, ritual, and distinctive material culture that distinguishes different civilizations; without them this conjunction of style, meaning, and politics unravels as these elements are reshaped in the face of changing circumstances. While difficult, if not impossible, to systematically assess, Andean civilization does appear to be more discontinuous than others, with what Moseley (1978) has termed distinctive "corporate styles" appearing rapidly after the formation of successive states. Why this should be the case – perhaps because of sustained periods of decentralization or the exceptionally rugged terrain and consequent difficulty of communication – is not clear.

Over the last few decades Andeanists have taken a critical stance towards a Cuzco-centric model of the Inka empire. They have turned their attention to the provinces and the examination of bureaucratic records in an attempt to penetrate the European and Inka biases inherent in the classic Spanish chronicles (e.g., D'Altroy 1992; Malpass 1993; Murra and Morris 1976). One of the findings to emerge from this scholarship is that rather than the monolithic state depicted by indigenous and Spanish elites, the Inka empire was a rapidly changing, and in some ways fragile, polity that was repeatedly challenged by both conquered groups and royal factions. While elites attempted to impose notions of order associated with the state and campaigned against alternative ideologies, they did not always succeed. Furthermore, although the high culture associated with the Inka state was a novel configuration of ideas and practices, its origins can be traced to less complex societies that existed prior to the expansion of the empire and that were eventually absorbed by it.

One might argue that the examination of an empire that was in the process of expanding when it was destroyed tells us little about the long-term processes that are characteristic of civilizations. However, the availability of information on the early development of the Inka empire and the fact that it is such a recent case allow us to see processes that might otherwise be obscured by the consolidation of power and the passage of time. The role played by non-elites in the transmittal of civilization is probably not unique to the Andes – only more visible. The Inka case thus suggests that approaches to the analysis of continuity in ancient civilizations should foster the examination of linkages as well as the ruptures between inner elites, provincial leaders, and their subjects.

# 8 Wealth and socioeconomic hierarchies of the Indus Valley civilization

JONATHAN MARK KENOYER

## Introduction

When archaeologists first began excavating the ancient cities of Harappa and Mohenjo-daro in the 1920s and 1930s, they did so in the shadow of unique discoveries being made in Egypt and Mesopotamia. The social and political organization of these civilizations set the standard against which other early state societies were compared. Furthermore, monumental stone architecture, sculptures made of stone or precious metals, elaborate grave goods, and royal tombs filled with gold and exotic treasures came to be used as a standard of ancient wealth. Based on the written records of Egypt and Mesopotamia, many scholars have assumed that indicators of wealth and socio-economic status were relatively uniform in the ancient world and that these indicators were used in much the same way in all early states.

The absence of comparable categories of wealth items and centralized architectural structures in the Indus cities has led most scholars to conclude that the people ruling the Indus cities had different values and possibly a different form of political organization from that seen in other early states (Kenoyer 1989; Fairservis 1989; J. G. Shaffer 1982). The lack of long texts and the fact that the Indus script has not been deciphered has remained a major obstacle in explaining these differences.

In contrast to other civilizations where written texts provide the foundation for discussion, it is necessary to look back to the first settlements of the Indus Valley in order to understand the ideology and hierarchy of order, the legitimation of that order, and the nature of wealth in the Indus cities. In these early settlements it is possible to trace the origins of specific objects that came to be used as wealth items and symbols of order and legitimation during the later Indus cities. The creation of these wealth items and the role of specific wealth items as indicators of socioeconomic status is based on a combination of economic and ideological processes that are highly variable, both regionally and temporally. Nevertheless, contextual and chronological studies of specific artifact types reveal the use of symbolic objects and the accumulation of wealth as a means of reinforcing social and economic hierarchies, beginning with the earliest Neolithic occupations at Mehrgarh (7000–6500 BC), continuing through the Chalcolithic occupation at Mehrgarh, Nausharo, and Harappa, and culminating in the Integration Era, Harappan Phase, 2600–1900 BC.

With the rise of the Indus cities around 2600 BC, technology and crafts appear to have become an essential mechanism for creating unique wealth objects to distinguish socioeconomic classes and reinforce the hierarchy of these classes in an urban context. Many of these wealth objects have strong ideological associations and appear to have been used as symbols that served both to unite as well as to differentiate socioeconomic classes living in the cities (Vidale 1989a; Kenoyer 1992a; Bhan *et al.* 1994). Merchants and artisans of the Indus cities appear to have played a significant role in power negotiations through restricting access to exotic raw materials and by the invention of new and more complex technologies requiring special knowledge of materials and manufacturing processes. Some of these technologies and their products were directly controlled by the rulers and powerful merchants (similar to what Baines and Yoffee call inner elites [Baines and Yoffee 1998; chapter 2 in this volume]), but there is little evidence for military coercion. Other technologies may have been subject to indirect control through taxation and limited access to raw materials.

While some of the wealth items used in the Indus Valley can be identified by comparison with contemporaneous cultures, other objects that may have been used as symbols of wealth can be identified archaeologically through quantitative studies combined with technological analysis and distribution patterns within the site (Kenoyer 1992b, 1997a). Through the use of stylistic studies and relational analogies with later cultures of the subcontinent and adjacent regions, it is also possible to identify symbolic objects that may have been used to communicate power and status. The nature of wealth that must have been used to support and legitimize power can also be identified. These studies have made it

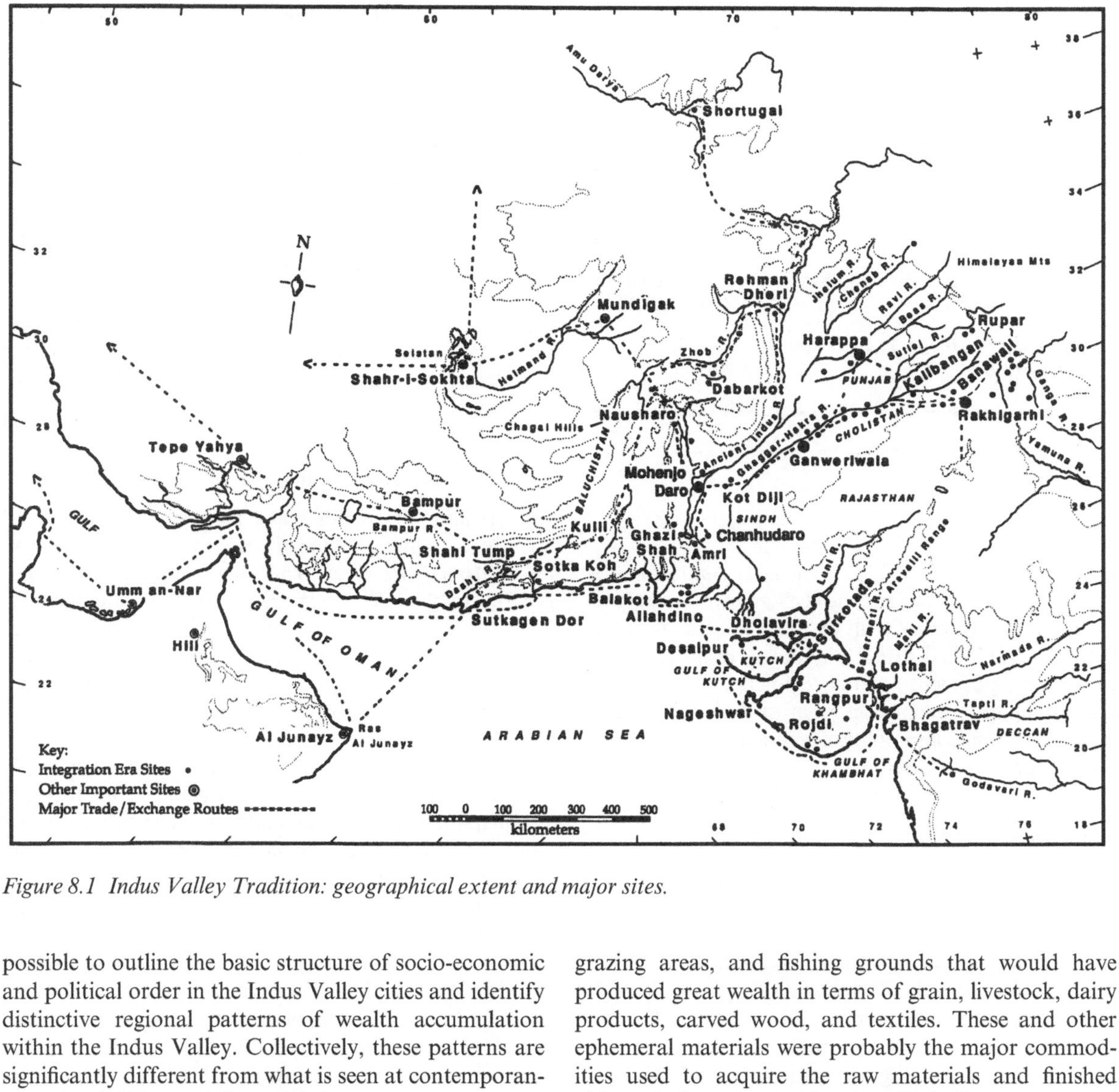


*Figure 8.1 Indus Valley Tradition: geographical extent and major sites.*

possible to outline the basic structure of socio-economic and political order in the Indus Valley cities and identify distinctive regional patterns of wealth accumulation within the Indus Valley. Collectively, these patterns are significantly different from what is seen at contemporaneous sites in West and Central Asia.

### Geographical setting and resource distribution

The geographical setting for the Indus Valley Tradition includes the piedmont and plateaus of Baluchistan to the west, and the mountainous regions of northern Pakistan, Afghanistan, and India to the northwest and north (Figure 8.1). Two major river systems formerly watered the greater Indus plain, the Indus and the Ghaggar-Hakra (now dry). The alluvial plains have abundant resources in terms of fertile agricultural land, grazing areas, and fishing grounds that would have produced great wealth in terms of grain, livestock, dairy products, carved wood, and textiles. These and other ephemeral materials were probably the major commodities used to acquire the raw materials and finished objects that are preserved archaeologically.

Except for clay used for pottery, and animal products such as bone, antler, and ivory, most of the permanent raw materials used in the production of other types of wealth items came from one or more source areas outside of the alluvial plain. Some of the chert and limestone used in the cities was obtained from outcrops in the alluvial plain, but most of the other lithic materials and mineral resources were brought from peripheral regions. The distribution of important natural resources along the edges of the Indus Valley was such that several alternative sources of specific materials

| | |
|---|---|
| ***Localization Era*** | |
| Late Harappan Phase | *c.* 1900–1300 BC |
| ***Integration Era*** | |
| Harappan Phase | 2600–1900 BC |
| *Harappa: Period 3C, Final* | *2200–1900 BC* |
| *Harappa: Period 3B, Middle* | *2450–2200 BC* |
| *Harappa: Period 3A, Initial* | *2600–2400 BC* |
| ***Regionalization Era*** | |
| Early Harappan (several Phases) | *c.* 5500–2600 BC |
| *Kot Diji Phase* | *2800–2600 BC* |
| ***Early Food Producing Era*** | |
| Neolithic | *c.* 7000–5500 BC |

*Figure 8.2 General chronology of the Indus Valley Tradition.*

existed. Lapis lazuli, agate, carnelian, steatite, ochre, copper, tin, gold, silver, marine shell and wood could all be obtained from more than one source area (Kenoyer 1995a). The unique distribution of these resources led to the early development of inter-regional trade networks that stimulated economic competition and more complex economic and political interaction between the early village communities.

## Chronology

The Indus Valley Tradition refers to the long cultural trajectory leading to the first urban state level society in South Asia (Kenoyer 1991a; J. G. Shaffer 1992). This trajectory is divided into four Eras (Figure 8.2), beginning with the Early Food Producing Era (*c.* 7000–5500 BC), when domestic plants and animals are first exploited by semi-sedentary communities in the Indus Valley region. The Regionalization Era (5500–2600 BC), is a period of cultural development on a regional scale with the emergence of distinctive artifact styles, burial practices, and settlement organization. At the site of Harappa there is new evidence suggesting the emergence of an Early Indus state around 2800 BC, but the major urban phase begins around 2600 BC during the Harappan Phase of the Integration Era (Kenoyer 1994a; Meadow and Kenoyer 1999).

The Integration Era sees the widespread use of the Indus script, inscribed seals and tablets, standardized weights, similar styles of pottery vessels and a wide range of other symbolic objects and wealth indicators. There is considerable evidence for economic and ideological integration throughout the vast regions of the Indus valley and some evidence for localized political domination by individual city states or republics (Kenoyer 1997b).

During the Localization Era (1900–1300 BC) there is a breakdown of integration and the reemergence of regional cultures that reflect localized trade networks and stylistic features of material culture. The disappearance of Indus writing, standardized weights, and the collapse of long-distance trade represents a major reorganization of social, economic, and political structures. In addition, there appear to have been major changes in the ideology used to legitimize elite control (Kenoyer 1995b).

## Symbols of wealth and status

The creation of wealth items in a specific culture is directly correlated to the distribution of specific raw materials and the accessibility of these materials to the general public. As summarized by Van Buren and Richards in the introduction to this volume, these wealth items form the basis for both order and legitimacy within a society. In order for symbols of wealth and status to be effective they must be commonly understood or legitimized by the society at large and by the smaller communities within which private symbols of wealth are viewed. Manufactured with permanent or ephemeral materials, these wealth items and their correlation with status or power can result from very different processes of cultural selection and use (Kenoyer 1995b). Although the mechanisms through which this association and its legitimation is achieved cannot be determined without recourse to textual records, it is possible to follow the changing role of specific objects over time.

The cultural selection of wealth items often results from long-term economic conditions and/or ideological associations, such as the rarity of gold and its immutable qualities. Other forms of wealth are short-term creations stimulated by the need for overt displays in a rapidly changing social system. For example, the creation of inscribed seals with animal motifs and script coincides with the emergence of Indus elites and disappears with the breakdown of the Indus economic and ideological system.

The use of wealth items is also quite complex in that some wealth items were meant for general public display, whereas others may have been privately displayed among elites or a more limited set of social groups (again, similar to what Baines and Yoffee refer to as inner elites). Examples of publicly visible wealth would be the vast herds or agricultural lands of ruling families, the massive architecture and cities in which the elites resided, or the occasional public displays of elites dressed in elaborate costumes. Private wealth can be defined as objects that are viewed by a limited number of individuals, generally restricted to the interior of habitation areas or sacred precincts, used in special rituals such as burial, or personal ornaments that are worn beneath the clothing or are not displayed ostentatiously. Private wealth displays among elites would be seen in the details of ornaments, utensils, textiles, and the ornamentation of private domestic furnishings, such as beds, tables, stools, and containers.

The differentiation between public and private is important because they often present contrasting views of a society. Public symbols may be used to unite people to a common ideology or political agenda, while private symbols may be used to reinforce smaller group identity, especially among elites. The identification of public and private symbols is quite difficult archaeologically since private wealth objects may intentionally or inadvertently be exposed for public viewing. Nevertheless, it is useful to differentiate between public and private use of wealth symbols for interpreting their role in legitimation of social order and ideology. Both public and private symbols of wealth are used by human societies as a form of non-verbal communication of status, ideology, and power. Once a child has become socialized or an outsider has become acculturated to a specific community, the visual effects of a wide range of cultural materials communicate meaning without the need for repeated verbal articulation. In the context of early state society, a secluded temple precinct with sacred sculptures and buried wealth offerings could be contrasted with openly worn ornaments and decorated buildings. Both sets of symbols provide important clues about the role of wealth and other symbolic objects in the reinforcement of social order and ideology within specific contexts (Hodder 1982; R. L. Anderson 1989).

Systematic recovery and documentation of preserved objects or symbols can provide unique perspectives on the socioeconomic structure of a society. Coercive power (military) or ritual power (ideology) also can be reflected in specific forms of utilitarian or symbolic items. For example, military power legitimized by ideology can be depicted in graphic displays depicting rulers supported by deities. When such narratives are carved in stone or incorporated into ornaments they also reflect the wealth in materials or labor that is at the disposal of certain elites. More often than not, where texts are available, economic wealth is directly linked with coercive power, both physical and ideological.

Competition for wealth is also an important factor in technological elaboration and exploration for new material resources. When objects that were once considered as wealth become accessible to the common people, new forms of wealth must be created. Illegal production and imitation are important factors that often result in expanded trade contacts and new technological achievements.

In the context of the ancient Indus Valley Tradition there is an absence of written texts that could provide culturally specific information on the value of different objects and their relationship to economic wealth, social status, and power. Furthermore there are no large narrative carvings that depict rulers or elites with symbols of power or wealth. Consequently the evaluation and ranking of wealth items must be approached from a more empirical perspective based on slightly overlapping assumptions that will be discussed below. These assumptions are central to understanding the creation of wealth and how wealth items are modified over time.

### Archaeological indicators of wealth and power

Generally speaking, a wealth item can be defined as an archaeologically preserved object that reflects relatively high levels of indirect or direct economic control of resources, labor, or technological knowledge. Archaeologically preserved objects, such as ornaments, architecture, or tools reflect other forms of wealth that are not preserved, for example, grain, foodstuffs, livestock, or even agricultural land. The relative value of preserved objects can be calculated on the basis of four major assumptions:

1. rare or exotic raw materials have relatively more value than locally available raw materials;
2. the overall wealth value of an object increases with the amount of labor required for production, where labor refers to time and/or numbers of artisans involved in production;
3. technological processes involving numerous stages, high degrees of skill and/or specialized technical knowledge increase the value of an object;
4. once an item has been accepted as a symbol of wealth within a society, elites will attempt to control the access to raw materials or knowledge in order to limit the production of specific wealth items and control their use.

The validity of these assumptions in the evaluation of economic wealth is well supported by cross-cultural studies of crafts and the relationships between long distance trade, crafting and power (Helms 1993). Within this framework it is possible to rank various crafts products used in a society and estimate the relative value of specific types of objects. This ranking can then be compared with the actual distribution of objects throughout the site or their frequency over time (Kenoyer 1992b).

These four assumptions can be further correlated with major groups of specialized crafts that are defined by two sets of variables: the accessibility of raw materials and the complexity of the technology required to process raw material into specific objects (Kenoyer 1992a). In the geographical context of the Indus Valley the craft technologies used to create objects can be divided into four major groups:

1 crafts processing from locally available materials using relatively simple technologies include woodworking, basket making, simple weaving, terracotta pottery production, and house-building;
2 crafts using imported materials with relatively simple technologies include stone-shaping for domestic purposes and chipped stone tool-making;
3 crafts using local materials and complex technologies and production processes include stoneware bangle manufacture, elaborate painted and specialized pottery production, complex weaving and carpet making, inlaid woodwork production and construction of decorative architecture;
4 crafts using imported materials and highly complex technologies include agate bead manufacture, seal production, copper/bronze metalworking, stone-carving, precious metalworking, shell working, and faience manufacture.

The production and distribution of objects made by crafts in the last two categories are the most easily controlled. Consequently, these are the crafts that tend to be used in the creation of wealth items, a process that began with the earliest Neolithic communities and became modified with each subsequent phase of development.

## Early technologies and wealth indicators

Beginning with the early Neolithic settlements of the Indus Valley region, around 7000–6500 BC, regional cultural identity and social complexity within specific settlements began to be represented by symbolic and utilitarian objects created by specialized craft technologies, such as metallurgy, ceramic production, lapidary, and glazing (J.-F. Jarrige 1982). The invention and initial development of these specialized technologies seems to have focused more on the production of symbolic objects representing wealth and power, rather than simply utilitarian objects, a pattern noted by C. S. Smith in his broad comparative study of early metallurgy (C. S. Smith 1976).

The site of Mehrgarh, at the western edge of the Indus valley, provides an excellent record of the early use of material objects as symbols to define social status and power (J.-F. Jarrige 1984). The Neolithic and early Chalcolithic occupations reveal a rich assemblage of material culture from both domestic and burial contexts which reflects changing economic strategies and possibly changing attitudes towards wealth.

In the Neolithic cemetery, during Period 1A (non-ceramic Neolithic), both juveniles and adults were buried with varying quantities and styles of ornaments and grave goods (Sellier 1988; Barthélémy de Saizieu 1990, 1992), but there is no clear patterning to suggest hierarchical social organization (J.-F. Jarrige 1995). Valuable ornaments of particular importance to this study are wide shell bangles made from the marine shell *Turbinella pyrum*, shell beads and pendants, and beads made from colored stones and soft steatite. These same materials continued to be used in later times and eventually came to be used as wealth items during the Harappan Phase. Over time, the number of burial goods interred with the dead decreased, such that the later Chalcolithic burials (Periods II and III, from around 5500 to 3300 BC) had very few ornaments or utensils (Samzun and Sellier 1983; Samzun 1988).

In contrast to the burials, the Neolithic figurines depict few, if any, ornaments. Later Chalcolithic period figurines show increasing amounts of ornaments, with a veritable explosion in the diversity of coiffure styles and body ornaments for both female and male figurines during Periods VI and VII, *c.* 2900–2600 BC (C. Jarrige 1988; C. Jarrige *et al.* 1995). These figurines undoubtedly reflect changing patterns of personal adornment as well as attitudes towards wealth.

Corresponding to the increases in ornamentation on figurines is a marked change in production strategies for ornaments and other objects at the site. During the Neolithic occupation (Period I), most of the ornaments were made of exotic materials that appear to have been traded to the site as finished objects (C. Jarrige *et al.* 1995; Kenoyer 1995c). In contrast, during the Chalcolithic there is a gradual increase in the importation and processing of non-local raw materials and local production of many ornaments and tools becomes the norm during Period III (around 4800 to 3300 BC).

The change to local production is quite significant because it reflects the direct control of production for items that would have been used to define ethnic identity, status, and power. The inhabitants of Mehrgarh no longer traded for finished shell bangles and beads through intermediaries, but had begun to acquire the raw materials and produce their own styles of ornaments. Steatite and other varieties of soft stone were brought to the site and processed there rather than at the source areas in the mountains.

Eventually steatite bead production became more complex through the addition of pyrotechnological components (Vanzetti and Vidale 1994; Vidale 1989b, 1995) that set the foundation for the later production of glazed quartz or faience, also referred to as siliceous faience (Barthélémy de Saizieu and Bouquillon 1994; H. M.-L. Miller 1997). These developments can be directly correlated with increasingly sophisticated pottery production and copper working (J.-F. Jarrige 1995: 67), technologies that were probably not accessible to all individuals of the community.

The increasing diversity of ornaments used by the living populations at Mehrgarh reflects an increased need to publicly display wealth and status indicators. This trend corresponds with the increase in settlement size and complexity, and also coincides with the gradual decrease in ornaments as a component of burial offerings. Although Jarrige has argued that there is nothing in the burials, architecture or spatial organization of the site during Period III to suggest a greater degree of hierarchy than in the Neolithic (J.-F. Jarrige 1995: 73), it is not unlikely that the overall decrease in the total number of grave goods in these later levels indicates a gradual change in social attitudes towards wealth. If this changing pattern of burial offerings reflects a change in attitudes towards wealth accumulation, it is probable that wealth items were being kept in circulation rather than being buried in the ground. The few burial offerings that were placed with the dead may represent ritual items or ornaments that were not transferable to other individuals, either in the family or clan.

Although the emergence of distinct socioeconomic classes at Mehrgarh cannot be documented through conventional data, such as burials and architecture, I would argue that the invention of glazed steatite and faience clearly reflect the need to create unique wealth materials for certain members of the community. No centralized structures for political, economic, or ideological control have been found at the site, and yet craft production was gradually transformed from relatively simple forms of processing to highly specialized industries involving both local and exotic materials and complex pyrotechnologies. The trend towards wealth creation through the control of technology rather than simply the centralized acquisition of exotic or rare materials reflects a basic pattern that is quite different from that proposed by Baines and Yoffee for Egypt and Mesopotamia (Baines and Yoffee 1998). These general trends in the production, display, and deposition of wealth items during the Neolithic and Early Chalcolithic period at Mehrgarh provide an important background for understanding later forms of wealth creation in the Indus Valley as a whole.

## Early Harappan transformations

In order to follow the subsequent developments in the Indus Valley Tradition it is necessary to focus on the site of Harappa, located in the center of the northern alluvial plain. Here it is possible to document the crystallization of social order and mechanisms for legitimation during the Early Harappan Phase, around 3500 BC to 2800 BC. The gradually standardized forms and orientation of architecture and the overall layout of the site are perhaps the most direct indicators of social and ideological order. These developments coincide with the emergence of writing, the use of inscribed seals and specific symbols on painted pottery and other objects. Together with major advances in craft production and shifting centers of trade networks these changes reflect more complex forms of social, political, and ideological organization in the Indus Valley. Some of these changes can be directly linked to the creation of new forms of wealth to distinguish hierarchical social and economic classes, while other changes can be indirectly associated with ideological developments and political-economic control (Kenoyer 1991a).

Unlike early Egypt, where rulers and ideologies can be identified on the basis of inscribed ivory tags and carved stone palettes (Fischer 1989), it is not possible to identify the individuals or groups who were responsible for the early economic and political development in the Indus Valley. Nevertheless, as will be demonstrated below, there is clear evidence for the creation of order through social and economic stratification and the accumulation of wealth, as well as the legitimation of order through the use of both exclusive and shared symbols.

At Harappa, the Early Harappan occupation (Harappa Period 1) represents one of the oldest village

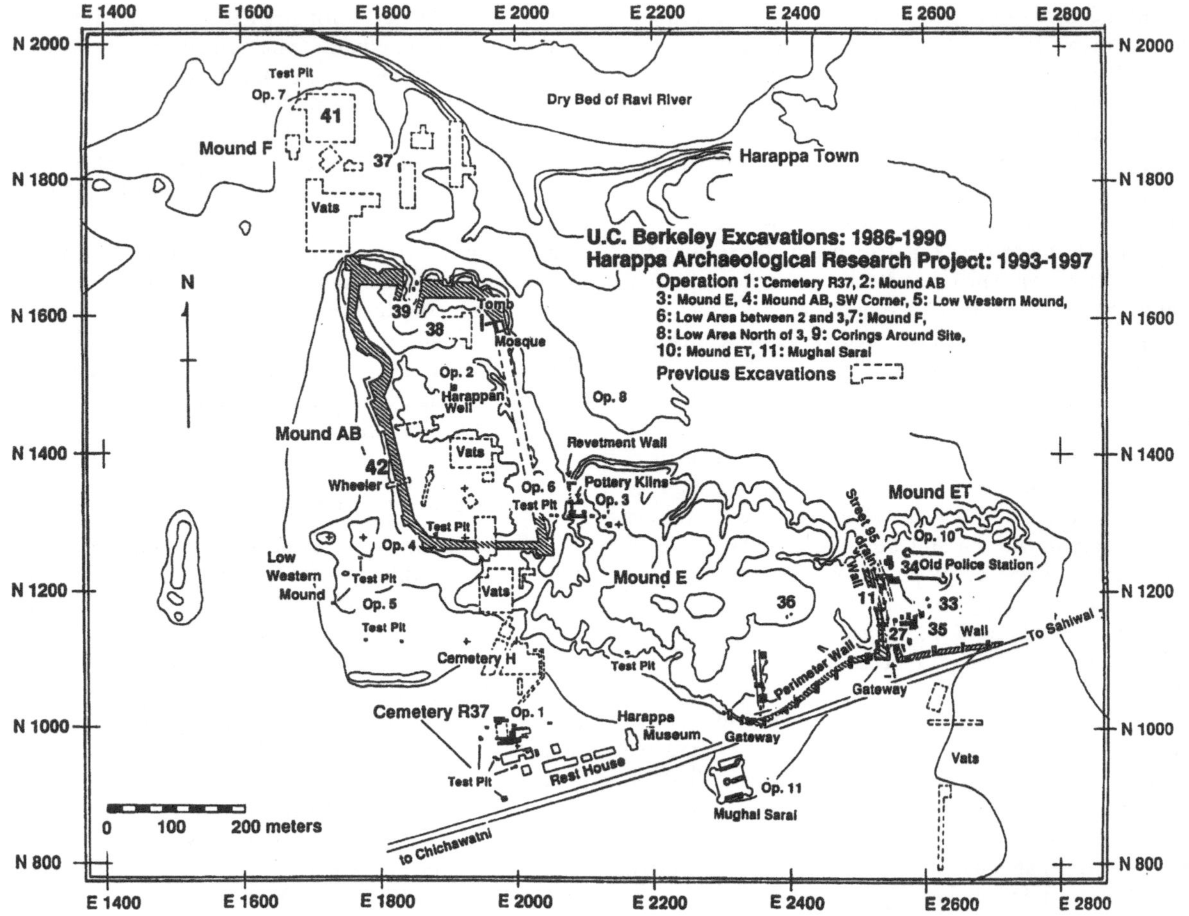


*Figure 8.3 Harappa 1997: site plan and excavation areas.*

settlements in the core area of the northern Indus valley, dating from around 3300–2800 BC (Figure 8.3). During this period Harappa is characterized by a small community, approximately 10 hectares in area, practicing wheat and barley agriculture, supplemented by animal husbandry, specialized crafts, and long-distance trade. Other settlements equivalent to Period 1 have been discovered to the south at Jalilpur (Mughal 1974) and at Rajanpur to the northwest (Mughal 1997; M. R. Mughal and Afzal Khan, personal communication). By Period 2 (2800–2600 BC) the settlement at Harappa had expanded to more than 25 hectares with numerous smaller sites in the surrounding hinterland (Mughal 1990; M. R. Mughal, Punjab Survey, personal communication). Although detailed regional surveys have not yet been completed, a multi-tiered settlement pattern can be expected, with Harappa being the earliest urban center of the northern Indus Valley.

The early levels at the site contain a wide variety of exotic materials indicating long-distance trade contacts with the Makran coast in the south, as well as with the mountain regions to the west and deserts to the east (Meadow and Kenoyer 1999). The strategic position of Harappa in a rich agricultural zone centered between major north–south riverine routes and east–west overland routes is quite significant. Over time, the manipulation of trade and subsistence resources, the invention of new technologies to create new forms of wealth, and possibly specific political and ideological factors led to its growth and eventual dominance as an urban center. A similar process may have been occurring at sites such as Mohenjo-daro, Chanhudaro, and Amri to the south, but concrete evidence for the initial phases of this important transition have so far only been recovered from Harappa. Contrary to previous models for the origin of Indus cities, which suggested a population movement from the piedmont to the central alluvial plains (Dales 1965; Fairservis 1967), it is more likely that communities which had been living in the alluvium for hundreds of years began a process of economic development similar to what had happened at Mehrgarh during Periods II and III. But unlike Mehrgarh, where, with the exception of pottery production, specialized craft activities appear to have fallen off after Period III (around 3500 BC), Harappa sees the gradual increase and elaboration of craft activities beginning at approximately the same time. Because of the larger agricultural base and potential markets to the east and south, Harappa was able to continue along a trajectory of economic and political growth that led to its eventual establishment as a dominant urban center. These developments at Harappa and presumably other sites such as Mohenjo-daro, resulted in major reorganizations of trade networks, political structures, and power relations, such that the new centers were in the alluvium rather than along the piedmont.

During the Early Harappan Phase increasing social stratification is reflected in the overall hierarchy of settlement sizes (Mughal 1982, 1990) and the internal divisions of sites into neighborhoods with localized craft activities. Perhaps most important is the creation of massive walls and gateways to protect the settlements and control movement into and out of the occupation areas (Kenoyer 1991a, 1991b).

Other indicators of social stratification are seen in the creation of new styles of wealth indicators which include decorated pottery, ornaments, metal tools, and symbolic objects such as seals. Of central importance is the fact that many of the same basic styles of objects were being created in materials of different relative value (as defined above). Presumably this pattern reflects socioeconomic stratification and some degree of ideological integration. It has been possible to identify specific examples of the types of artifacts that were being developed into symbols of status and wealth during the Early Harappan Phase. Some of these objects, such as painted pottery motifs, beads, bangles, and carved seals may also have served as symbols of ethnic and/or ideological identity.

Painted pottery is a common artifact in the earliest occupation at Harappa (Period 1) when there is a great diversity in motifs and color combinations, but a relatively low number of vessel shapes. The earliest examples of the intersecting circle design and the fish-scale motif appear during this period (Figure 8.4). Later, in Period 2, most of the polychrome painting and the diversity of geometric and floral motifs is replaced by black/brown designs or horizontal bands, on red slipped surfaces. The development of wheel-thrown pottery results in a greater diversity of rim, body, and base forms. Although most of the earlier shapes and designs disappear, two notable exceptions are the intersecting circle motif and the fish-scale design (Figures 8.4 and 8.9).

At Harappa these two motifs continue to be executed on pottery vessels using black paint on red slip and at this same time begin to appear at sites throughout the Indus Valley and Baluchistan. These painted designs are certainly more than simple decorative motifs and most likely represent important rituals or ideologies that are gradually spreading or crystallizing throughout the Indus Valley. In later times, the circle, and by extension the intersecting circle motif, is associated with concepts of unity, interconnectedness, protection, and strength (Parpola 1990, 1994). The fish motif is commonly associated with fertility in later iconography and hence the fish-scale design may reflect abundance or fertility. When painted on large vessels that were used in the home as well as in rituals, such as weddings or harvest celebrations, these motifs would have served as both private and public reinforcement of an ideology that was shared by communities throughout the Indus Valley.

The lower proportion of decorated to plain vessels during Period 2 (Early Harappan Phase) suggests that painted vessels may have been more valuable than plain wares, but there is no evidence that these painted vessels were being traded as a form of wealth. More important is the fact that only wealthy people can afford to fill large vessels with beer or grain. Consequently, the display of large vessels with painted designs during a ceremony or simply as a part of daily use in the home can be seen as a form of legitimation and reinforcement of status and ideology.

More specific indicators of wealth can be seen in ornaments made from different types of raw materials and complex manufacturing processes. Exotic raw materials such as marine shell, lapis lazuli, carnelian, and banded agate were being processed at Harappa using a variety of techniques and finished objects made from these materials can be identified as valuable wealth items based on the assumptions stated earlier. Gold and silver ornaments have not yet been found at Harappa during this early period, but they are reported from other sites such as Rehman Dheri (Durrani 1988), Jalilpur (Mughal 1974), and Kunal (Khatri and Acharya 1995). In addition to these more commonly identified materials, stea-

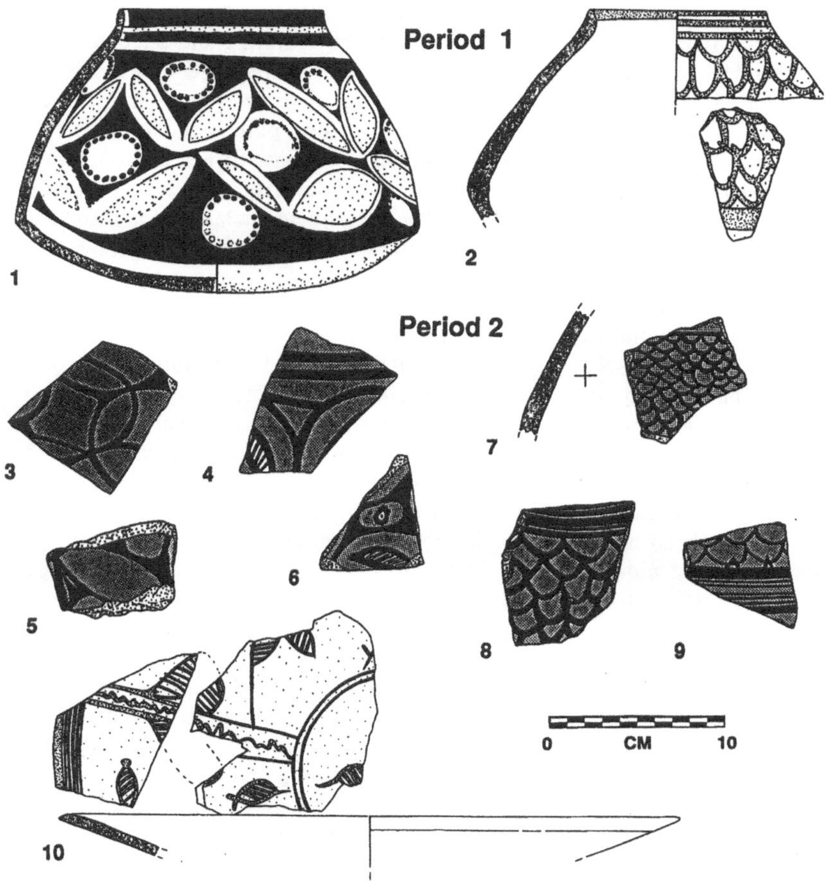


*Figure 8.4 Early Harappan painted ceramics. 1–2: period 1; 2–9: period 2; 10: non-local ware with pipal leaf design.*

tite is one of the critical raw materials used in the creation of wealth objects at Harappa and presumably at other sites throughout the Indus Valley.

Unlike the site of Mehrgarh, where steatite was available in the nearby hills and may have been accessible to a large number of individuals, the steatite lumps used at Harappa were a valuable commodity obtained through long-distance trade networks extending over 500 kilometers and across several major rivers, including the Indus. A very thin copper saw that may have been designed specifically to conserve the raw material was used to saw the bead blanks. A wide variety of bead shapes was produced (Figure 8.5) and perforated with a thin copper drill that had a beveled tip (Kenoyer 1997b).

Whereas the technology for heating and hardening steatite appears to be similar between Mehrgarh and Harappa, the glazing at Harappa reflects a more complex technology of production (Kenoyer 1997a). Green glazed steatite may have been used to imitate turquoise or amazonite, both of which are natural raw materials that are difficult to make into shiny beads. During Period 2 at Harappa (2800–2600 BC) the white colored silica glaze on steatite was replaced by the manufacture of white fired steatite that does not have a preserved layer of silica glaze. Green glazed steatite is replaced by green and blue-green colored faience beads, many of which were extremely small and made with a glassy, fine-grained structure referred to as compact faience (McCarthy and Vandiver 1990; Kenoyer 1994b).

Square or circular seals carved with geometric designs were also made from glazed and hardened steatite during the Early Harappan Phase (Figure 8.5). The circular seals are similar to button seals found at other Early Harappan sites such as Rehman Dheri and Kunal. A new form of seal at Harappa is seen in the square glazed steatite seal with a perforated boss (Figure 8.5). Square seals with script and other motifs were also first used during this period. Excavations in 1998 uncovered a square-seal impression on a broken lump of clay that may have been used to seal a storeroom or bundle of

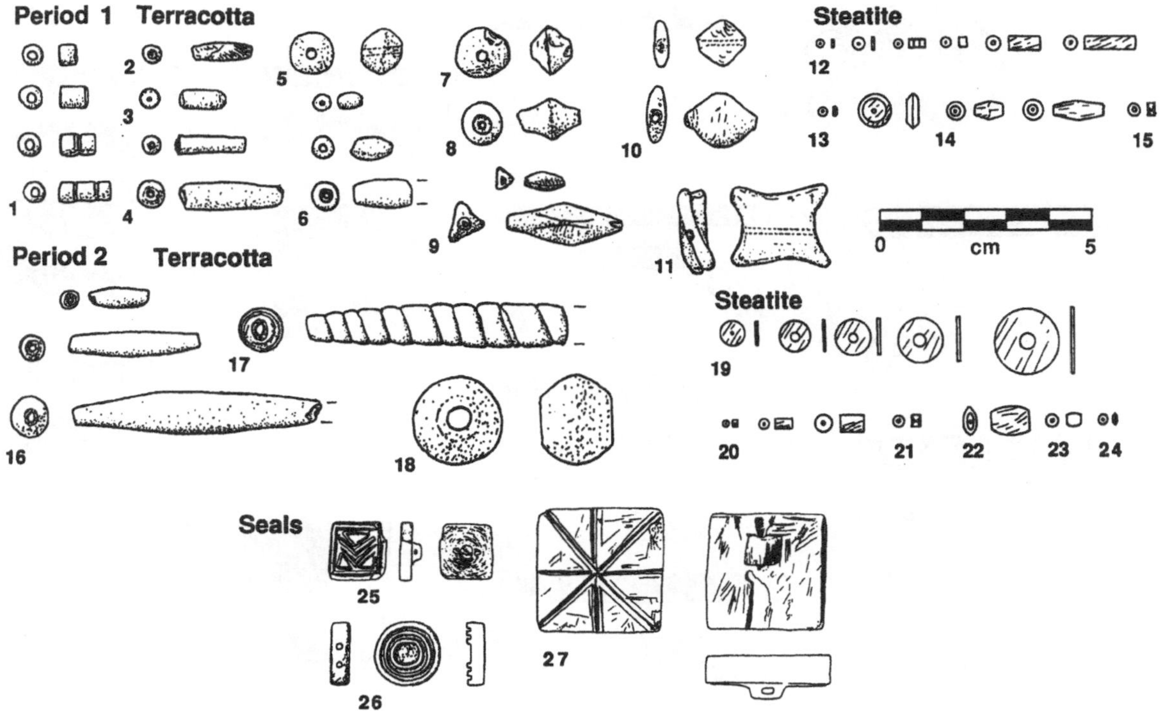


*Figure 8.5 Early Harappan beads and seals. 1–11: period 1, terracotta beads; 12–14: Period 1, fired and glazed steatite; 15: carnelian; 16–18: Period 2, terracotta beads; 19, 20, 22: fired steatite; 21: carnelian; 23: amazonite; 24: lapis lazuli; 25–27 square and circular seals.*

goods. Such sealings are very rare because they are usually not preserved, but this one example is proof that someone at Harappa was receiving or controlling the distribution of a commodity that must have had considerable value. These early square seals appear to be prototypes for the square seals that are distinctive of the Harappan Phase and are associated with high economic status and political power.

The use of similar technologies to produce two different types of objects, beads and seals, provides some insight into the early role of economics and ideology in the creation of wealth items. Although the sample size from Harappa is quite small, glazed steatite *beads* are relatively more numerous and may have been used by more than one socio-economic group, possibly as a form of wealth or some unifying ideology associated with white beads. On the other hand, glazed steatite *seals* appear to be extremely rare and may have been used only by a limited number of individuals. Since the technology for production is basically the same, except for the carving of geometric designs and script, the only thing stopping bead makers from making seals would be ideological or political control. This control is more clearly exercised during the following Harappan Phase, but its origins may be traced to the Early Harappan Phase.

Another important wealth item that was being created during the Early Harappan Phase is bangles made from circlets of terracotta, shell, and copper (Figure 8.6). Beginning in Period 1A and continuing into Period 2 there is a gradual increase in the variety of bangle styles made from terracotta, many of which were decorated with red and black paint. Reduction firing was used to create distinctive black or gray colored bangles which were highly burnished and incised with hatched designs.

In both bead and bangle production new technologies and more complex manufacturing processes were employed to create more varieties of ornaments each of which probably had specific cultural meaning, and presumably some of these ornaments would have been more valuable than others. It is not possible to deter-

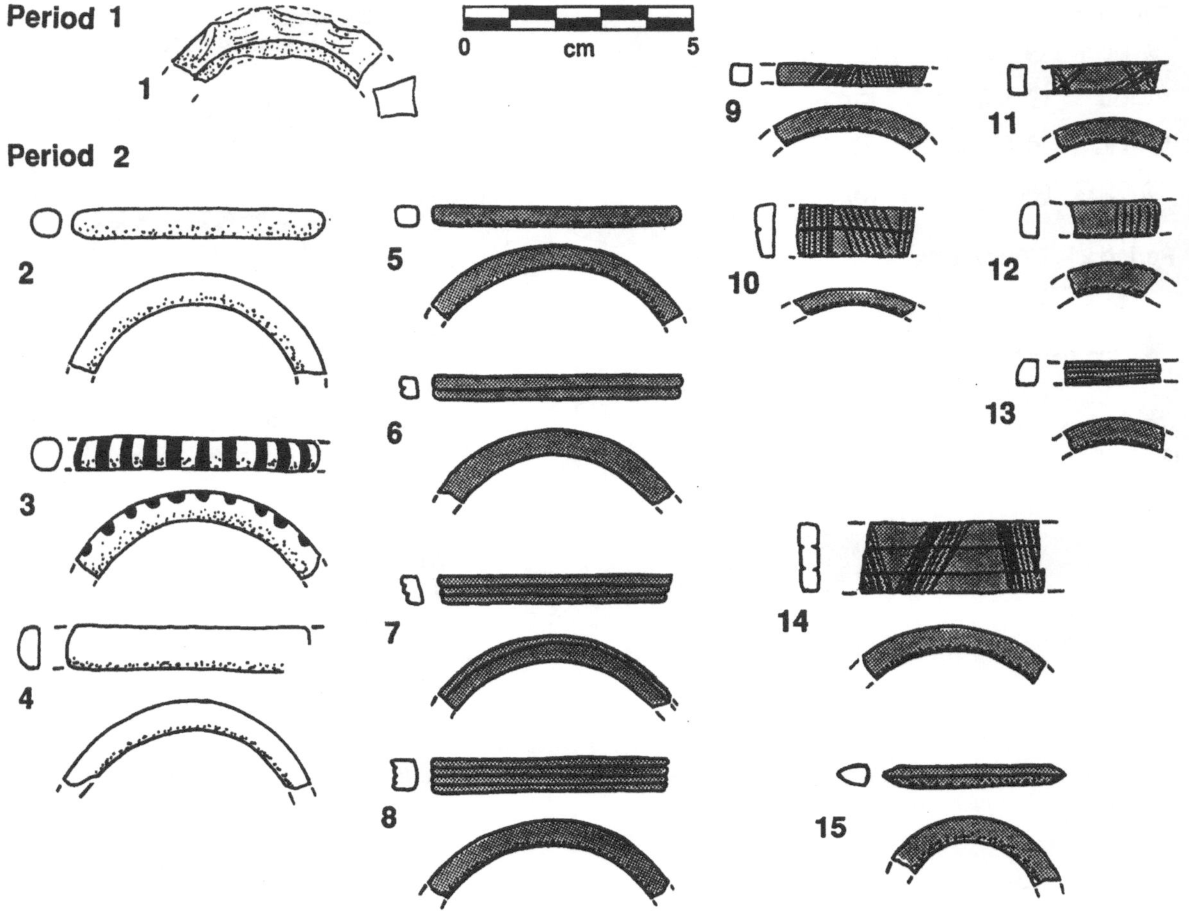


*Figure 8.6 Early Harappan bangle types. 1: period 1; 2 and 4: period 2, terracotta; 3: painted with black bands; 5–15: gray-fired, burnished and incised.*

mine if any of these crafts were being directly controlled by elites during the Early Harappan Phase, but the identification of massive walls enclosing portions of the site where these crafts were practiced suggests some degree of indirect control (Kenoyer 1991b, 1992a).

During the Early Harappan Phase this mechanism for creating wealth items appears to have become well established at Harappa and a similar process was probably going on at other major settlements such as Nausharo (J.-F. Jarrige 1988, 1990), Rehman Dheri, and Mohenjo-daro. More specifically, the basic types of ornaments associated with wealth and stratification that begin to emerge in the Early Harappan Phase set the foundation for the creation of unique forms of wealth that were necessary to reinforce the socioeconomic stratification of the Harappan Phase as seen in the Indus State.

### Harappan order and wealth

During the Harappan Phase (2600–1900 BC), the cities of Harappa, Mohenjo-daro, Dholavira, Ganweriwala, and Rakhigarhi (Figure 8.1) appear to have been relatively independent city-states that would have had direct control over a limited hinterland. The absence of centralized palaces or temples suggests that these cities were not organized as monarchies or theocratic city-states, but were probably more similar to the republics and oligarchies of the Early Historic Period (Kenoyer 1994a, 1997b). Rulers or dominant elites in the various cities would have included traders and merchants, ritual specialists, and individuals who controlled subsistence resources. The elites at each of the major cities appear to have shared a common ideology and economic system as represented by symbolic objects such as seals, ornaments, pottery, and other artifacts. Occupational specialists and service communities (such as sweepers, porters, etc.), who appear to have been organized in loosely stratified groups, were also actively integrated into the overall ideology and contributed to its legitimation through the continued production of symbolic objects and wealth items that were used by the different social classes. In contrast to the large cities, the rural settlements may have been less rigidly stratified and segregated, and would have included larger numbers of farmers, pastoralists, fishers, miners, hunters, and gatherers, etc. The precise degree of political integration probably fluctuated over time, but trade and exchange of important socio-ritual status items demonstrates that the cities and villages were economically integrated, and therefore appear to be integrated on a general ideological level as well.

In contrast with earlier periods, the control of craft production through both indirect and direct means is better documented during the Harappan Phase (Bhan *et al.* 1994). Not surprisingly, the major crafts being controlled were those that used complex technologies and either imported or locally available raw materials. In recent excavations at Harappa, stone bead making, stone weight manufacture, shell, bone and ivory working, inlay manufacture, steatite bead and seal manufacture, copper working, and possibly glazed faience and gold working are all found in close proximity in a distinct craft activity area of Mound ET (Meadow and Kenoyer 1997) (Figure 8.7). The presence of more than one craft in a single area can result from factors other than state control (Kenoyer 1992a), but in this case the craft area is situated inside a walled suburb of the larger Mound E and is located just inside the major southern gateway. Indirect control by urban elites can be inferred because of their localization inside a walled area of the city, but the relatively high concentrations of inscribed tablets and seals in association with the craft area also suggests that there may have been some direct control of specific crafts.

All of these crafts produced objects that can be considered wealth indicators, or, as in the case of cubical stone weights, economic indicators (stone weights were not used as symbols of wealth but would have been used to evaluate wealth economically). Some evidence for seal making is found in this area as well, but copper smelting and stoneware bangle production were being carried out in other areas (Dales and Kenoyer 1991; H. M.-L. Miller 1999). Pottery making, which is found in numerous widely scattered areas of the site, is also noticeably absent from this area of specialized crafts; apparently it was not being directly controlled even though it produced important forms of decorated pottery that had culture-specific symbolic meaning.

When compared with the previous phase of regional development, during the Harappan Phase we see a decrease in the overall variation of certain symbols, such as painted pottery motifs, but an increase in the variety of materials used to make wealth objects and new variations on symbolic themes, specifically in the context of ornaments. We also see the creation of new symbolic objects and wealth indicators, such as seals and weights, that are distinctive for the period of urban integration.

The overall decrease in the heterogeneity or variability of painted pottery designs and the general uniformity of other symbolic objects such as seals and weights probably indicates ideological integration. On the other hand, the increase in variability of ornament styles (Figure 8.8) and raw materials could be the result of several factors, such as diversification of subsistence practices, development of new technologies, and fragmentation and agglomeration of social groups, all of which contributed to the establishment of more stratified social organization. Preliminary comparisons between Indus sites in different geographical regions suggests that there are distinctive regional patterns in certain artifact categories, such as pottery (Dales and Kenoyer 1986) and seals (Rissman 1989), but due to limitations of space it is possible to discuss only a few of the most important categories of artifacts that reflect the wealth and socioeconomic hierarchies of the Harappan Phase. Distinctive seals with Indus script and cubical stone weights represent the important new types of objects that reflect wealth and order. Pottery and ornaments provide examples of socioeconomic stratification, ideological integration, and legitimation.

## Seals

The Harappan Phase and the beginning of the Indus state coincide with the widespread use of a unique form of intaglio seal with Indus script and various symbolic motifs (Figure 8.9). These intaglio seals had a perforated boss on the back and were made from steatite that was whitened and fired at high temperatures to create a hardened surface. Seals were engraved by highly skilled

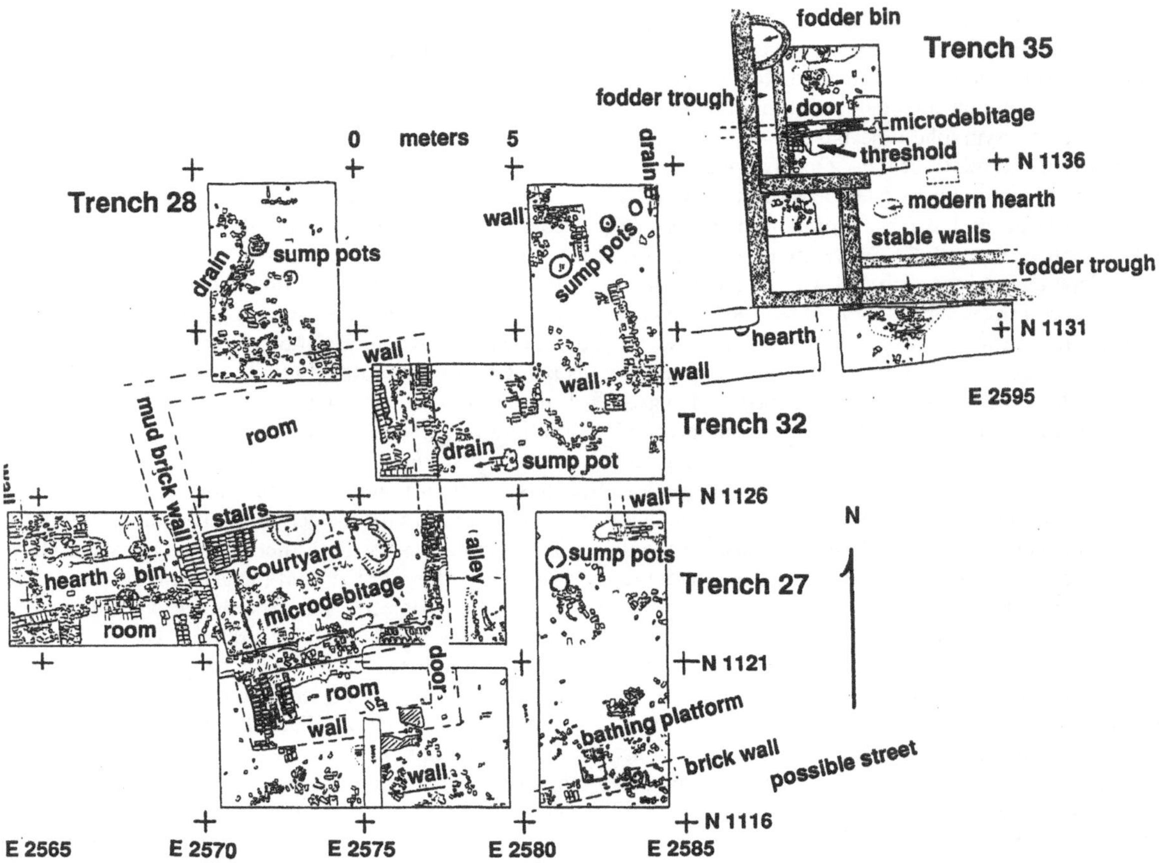


*Figure 8.7 Harappan craft activity area: Mound E/ET.*

artisans, with script as well as zoomorphic and occasionally anthropomorphic figures. Numerous impressions on clay lumps, bullae, and pottery attest to their function as actual seals, though they would have been effective as visible symbols or badges of office as well.

Button seals such as those found in earlier periods are found in association with the intaglio seals, but the geometric designs are generally different from those of the earlier period. The Harappan Phase motifs include the swastika, the endless knot, and various stepped cross designs (Figure 8.9).

All seals can be considered wealth indicators because of their use in the identification of individuals or commodities, but they also served as symbols of ideology and legitimation. The use of intaglio seals appears to have been limited to a relatively small proportion of the population who would have included merchants or political administrators, and in some cases possibly ritual elites. Current research at Harappa has demonstrated that although discarded seals became distributed throughout the settlements, the people who controlled and used the seals were probably living in distinct areas of the cities (Dales and Kenoyer 1990).

Even though only the dominant literate elite used the seals, both literate and illiterate persons would have been able to recognize the message of the seals because most seals contained two levels of information. The script along the top of the seal could have been read by literate elites, while the animal symbol or geometric designs would have informed the illiterate commoners or laborers about the social or ritual affiliation of the seal's owner.

The unicorn motif is the most common symbol used on the seals, while the humped bull and various forms of composite animals are the least common. Due to the lack of stratigraphic and chronological control of seals collected in the past, it is premature to try and sort out the hierarchy of these symbols, but they probably reflect

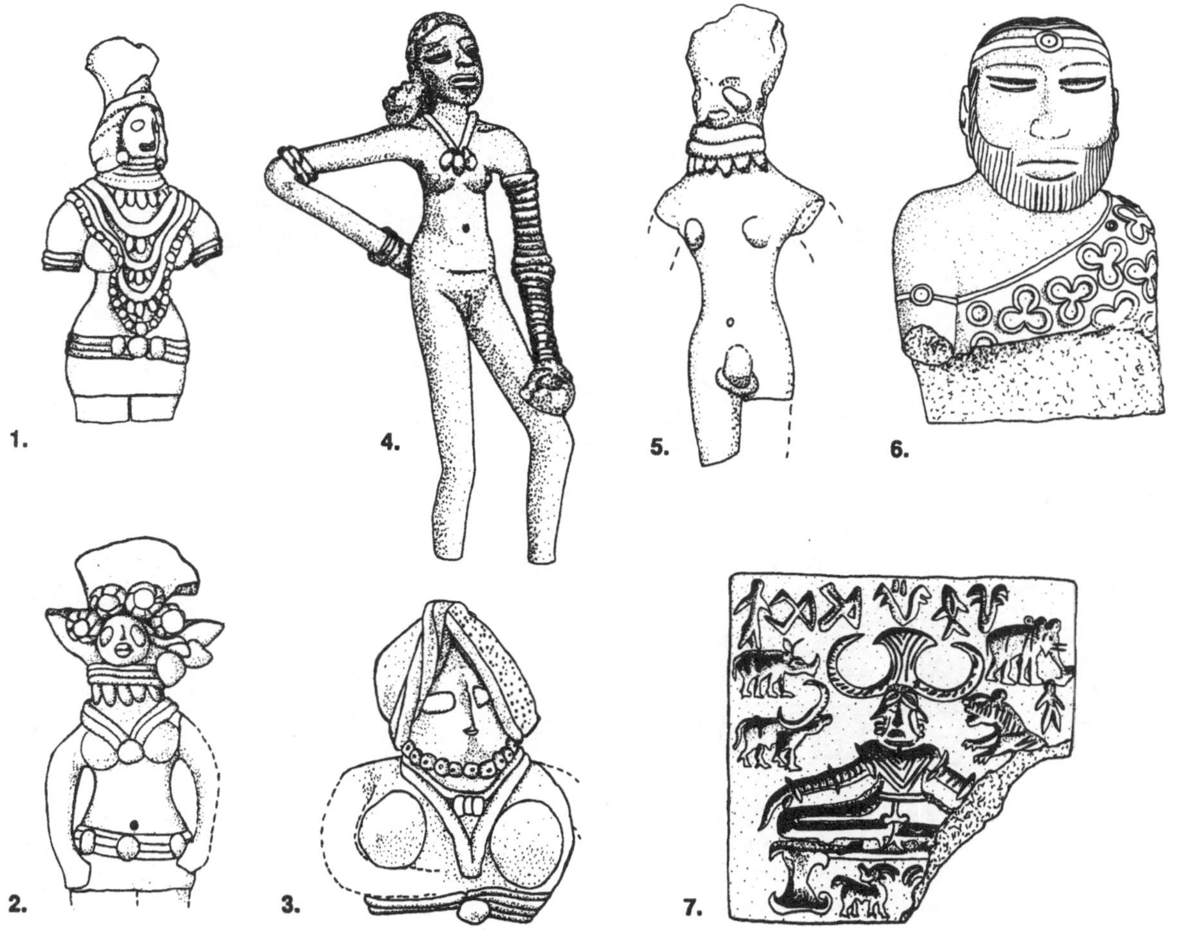


*Figure 8.8 Ornament styles of the Harappan Phase. 1–3, terracotta female figurines from Mohenjo-daro and Harappa; 4, copper/bronze female figurine from Mohenjo-daro; 5, terracotta male figurine from Harappa; 6, white steatite male figurine from Mohenjo-daro; 7, fired steatite intaglio seal from Mohenjo-daro.*

hierarchy within the elites, and may identify hereditary merchant communities, sodalities, clans, or even different classes of administrative officials.

Regardless of the actual meaning of seals, we can suggest that the visual impact of a seal worn openly by an individual or the impression of a seal on a commodity, would serve to reinforce the social and economic hierarchy of the society. Furthermore, the ritual symbolism of the animal or geometric designs might serve to legitimize the social order. The presence of seals throughout the extent of the Indus State indicates that the individuals who used them were widespread and were present at both large urban centers as well as at smaller villages and outposts. This widespread presence of administrative elites or literate merchants may indicate an important mechanism that was used to support the Indus State. The lack of evidence for overt military coercion would indicate that the state was legitimized primarily by economic and/or ritual coercion. A wide range of artifacts can be cited as evidence for the presence of both ritual and economic coercion, but only a few of the most important will be presented here.

## Weights

The Indus weight system is one of the most highly standardized weight systems in prehistory (Marshall 1931) and indicates the existence of a centralized

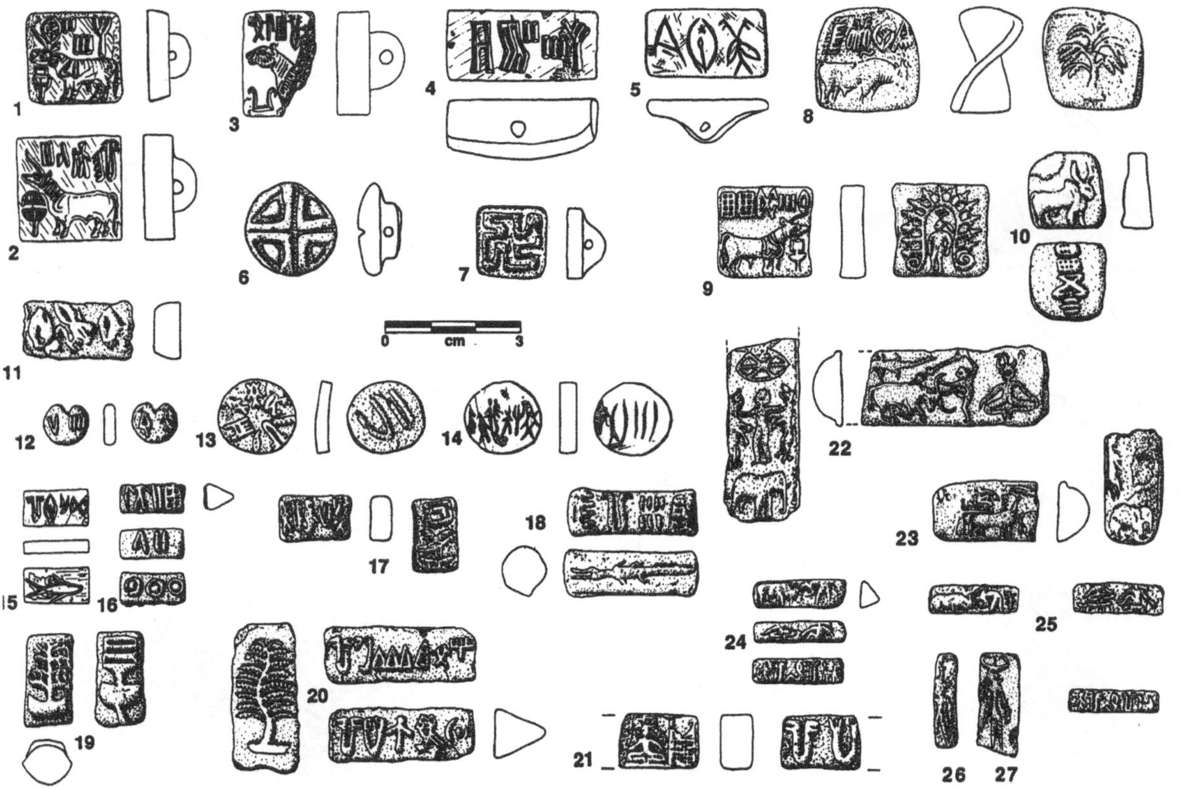

*Figure 8.9 Harappan seals and tablets. 1–3: fired steatite intaglio seals; 4–5: fired steatite intaglio seals with script only; 6–7: molded faience button seals; 8–9 molded terracotta tablets; 10: molded faience tablet; 12–18: various shapes of faience and steatite tablets with script and animal motifs; 19–20: faience and terracotta tablets with sacred tree motifs; 21: seated deity with reed hut or shrine; 22–27 terracotta and faience tablets with narrative motifs.*

authority or coalition of merchants that taxed or controlled the trade of specific commodities. The distinctive cubical chert or agate weights, usually in several graduated sizes, have been found in most settlements of the Indus region as well as in settlements on the periphery where Indus merchants may have obtained raw materials or traded finished products. However, the manufacture of these weights is only confirmed at the largest sites of Mohenjo Daro and Harappa, and the smaller specialized site of Chanhudaro. These three sites also have the largest range in weight categories while the smaller rural settlements tend to have only the middle weights.

The strict adherence to a standard weight system was probably reinforced from the major cities through centralized workshops that produced the weights and through officials who would periodically check the value of the weights to maintain standardization and discourage cheating. This pattern of control may have been similar to the later practice during the Early Historic Mauryan State (*c.* third century BC) in which the state-appointed Minister of Weights and Measures and his officers would travel to smaller towns and check weights being used in the markets and ensure that taxable items were being properly assessed (Prasad 1984, 1987).

The use of cubical stone weights can be seen as an economic indicator of wealth and a symbol of ideology regarding the economic systems of the Indus state. In the absence of evidence for military coercion, the economic system was most probably supported by a common ritual ideology that legitimized the enforcement of such rigid standards. Whether used specifically for taxation or ritual tithe, or simply for the weighing of special commodities, these weights and the fact that they were highly standardized provide evidence for a coercive economic authority that reached almost every settlement

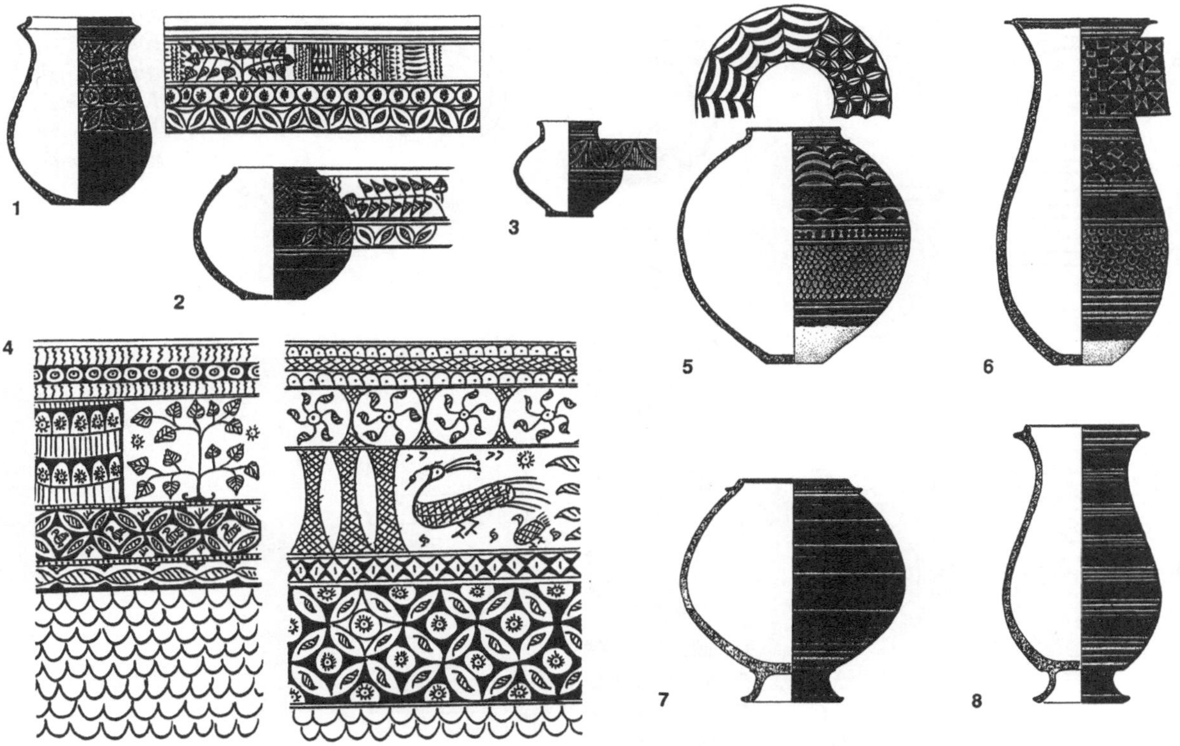


*Figure 8.10 Harappan painted ceramics. 1–4: classical Harappan painting styles; 5–6: Harappan geometric painting style; 7–8: Harappan banded painting style.*

of the Indus region. In combination with the evidence from the seals mentioned above, we can visualize literate merchants or elites, who, along with their seals and standardized weights, represented the authority of the Indus state. Seals and weights, as symbols of wealth and authority, would have been visible to the general public but would have been used exclusively by elites.

The ideology that legitimized economic coercion appears to have been reinforced through a wide range of symbols that are found distributed throughout most Indus sites and were apparently accepted and used by all segments of the population. Of these, pottery vessels and ornaments are the most easily identified and were used by numerous different hierarchical segments of the population, reflecting the vertical integration of the ideology.

## Pottery

With the rise of major cities we see a synthesis of some shapes and motifs from the earlier pottery traditions and the introduction of new shapes and some new painted designs. Most of the Harappan pottery is undecorated, but the small percentage of painted types is dominated by black painting on red slip (Figure 8.10). The painting is organized in horizontal panels and the most widespread motifs, usually found on the lower panel, are the intersecting circle and fish-scale designs. Other symbols occurring on the upper panels include peacock, bull, fish, and floral motifs such as the pipal tree or leaf.

During the Harappan phase an important new development is the reproduction of many of the pottery motifs in other materials. For example, the intersecting circle, fish-scale, pipal leaf and other ritual symbols are found in shell inlay, carved ornaments, decorated beads, floor tiles, and even in the Indus script. It is not unlikely that they were also incorporated into textiles and carved wood, but unfortunately these have not been preserved. The addition of these motifs as decoration would certainly have increased the value of an object as well as its overall symbolic impact.

As mentioned earlier, painted pottery itself may not have been of significant wealth value, but since such pottery would have been needed for domestic use and public rituals, anyone desiring to emulate, affiliate, or

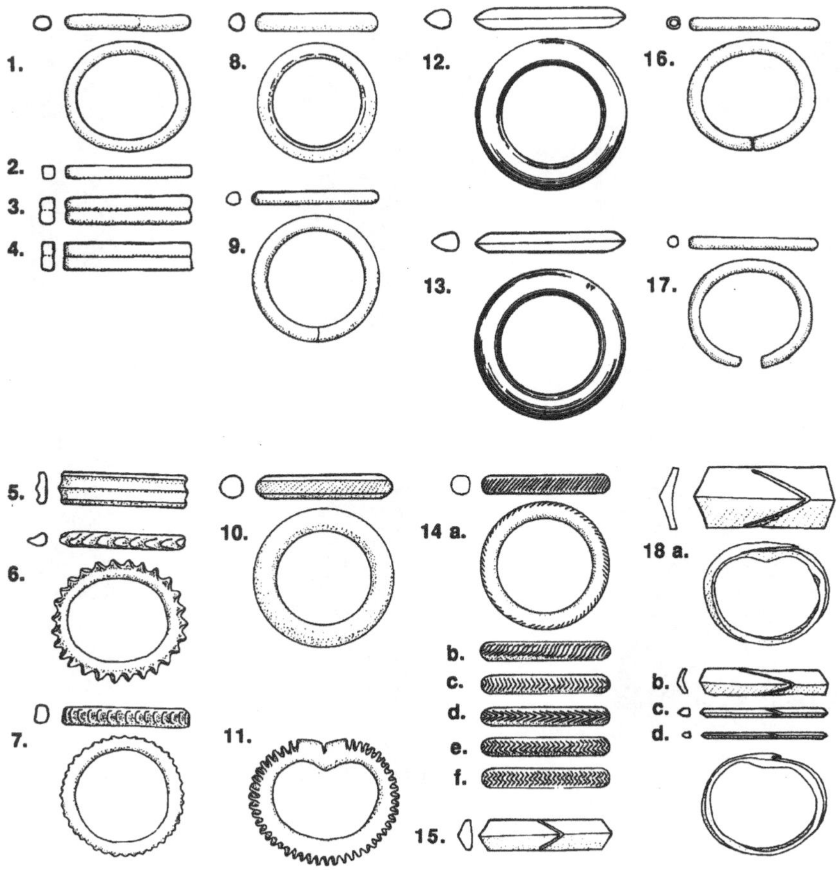


*Figure 8.11 Harappan bangle types. 1–7: terracotta; 8: faience; 9: copper/bronze; 10: fine terracotta; 11: faience; 12: fine terracotta; 13: stoneware; 14–15: faience; 16–17: gold/silver; 18: shell.*

integrate to this social–ritual–political system would need to acquire and visibly display pottery with appropriate decorative elements. These painted vessels are not limited to specific areas of the cities and it is highly unlikely that they were used only by one community or only by the elites. Such a pattern would indicate that the ideology reflected by the painted pottery was embraced by the many different stratified communities present in the cities. Furthermore, the presence of these distinctive vessels in both large and small settlements indicates the widespread acceptance of the ideology that served to integrate the society vertically within settlements, as well as horizontally across previous regional boundaries.

### Ornaments

During the Harappan phase, new styles of bangles and beads were created using different raw materials and in many cases different technologies. Many of the same basic styles of beads and bangles were made with raw materials or technologies of relatively different values. In contrast with painted pottery, which reflects horizontal integration, Harappan phase ornaments reflect the distribution of identical, shared symbols along the vertical socioeconomic axis. At the same time that these shared symbols reinforce the shared ideology through symbols, the ornaments have different values due to the nature of the raw material or technology. Such ornaments reinforce the stratification of Indus society by the fact that only certain classes of merchants or land owners could afford beads of high value.

For example, bangles with the same shape and design were made from common terracotta, fine processed clays, stoneware, glazed faience, copper/bronze, ivory, shell, silver, and gold (Figure 8.11). Identical shapes of beads were made from terracotta, faience, agate/carnelian, copper/bronze, shell, steatite, silver, and gold (Figure 8.12). Circular and banded designs found on natural stones were copied in terracotta, inlaid stone, shell, faience, and steatite. On the basis of later cultural

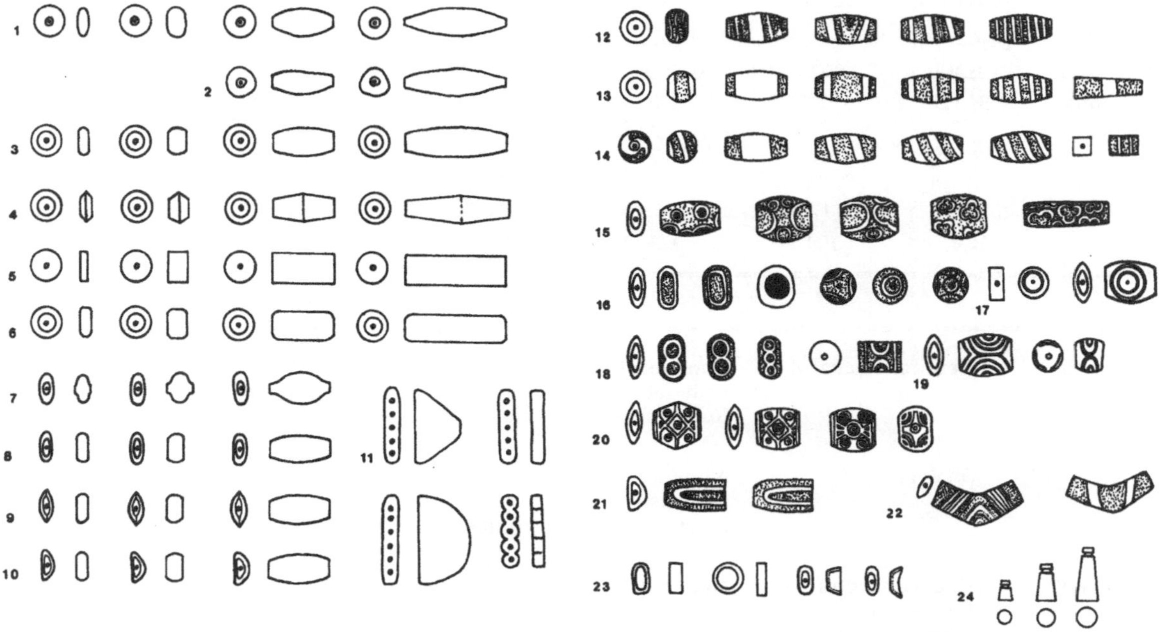


*Figure 8.12 Harappan bead designs and amulets. 1–11: terracotta beads; 12–22: natural stone beads and imitation beads made from steatite and faience; 23: gold bead caps; 24: pendants (amulets) made from stone or faience.*

traditions in South Asia, the ornament shapes and styles reflect the use of symbols that communicated socio-ritual status and identity. The use of natural and artificial materials allowed for the differentiation of individuals on the basis of economic, social, and ritual affiliations.

Although many of the basic bead types are found distributed horizontally among many different sizes of settlements throughout the Indus valley, there is a greater range of raw materials and a higher degree of stylistic variation within the larger urban settlements of Mohenjo-daro and Harappa (Kenoyer 1992b), or specialized settlements such as Chanhudaro (Vidale 1989a). This would suggest that the larger urban centers contained a more diverse set of consumers representing a greater number of social strata than was present at rural settlements. Current studies at Harappa are focused on determining if these different communities lived in different areas of the city or in distinct neighborhoods.

The manufacture of similar types of beads or bangles from different raw materials is not unique to the Indus civilization, but is seen in all societies where valuable raw materials are not equally accessible to all members of a community. For example, in Mesopotamia, cylinder seals were made from marine shell, as well as both soft and hard stones. Exotic lapis lazuli and agate/chalcedony were among the most prized raw materials and elaborately carved cylinder seals made from these materials appear to have been used primarily by elites based on their inclusion in burials (e.g., Woolley 1955) and from the value ascribed to these materials in texts (see Moorey 1994).

Since the Harappans did not include large quantities of wealth items in burials and there are no deciphered texts, the value of different raw materials can only be gauged on the basis of their relative availability to the general public using the assumptions outlined at the beginning of this chapter. Initial studies of beads and bangles from the 1986 to 1990 excavations at Harappa indicated that the most valuable materials were probably precious metals, but due to the fact that metals can be recycled, they may be somewhat under-represented when compared with materials that are less easily recycled, such as terracotta, faience, or shell. In the following tables, the bangles and beads from excavations conducted from 1986 to 1990, primarily from the cemetery and Mound E (Kenoyer 1992b), are contrasted with the totals from 1986 to 1996, which represent a larger sample that has been collected from excavations on each of the major mounded areas, in addition to the Har-

| BANGLES Raw Material | 1986–1990 Excavations | Percentage | 1986–1996 Excavations | Percentage |
|---|---|---|---|---|
| Terracotta | 34,127 | 97.72% | 120,612 | 97.92% |
| Faience | 390 | 1.12% | 1,092 | 0.89% |
| Shell | 340 | 0.97% | 1,230 | 1.00% |
| Stoneware | 48 | 0.14% | 198 | 0.16% |
| Copper | 17 | 0.05% | 39 | 0.03% |
| Total | 34,922 | 100.0% | 123,171 | 100.0% |

*Figure 8.13 Harappan Phase bangles (2600–1900 BC), sorted by raw material type.*

| | | |
|---|---|---|
| Lowest rank | Terracotta bangles | Common, locally available raw material<br>Relatively simple technology |
| | Shell bangles | Non-local raw material (except on the coast)<br>Relatively simple technology |
| Highest rank | Faience bangles<br>Copper bangles<br>Stoneware bangles<br>Gold/silver bangles | Non-local and locally available raw materials<br>Relatively complex technology and high temperature kilns |

*Figure 8.14 Ranking of bangles by raw material and technology.*

appan cemetery. These data represent the total number of bangles and beads recovered from Harappan Phase stratigraphic units (2600–1900 BC) using a standardized procedure for all seasons of excavation (Meadow and Kenoyer 1993).

In the category of bangles, the most rare forms of bangles are metal, gold/silver, and copper. As pointed out above, the very low percentage of metal bangles probably reflects a high degree of recycling. The next ranked raw materials include stoneware, faience, and shell, while the most common and lowest-ranked are terracotta bangles. It is interesting to note that when comparing the results of the two different samples the most common and most rare materials have remained unchanged, but some of the middle ranked raw materials have very different percentages (Figures 8.13 and 8.15). Nevertheless, the overall ranking combining both raw material type and technology remains unchanged (Figures 8.14 and 8.16).

Most Harappan ornaments would have been worn openly, providing public information about one's status and social affiliation, but some beads and pendants appear to have been worn hidden from view under clothing or separate from the more elaborate ornaments. Such ornaments would have functioned as private symbols that informed and reinforced ideologies or legitimation of the social order on a more intimate level.

Excavations in the Harappan cemetery have revealed that certain men and women were buried with a few beads of carnelian, lapis, and/or copper generally found on the pelvis or at the lower back (Dales and Kenoyer 1990). These beads appear to have been worn beneath the clothing and next to the skin, functioning as protective amulets or personal ornaments that could not be passed on to their descendants. The absence of more elaborate ornaments of gold, silver, and precious stones suggests that they were passed on to the next generation.

Truncated conical stone pendants are also found among burial ornaments and are almost exclusively associated with adult women. Probably worn alone on a cord around the neck these pendants would have been obscured by clothing or the massive bead collars and torques that were commonly worn by Harappan ladies.

In contrast with other ornaments which were removed at death and probably represented wealth and status, the single pendants and beads in the Harappan burials probably represent amulets that were worn, not for public display, but rather for protection or to define personal ritual status. Their inclusion in the burial may indicate the continued need for amuletic protection

| BEAD / PENDANT Raw material | 1986–1990 Excavations | Percentage | 1986–1996 Excavations | Percentage |
|---|---|---|---|---|
| Steatite / paste | 3,842 | 77.32% | 8,688 | 69.43% |
| Terracotta | 693 | 13.95% | 2,111 | 16.87% |
| Other stone | 225 | 4.53% | 667 | 5.33% |
| Faience | 95 | 1.91% | 832 | 6.65% |
| Shell | 54 | 1.09% | 94 | 0.75% |
| Copper | 39 | 0.78% | 98 | 0.78% |
| Gold / silver | 21 | 0.42% | 23 | 0.18% |
| Total | 4,969 | 100.00% | 12,513 | 100.00% |

*Figure 8.15 Harappan Phase beads (2600–1900 BC), sorted by raw material type.*

| | | |
|---|---|---|
| Lowest rank | Terracotta | Common, locally available raw material<br>Relatively simple technology |
| | Shell<br>Unfired steatite<br>Other stone (soft) | Non-local raw material<br>Relatively simple technology |
| Highest rank | Fired steatite / paste<br>Faience<br>Other stone (hard)<br>Copper<br>Gold | Non-local and locally available raw materials<br>Relatively complex technology and high temperature kilns |

*Figure 8.16 Ranking of beads by raw material and technology.*

and/or the fact that such personalized ornaments could not be transferred to living relatives. Although these private ornaments may not have been used to communicate to the general public, members of the immediate community would have recognized and understood their significance as status or wealth items. The presence of stylistically similar private ornaments and amulets in widely distributed settlements is an important indicator of a shared ideology among elite communities that helps to define the general order of the social hierarchy and also integrate the society.

These examples of both private and public ornaments illustrate the hierarchical use of wealth items which in turn reflect the stratification and social order of Indus society. After around 1900 BC, all of the distinctive styles of Indus ornaments mentioned above disappeared, presumably because they were specifically associated with the legitimation of a socio-ritual order that was no longer tenable.

During the Late Harappan and subsequent Early Historic Period, the Harappa ornaments were replaced by stylistically different forms but in most cases there was a continuity in general function and technology of production. Shell bangles continued to be worn in some regions but they had new forms of decoration. Faience and eventually glass or ivory bangles became quite common in other regions of the subcontinent (Kenoyer 1983). Beads with specific designs or motifs continued to be produced in a wide range of materials that can be ranked and correlated to socio-economic or ritual status (Kenoyer 1986). Private ornaments that were used to define social sub-sets continued to be produced and are still an important feature of ornamentation in Pakistan and India (Kenoyer 1992b).

## Conclusion

Specific aspects of ideology and legitimation, along with the precise mechanisms that helped to maintain social order in the Indus cities, are difficult to identify without the aid of written texts. Nevertheless, as outlined above it is possible to identify some objects that were used as symbols of wealth and see how these objects were used to reflect and reinforce the social order.

Many of the wealth indicators, such as painted pottery, bangles, beaded ornaments, and even the layout of the cities show marked stylistic and technological changes at the end of the Harappan Phase. In addition, the use of seals, writing, weights, and specific narrative scenes ends with the period of urban integration. The correlation between the end of the Indus cities and the disappearance of these characteristic artifacts suggests that they were critical to the legitimation of the elites who were maintaining order and socio-economic integration. The fact that such objects do not reemerge for another 300 to 400 years, when they are associated with a new set of elites in the Indo-Gangetic Regionalization Era (Kenoyer 1995a), further supports the role of these objects as symbols of wealth and socioeconomic stratification. Finally, with the reemergence of cities in the Early Historic Period, certain parallel developments occur that provide a historical link to reinforce the interpretation of specific objects as wealth and status indicators.

In historical South Asia, the legitimacy of the state, whether ruled as a republic, by a king, or as an oligarchy, was derived from *dharma* – the sacred order or the sacred duty – of the ruler. The duty of the ruler was to maintain and protect the order of *varna* or socio-ritual organization (Wink 1986: 17–18). This was achieved through the promotion of *dharma* (right action, encouraging virtue, and morality), *artha* (wealth, through the encouragement of trade, industry, and agriculture), *kama* (worldly pleasures, peace, and order) and *moksha* (release from the cycle of rebirth) (Altekar 1984; Ragaranjan 1992; Scharfe 1989). One mechanism through which the state was able to grow strong and remain stable was the promotion of wealth and creation of new forms of wealth that served to maintain social differentiation and at the same time reinforce ideological integration.

Based on the evidence presented above, I feel that the order and legitimation of the Indus State were maintained through the creation of wealth items that had strong ideological associations. These objects changed over time and were modified through technological advancements or changing trade patterns, resulting in regionally distinctive patterns of wealth accumulation. Collectively, these patterns are significantly different from what is seen at contemporaneous sites in West and Central Asia. The most obvious difference between the Indus and cultures to the west is that large quantities of portable wealth were not interred with the dead and wealth was not used to create permanent public monuments that had no direct economic function.

In the past, studies of ancient civilizations have focused on the most obvious differences in wealth, ideology, and order, with a disproportionate emphasis on the uppermost social strata (i.e. high culture and inner elites). Such general characterizations have limited value for understanding the diversity of socioeconomic hierarchies that were part of early state society. Subtle differences or perhaps similarities in the concepts of wealth and socioeconomic hierarchies between these major regions can only be understood through more detailed comparative studies of raw material and artifact ranking. By changing our levels of analysis to investigate these more subtle patterns that reflect the complex infrastructure within each culture, it will also be possible to begin to understand the multiple levels of interaction between elites and the general population. Initial comparisons between this study and others presented in this volume suggest that there are in fact important similarities in the ways in which the common people were integrated through the use of wealth and ideology.

## Note

This chapter is a revised and considerably expanded version of an earlier paper titled "Ideology and Legitimation in the Indus State as revealed through Public and Private Symbols" that was presented at the 13th International Congress of Anthropological and Ethnological Sciences Mexico City, July 28–Aug. 5, 1993, and subsequently published in 1995 in *The Archaeological Review: Pakistan Archaeologists Forum* 4 (1&2): pp. 87–131. I would like to thank the editors for their incredible patience in putting this volume together and their helpful comments on the final version of my paper.

Support for my ongoing research at Harappa and the Indus Civilization has been provided by numerous organizations, and I would like to thank the National Science Foundation, the National Endowment for the Humanities, the National Geographic Society, the Smithsonian Institution and the University of Wisconsin for their long-term commitments to my research. Other support has come through private donations. I would like to acknowledge my great debt to the late Dr. George F. Dales for his encouragement in my early research and also for inviting me to work with him at Harappa as Field Director. I would also like to thank my colleagues Dr. Richard Meadow (Harvard University and Co-Director at Harappa), Dr. Rita Wright (New York University and Assistant Director at Harappa), Dr. Rafique Mughal and my students William R. Belcher, Heather M. L. Miller, Seetha Reddy, and Chris Jenkins for their stimulating discussions on the Indus Civilization. Special thanks to Dr. J.-F. Jarrige, C. Jarrige, and G. Quivron for sharing information on the recent work of the French Archaeological Mission at Mehrgarh/Nausharo. Much of the data presented in this paper derives from the recent excavations at Harappa and I would like to thank all of the colleagues who have participated in the research at Harappa and have helped to collect and analyze data.

# 9 Classical order, alternative orders, and the uses of nostalgia

SUSAN E. ALCOCK

To the global perspective of this volume, the ancient Mediterranean world could have offered many settings through which to analyze the arguments presented by Baines and Yoffee. Of these, perhaps most conspicuous would have been the city-states of Greece, Italy, and Asia Minor in the fifth and fourth centuries BC. Politically independent, yet culturally unified, these congeries of city-states would sound familiar to students of other cultures (Nichols and Charlton 1997). Somewhat less recognizable, from the model presented by Baines and Yoffee, are other aspects of their political and social ordering.

First and foremost, order and legitimacy within these communities rested on the preservation and glorification of the city (or *polis*) as a whole, normally emphasizing communal (not elite, not individual) values and goals. Second, many *poleis* were democratic in governance (while not embracing groups such as women or slaves), or at least possessed a policy of widespread citizenship. Finally, profound separation of wealthy elite families from the rest of society was frequently denied. Indeed, the existence of any obvious elite was much masked through a variety of "leveling mechanisms," manifest in areas such as mortuary practice or domestic architecture (e.g. Hoepfner and Schwandner 1986; I. Morris 1992: 103–155). One corollary of these phenomena is a lack of what Baines and Yoffee would define as "high culture" in its exclusive, elitist sense. Instead, "high culture" in this world appears as a more shared domain, designed to showcase and celebrate the citizen body at large. Arenas for performances included theatrical displays and the rituals surrounding them, religious festivals for both local and panhellenic cults, and athletic contests.

Any closer look at this world of *poleis* (which, incidentally, numbered in the hundreds) would reveal a plethora of regional and temporal distinctions and differences, variations on the fundamental pattern here outlined. One version of a "classical case study" for this volume, then, might have expanded upon these distinctions, have teased out more and more subtle nuances in the relationship between order, legitimacy, and wealth in this society, and have analyzed it within the global framework presented here. Such comparative work would certainly be salutary for all concerned. On the one hand, the classical *polis* is – as Baines and Yoffee note – a "society with a different orientation" from the Egyptian and Mesopotamian civilizations which formed the focus of their analysis (Baines and Yoffee 1998: 258). On the other, such research would add another approach to the growing body of comparative city-state studies (Snodgrass 1986; Runciman 1990; I. Morris 1997; Small 1997).

Despite the attractions of such a study, this chapter will follow a different and more unfamiliar course, one that offers an alternative way to explore the nexus of order, legitimacy, and wealth in Greek society. To begin, we can "fast-forward" in time some five centuries or so, to approximately the first century BC/first century AD – the period immediately following the Roman conquest or appropriation of the eastern Mediterranean (including the territory of modern-day Greece and Turkey; Figure 9.1). Several profound social and political dislocations accompanied this annexation. Independent city-states were transformed into administrative, tax-paying components within a larger imperial system. Democracies were by and large transformed into oligarchies, with political authority now more directly and openly linked to the possession of wealth. Responsibilities once shared communally were now discharged in a more "normal" manner, with a dominant local elite in charge of civic affairs, of tax collection, and the behavior of the rest of the population. Although this restricted elite group worked under the overall control of provincial governors, the imperial administrative staff was remarkably small, leaving day-to-day matters very much in the hands of local authorities. Reorganization in favor of, and co-optation of, the few and the wealthy, together with visible and increasing social polarization, are hardly unpredictable developments within new imperial provinces.

What may have been less anticipated are the cultural developments that accompanied these social and political transformations. During the early imperial era, a powerful and retrospective "classicism" emerged in art

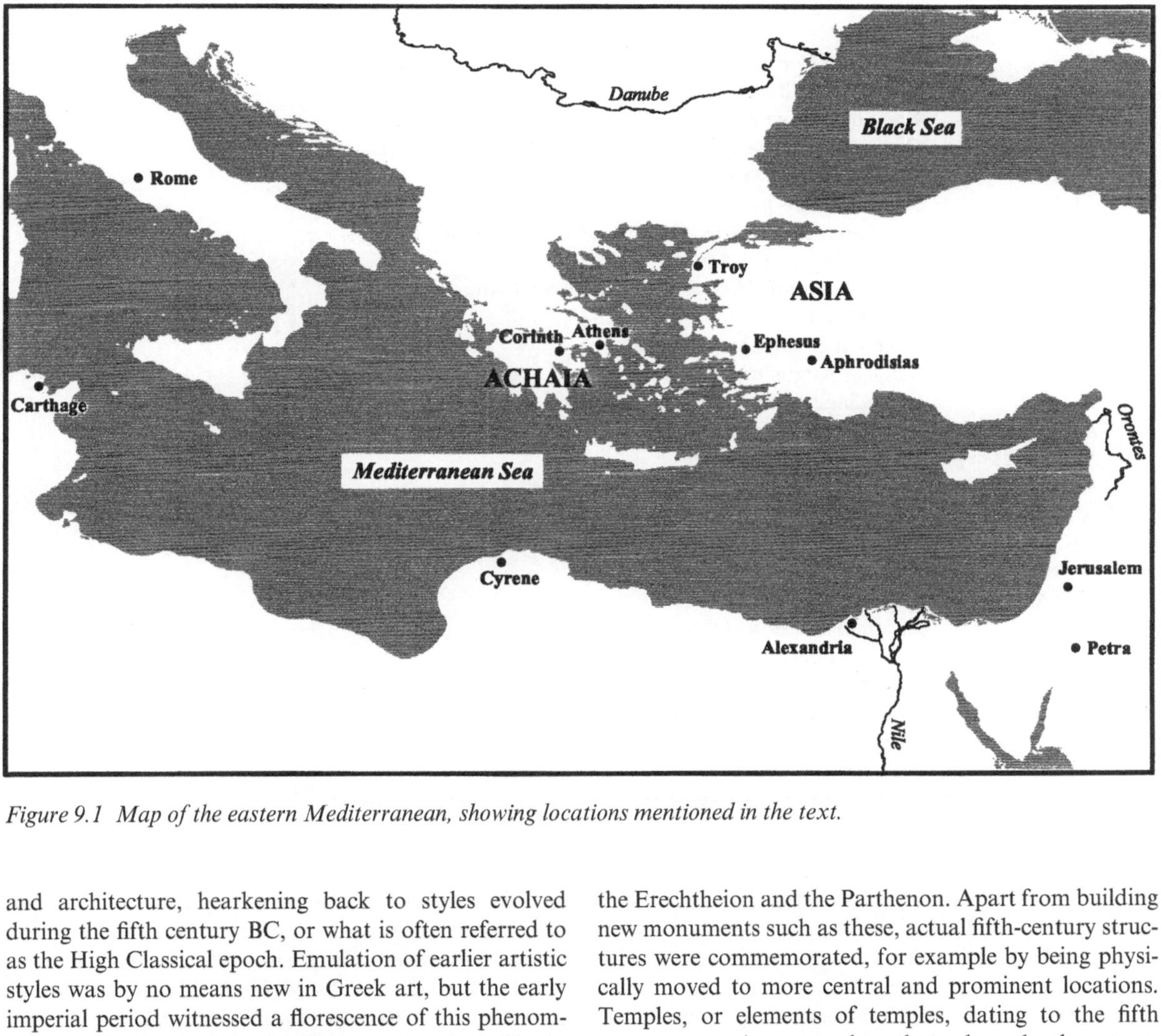


*Figure 9.1 Map of the eastern Mediterranean, showing locations mentioned in the text.*

and architecture, hearkening back to styles evolved during the fifth century BC, or what is often referred to as the High Classical epoch. Emulation of earlier artistic styles was by no means new in Greek art, but the early imperial period witnessed a florescence of this phenomenon (Pollitt 1986: 164–184; Elsner 1995: 125–155). At this time, a dependence on the classical past for legitimacy served a variety of political and social agendas, not only in the Greek east, but in Rome itself (Zanker 1988); the subject here, however, will be the east's own turn to "nostalgia."

Many signs of this development can be seen in the city of Athens, in the Roman province of Achaia, which ranks among our best explored and documented urban centers. In early imperial Athens, contemporary buildings were designed to echo older monuments in conception or placement. Thus, a small round Ionic temple dedicated to the goddess Roma and the emperor Augustus appears to have been designed and positioned to relate architecturally to two fifth-century BC temples, the Erechtheion and the Parthenon. Apart from building new monuments such as these, actual fifth-century structures were commemorated, for example by being physically moved to more central and prominent locations. Temples, or elements of temples, dating to the fifth century were thus transplanted to adorn the downtown public space (*agora*) of first-century AD Athens (e.g., the Temple of Ares, the South West (S.W.) and South East (S.E.) Temples: Shear 1981; Alcock 1993: 191–196; Spawforth 1997; Walker 1997; see Figure 9.4). The end result of this development, together with other Roman-period constructions (e.g., the music hall or Odeion of Agrippa, see Figure 9.4), was to "fill in" what had once been an open space for civic activity. The degree of urban transformation, if one compares the agora during the fourth century BC with its second-century AD manifestation (Figures 9.3 and 9.4), is remarkable, as is the degree to which so much of this "new building" is old.

This kind of retrospective classicism was not confined

*Figure 9.2 Chronological chart.*

| | |
|---|---|
| 146 BC | Sacking of Corinth by Mummius; end of Achaean War between Greek states and Rome |
| 133 BC | Creation of the province of Asia |
| 1st century BC | Conflicts in the eastern Mediterranean: Mithridatic Wars; Roman Civil Wars |
| 87/86 BC | Sack of Athens by Sulla |
| 44 BC | Refoundation of Corinth by Julius Caesar; Assassination of Julius Caesar |
| 31 BC | Battle of Actium; Victory of Octavian over Antony and Cleopatra |
| 27 BC | Octavian given the name 'Augustus' |
| 27 BC – AD 14 | Reign of Augustus |
| AD 14–68 | Julio-Claudian Dynasty |
| AD 14–37 | Tiberius |
| AD 37–41 | Gaius Caligula |
| AD 41–54 | Claudius |
| AD 54–68 | Nero |
| AD 69–96 | Flavian Dynasty |
| AD 96–192 | Antonine Age |
| AD 193–235 | Severan Dynasty |
| AD 267 | Herulian invasion of Greece |
| AD 410 | Sack of Rome by Alaric the Visigoth |
| AD 476 | End of Roman Empire in West |
| AD 1453 | Constantinople falls to Turks; end of Eastern Roman (Byzantine) Empire |

to the realms of art and architecture, but extended into other cultural domains as well. Literary and rhetorical works were affected by a strong contemporary interest in, and emulation of, earlier authors; indeed the literary culture of the early eastern empire has often been referred to as the 'Second Sophistic' (Bowersock 1969; 1974; G. Anderson 1993; Gleason 1995; Swain 1996). Admiration for the past and its "classic" style was also enthusiastically expressed by Romans, not least when visiting as tourists. Such individuals, often clad in Greek garb, visited and studied in cities such as Athens, seeking out landmarks such as the tomb of Perikles or Plato's Academy, and participating in such ancient rituals as the Eleusinian Mysteries (e.g., Cicero, *De Finibus* 5.1.2; Alcock 1993: 224–227; Cartledge and Spawforth 1989: 207–211; Habicht 1997).

The attitudes of conqueror towards conquered were markedly ambivalent in the case of Romans and Greeks, where strong traditions of philhellenic respect were combined with contempt for the loquacious, mendacious, and defeated *Graeculi* (or "Greeklings"; Petrochilos 1974; Wardman 1976). The former attitude typically receives more attention, bolstering as it does later Western admiration for classical Greek culture and leading to a scholarly emphasis on what could be termed reverse imperialism – the cultural triumph of Greek refinement over Roman crudity. One consequence of this conviction has been the tacit assumption that the cultural antiquarianism on display in imperial Greece was principally a response to a Roman need for Greece to become a kind of museum, even a fantasy land, catering to imperial desires.

This tacit assumption is also a dangerous one. It is misleading in the extreme to divorce this development entirely from the needs and desires of the Greek people themselves. Nor is it very helpful to perceive this hearkening back, this apparent nostalgia (a word with sound Greek roots), as a passive retreat into a more glorious history, hiding in memories of the good old days. As Gleason recently put it: "To see educated Greeks as seeking consolation in the past for their political impotence in the Roman present, however, does not quite do

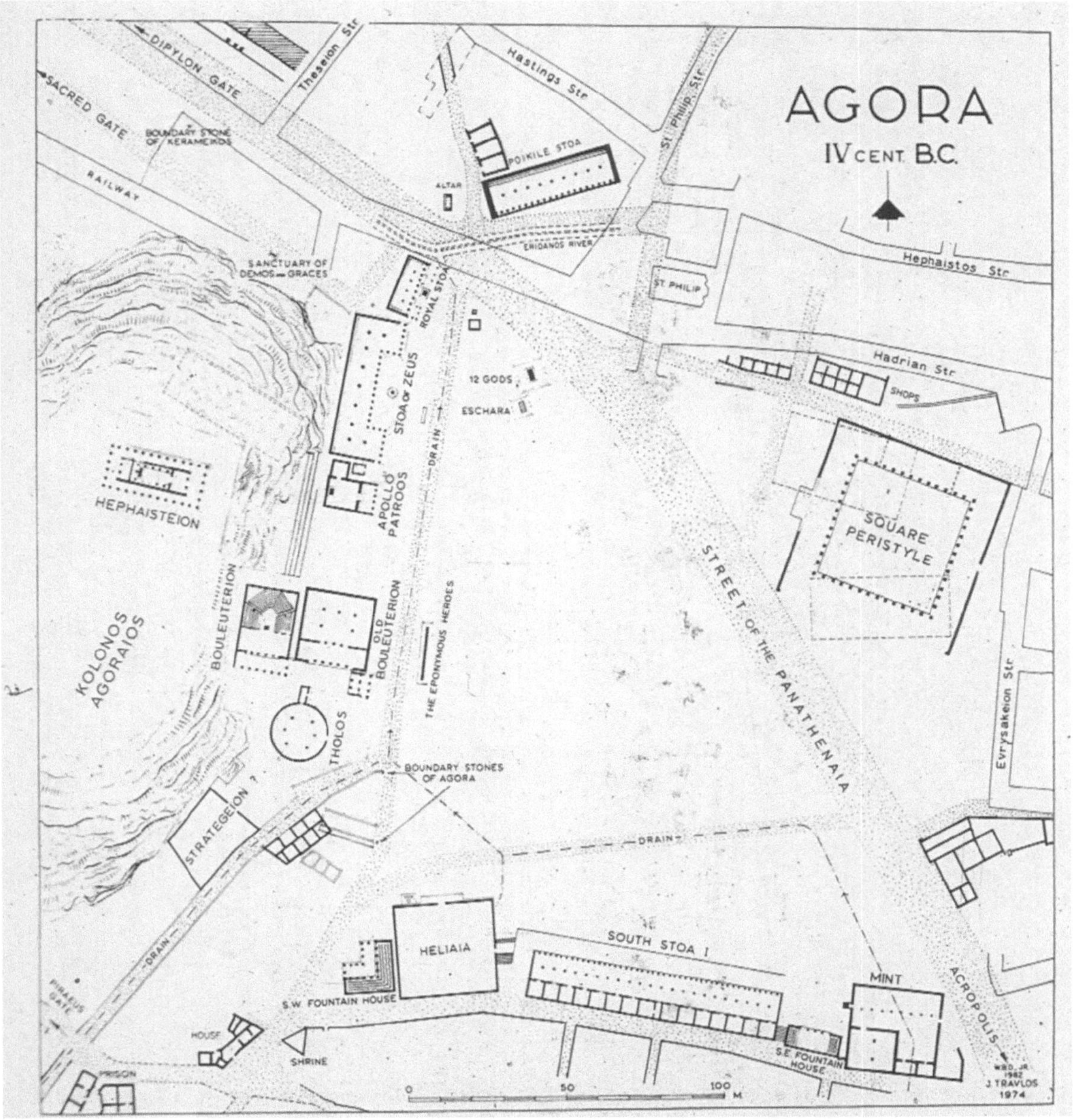


*Figure 9.3 Plan of the Athenian agora in the fourth century BC (courtesy of the American School of Classical Studies at Athens).*

justice to the vitality with which they experienced their continuity with tradition" (Gleason 1995: xix, n. 5; Bowie 1974; Woolf 1994). So how then to understand this emphasis on the past?

One answer would be to argue that if Roman conquest shook, even destroyed, established Greek perceptions of themselves and their world, then classical styles and the classical past were employed to bridge and to survive that dislocation. Nostalgia served as a means to negotiate an alternative framework of order and legitimacy, one that provided Greek elites with a cultural claim to power and authority, despite their newly

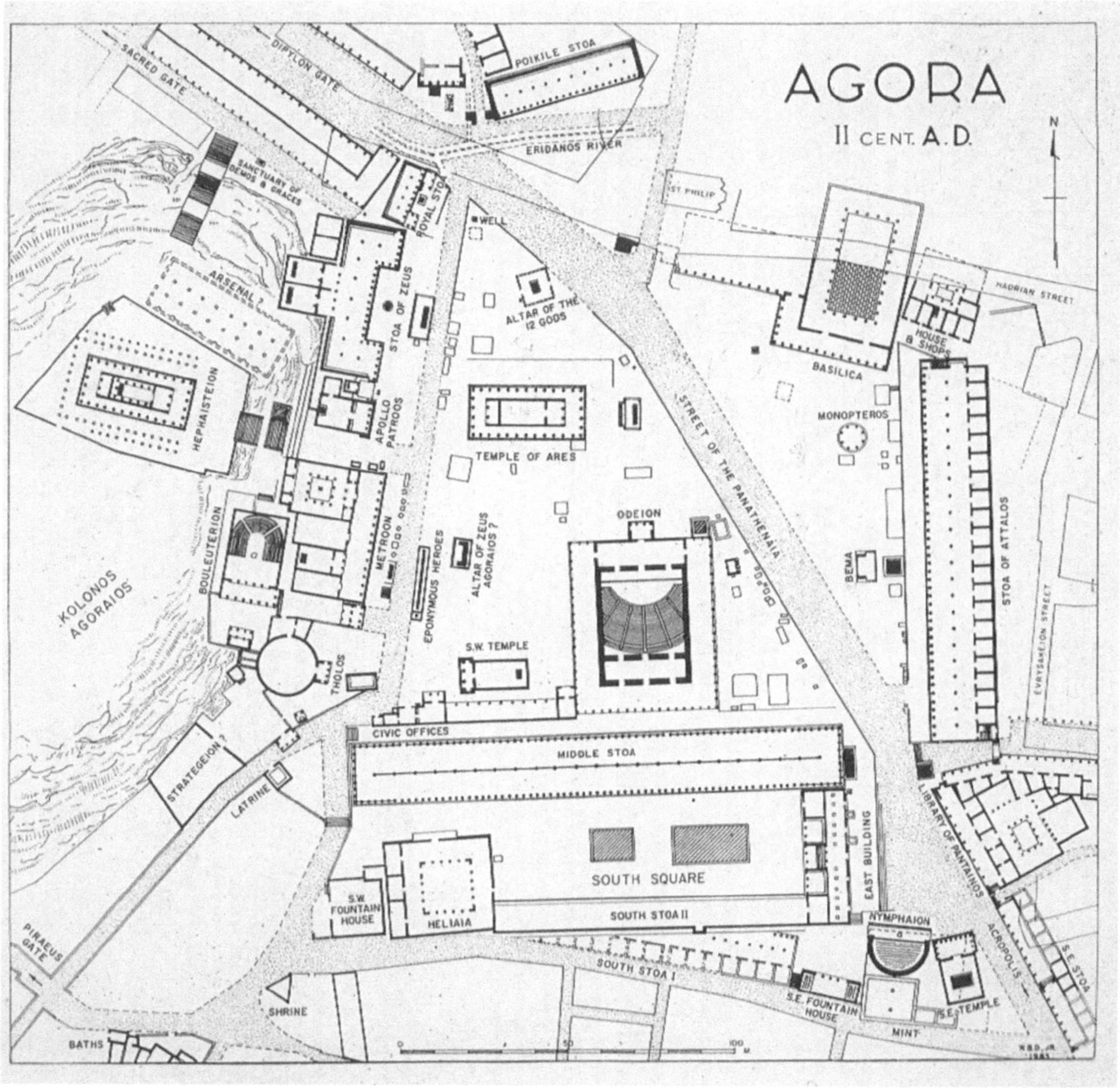


*Figure 9.4 Plan of the Athenian agora in the second century AD (courtesy of the American School of Classical Studies at Athens).*

circumscribed, politically insignificant position within the empire. This lack of congruity between ideological claim and political reality, as we shall see, poses a challenge to unitary definitions of "order" and "legitimacy" within an ancient empire – a challenge issued by other chapters in this volume as well.

One remarkable illustration of such an alternative order is to be found in the city of Aphrodisias in modern-day Turkey. The link, reflected in its name, of this city to the goddess Aphrodite (the Roman Venus) led to the development of a special relationship between the city and the imperial family, which traced its genealogy back to Venus. The granting of freedom and of allied status to Aphrodisias was one consequence of this, making the city formally (if perhaps not always practically) independent of the imperial province of Asia.

In recent years, Aphrodisias has been the subject of intensive archaeological exploration (e.g., Erim 1986; de la Genière and Erim 1987; Reynolds 1982; Roueché and Erim 1990; R. R. R. Smith and Erim 1991; R. R. R. Smith 1993; R. R. R. Smith and Ratté 1995, 1996, 1997, 1998). In the course of this research was discovered a temple and sanctuary complex dedicated to Aphrodite, to members of the then ruling dynasty, the Julio-Claudian emperors (worshipped as the *Theoi Sebastoi*, or Savior Gods), and to the *Demos*, or People, of Aphrodisias (R. R. R. Smith 1987: 90 for details of these dedications). This complex, which probably would have been termed a Sebasteion, was constructed during the course of the first century AD. Its plan was formal and impressive. A worshipper would enter at the west end through a monumental, two-storey entrance gate (or propylon), and proceed to the temple at the east end (*c.* 90 meters away), passing between two *c.* 12 meter-tall, three-storied porticos (Figure 9.5). The experience of moving through a symmetrically planned, colonnaded court to reach a temple placed axially at its end seems clearly derived from Roman models, not least from the imperial fora of Rome itself. The temple at the end was also in the Roman style: raised on a podium, with a frontal emphasis highlighted by tall Corinthian columns. As for the side porticoes, these were decorated on the second and third level with large sculpted relief panels. In all, the design allowed for 190 sculpted panels, of which less than half remain today. From what survives, however, it can be seen that this large-scale sculptural program presented one vision of a new cosmology: "the Roman empire, the Greek world within it, and the imperial family" (R. R. R. Smith 1987: 95).

The south portico is better preserved than the north. On its second storey appeared an extraordinarily wide selection of Greek mythology, with panels depicting (among other scenes) Leda and the Swan, Meleager and the boar, drunken Dionysos, Achilles and Penthesilea, the rescue of Prometheus by Heracles, and Bellerophon and Pegasus. The myths selected appear by and large to have been "mainstream" familiar tales, the common and shared property of an educated Greek audience; none appear to have been labeled so as to identify the myth involved. While the sheer number of myths represented, and the uncertainty of the order of many panels, makes it difficult to discern any tight programmatic coherence, at least one pattern seems clear. As a worshiper (and viewer) moved closer to the temple dedicated to Aphrodite and the *Theoi Sebastoi*, some panels seem to have reflected this proximity by turning attention to the relationship of Aphrodite and Rome. Subjects now appear – Aphrodite and the birth of Eros, Aeneas fleeing Troy, Romulus and Remus – which are related to the origins of Rome itself. This increasing emphasis on the link between Rome and Aphrodisias is echoed in the panels above as well (R. R. R. Smith 1987: 132–133).

These second-storey myths architecturally supported a third tier of images: "of imperial victory, the divine emperors, and the gods" (R. R. R. Smith 1987: 97). Olympian gods were shown as single figures, as were personifications of Nike (Victory). The most striking panels, however, depict the emperor and his imperial family. One well-known panel represents Augustus by Land and Sea, with the emperor receiving the bounty of earth and the command of seas, symbolized by a cornucopia and an oar (Figure 9.6). The nudity of the emperor in this panel, and indeed in the majority of those that survive, is interesting, reflecting an independence of choice in imperial representation. In Rome itself, naked emperors might appear in free-standing statue form, but in the type of narrative compositions seen in these panels, an emperor would be clothed or in military garb. Imperial nudity at the Sebasteion emerges instead in "the time-honored Greek manner" (R. R. R. Smith 1987: 135).

There are other, more specific scenes of imperial triumph. Over the female personification of the province of Britannia looms the emperor Claudius, pulling back her head to deliver the *coup de grâce* (Figure 9.7). Nero, wearing only a short cloak and baldric, stands dominatingly over a collapsing Armenia, with her oriental cap and "barbarian" hair. Both these representations bore labels identifying the protagonists, suggesting a concern with audience familiarity with the subjects. In the art of Rome itself, emperors are normally shown extending clemency to, or accepting homage from, defeated peoples; in these scenes, at any rate, imperial clemency gives way to an unusual violence. Parallels for depictions of triumphant males and broken women are, however, to be found in the mythic struggles of Greeks and Amazons, long-lived and popular representations in Greek art.

Opposite this complex of images, on the second storey of the less well-preserved north portico, was found a series of reliefs depicting female personifications of the numerous peoples (*ethne*) caught up in the Roman world. Such a sculptural program, Smith argues, must have been closely modeled on Augustan monuments in Rome, where images of personified peoples are known to have been placed (R. R. R. Smith 1988: 50, 70–77).

*Figure 9.5 Reconstruction of the Sebasteion at Aphrodisias, looking east from the propylon to the temple and showing the side porticoes decorated with sculpted reliefs (courtesy R. R. R. Smith).*

The *ethne* are shown as single, statue-like figures standing between columns on an inscribed base. Preserved inscriptions name thirteen foreign peoples and three islands scattered across the extent of the empire: from the Callaeci in Spain, to the Rhaeti near the upper Danube, to the Bosporans above the Black Sea, to the Egyptians and Judaeans in North Africa and the Levant. The islands named are Sicily, Crete, and Cyprus. All these peoples and places lay either within or at the border of the empire. All were to be perceived as subordinate to Rome, even if, as Smith avers, they were depicted in different categories of subjugation: "from near-equal partners to conquered subjects and neighbors" (R. R. R. Smith 1988: 59). On the third level, above the *ethne*, there appear to have stood allegorical representations and (probably) further images of emperors. The two preserved panels are personifications of cosmic significance – "Day" and "Ocean" – figures

*Figure 9.6 Panel from the south portico of the Sebasteion: Augustus by Land and Sea (courtesy of the Society for the Promotion of Roman Studies and R. R. R. Smith).*

*Figure 9.7 Panel from the south portico of the Sebasteion: Claudius and Britannia (courtesy of the Society for the Promotion of Roman Studies and R. R. R. Smith).*

intended to place the far-flung imperial peoples shown below within the timeless sphere fitting for an eternal empire.

In this impressive series, however, it is notable that the people of the Greek mainland or Asia Minor are not themselves explicitly identified. Admittedly, more than half of the inscribed *ethne* bases are still missing; it is also true that the islands named possessed, to a greater or lesser extent, a Greek population and identity. The choice to name islands, rather than particular peoples, is intriguing; as Smith notes "it was desirable that the older, Greek subjects of Rome be included not in person, as it were, but obliquely in terms of physical geography" (R. R. R. Smith 1988: 57). Very few of the actual personifications survive, but it is clear that different styles were employed to convey something of the characteristics of the *ethnos* or island involved – for example, by the use of "warlike" or "barbarian" attributes. One image (Figure 9.8) has been tentatively identified as one of the islands, possibly Sicily; "Hairstyle, pose and dress seem designed to characterize the figure as unambiguously Greek and 'free', as opposed to barbarian and captive" (R. R. R. Smith 1988: 65). Together with providing a "visual account" of the empire's extent, these personifications expressed different categories of subordination, from being depicted as captive, to "free", to perhaps not being named explicitly at all.

Taken as an expression of "the grandeur that was Rome," the Sebasteion at Aphrodisias is a stunning monument. Yet inscriptions discovered at the site reveal a twist in the tail. The Sebasteion was neither an imperially commissioned, nor a centrally decreed structure. Instead, this complex was paid for and dedicated by two wealthy families from Aphrodisias itself, members of the local elite now responsible for civic affairs. In artistic terms as well, despite its emulation of imperial fora design and certain Roman sculptural motifs, the case has been made convincingly by Smith that the overall conception and sculptural program of the complex was of local origin.

This information makes the Sebasteion, already an astonishing monument, even more astonishing – not

*Figure 9.8 Panel from the north portico of the Sebasteion:* Ethnos *or Greek island, possibly Sicily (courtesy of the Society for the Promotion of Roman Studies and R. R. R. Smith).*

only in its apparent celebration of a triumphant and serene Roman world order, but also in the way it apparently dwells upon (and glorifies) the conquest and submission of provincial peoples. In political and military terms, the Greek peoples were not, after all, that far distant from the position of a Britannia or Armenia. It is here that the employment of traditional myths and motifs announces another agenda and other intentions behind this monument.

What the Sebasteion defines is the place of the Greek peoples within what was, at that time, a new imperial order. In its sculptural program, Greek myths precede and are related to Roman aetiological tales. Greek mythic history offered (literally and figuratively) a foundation for the glories of imperial conquest over other, non-Greek peoples. Emperors are represented as glorious and omnipotent, yet their glory is depicted in a manner laden with particular overtones and memories containing emperors within a Greek frame of reference (R. R. R. Smith 1987: 136). Far from being members of a peripheral and defeated people, the Sebasteion offers a view of order and of legitimacy in which Greeks formed an integral part of the imperial core, essential to its mythic origins and cultural expression. A Roman imperial cosmology may have been expressed through the program of the Sebasteion – but only in terms of Greek choosing. This appropriation of political power, this culturally based claim to continued significance and continued legitimacy, can be extended from the Sebasteion to those other manifestations of "classical order" mentioned previously.

In one sense, this use of traditional myths and retrospective artistic styles to articulate an altered world order accords well with Baines and Yoffee's argument that change is often symbolized as a return to older and more conservative forms, and that appeals to "high culture" could validate claims to legitimacy. Yet just whose conception of order and legitimacy does the "neoclassicism" of early imperial Greece and Asia Minor represent?

One thing seems clear: it does not directly represent the conceptions of the empire's genuine "inner elite" based in Rome. Certainly these individuals imitated, employed, and enjoyed Greek artworks; the early imperial core evolved its own uses for classical styles and traditions. Nonetheless, this did not extend to including Greeks as integral and essential sharers in imperial power. Instead, the claims expressed are those of wealthy local elites, working to establish a closer harmony of interest with their Roman counterparts. Paradoxically, in terms of this volume's debate, it could be argued that only in the early imperial era does the use of classical styles and of the classical past pass into the realm of "high culture": that is, only then is it turned to the control, and used for the benefit of self-defined elites, their rulers, and their gods.

Yet if monuments such as the Sebasteion represent one version of an elite self-image, it remains only one version, and an optimistic one at that. As R. R. R. Smith remarks: "the relief panels as a whole present a detailed and broadly expressed vision of the fortunate position of the Greek world under Roman imperial rule" (1987: 138). In this context, it is worth recalling the favored status of Aphrodisias, a city particularly eager to celebrate its "special relationship" with Rome. Other less sanguine views of the Greek place in a Roman world were also expressed at this time. Anti-Roman feelings sometimes led to violence, including the sacking of cities such as Athens which periodically sided with Rome's enemies; or to symbolic gestures of rejection, as when a statue of Athena on the Athenian acropolis was reported to have turned and spat blood to the west, in the direction of Rome (Cassius Dio 54.7.2–3; Hoff 1989; 1997). Greek misgivings about the presence and power of Rome can be traced in literary accounts of the period, usually composed by wealthy individuals who in other ways accommodated to altered circumstances (for one such author, Pausanias, see Alcock 1994; more generally, Swain 1996). Perceptions of what constituted order and legitimacy were not unitary phenomena within the empire, or even among local elites within a portion of that empire. The two concepts must be viewed as more contested, more fractured, concepts than Baines and Yoffee allow.

If that observation is one larger point that can be extracted from this case-study, I would end with another reflection pertinent to the wider issues of this volume. The nostalgic self-presentation of early imperial Greeks warns us that the use of "high culture" to define order and legitimacy was not solely the prerogative of, nor solely in the interest of, the ultimate ruling power. In the Sebasteion, or in the Athenian agora, it is to a great extent the subject provincial peoples themselves who create their own world order, their own place in the imperial hierarchy. Yet what they choose to represent is an unreal hierarchy, an illusory cosmic order: illusory, that is, from a central, Rome-based perspective; illusory from the perspective of twentieth-century scholars assessing the actual balance of power and authority within the Roman empire. Yet does that invalidate what the Sebasteion expressed for those who worshipped within it? We may have to consider more carefully the questions – whose notions of order? whose sense of legitimacy?

## Note

I would like to thank the editors for inviting me to participate in this volume, as well as Janet Richards for her original invitation to the American Anthropological Association session in 1994. The editors, John F. Cherry, and the anonymous reviewers all offered helpful advice. My debt to the excellent work of R. R. R. Smith on the sculptural program of the Sebasteion at Aphrodisias must be especially acknowledged.

# 10
# Order, legitimacy, and wealth in ancient China

BENNET BRONSON

## Introduction: Han Gaozu and legitimacy

This chapter discusses the issues of legitimacy, order, and wealth as these were manifested at a crucial time in Chinese history: the late third century BC, when a rebel, Liu Bang (256–195 BC), seized imperial power from the short-lived Qin Dynasty and founded his own dynasty, the Han. He is known to history by his posthumous name, Han Gaozu.

Times of major political change, when new individuals and groups gain power in a governmental system which may itself be undergoing transformation, are almost by definition times when institutions and authority structures are likely to be reviewed and challenged. This is true even when the incoming rulers have reached their position by following accepted rules of succession: in China, for example, the designated heirs of emperors routinely sought to reinforce perceptions of their legitimacy by publicizing omens and engaging in appropriate ceremonies.

Authority structures are of course especially visible and vulnerable in cases where succession is not routine. The accession of Han Gaozu provides a prime example of this. He was a usurper who seized the throne by force. His origins were emphatically non-elite: born of poor parents, he began as a minor village official. During his rise to power he showed neither knowledge of nor sympathy for "high culture." His attitude in that regard is epitomized by the story of his reaction to a discussion with two distinguished Confucian scholars: he snatched the hat of one and urinated into it.

None of this was conducive to convincing others of Han Gaozu's legitimacy as emperor. Further, the throne he seized was itself not as legitimate as it might have been. Only twenty years had passed since Qin Shi Huangdi formally established the first pan-Chinese empire, ending centuries of political division. One reason why the Qin empire fell, in spite of Shi Huangdi's extraordinary creativity and ruthlessness, was that elite and commoners alike had not been convinced that the Qin or anyone else could legitimately wield a true emperor's power.

Yet Han Gaozu overcame these obstacles with outstanding success. He established a dynasty that would last more than four centuries, and a political system that would last 1,700 years beyond that. Under him and his immediate successors, the Chinese economy experienced an unprecedented boom. Moreover, unlike the execrated Qin Shi Huangdi, Han Gaozu was seen positively by future generations. Later emperors and would-be emperors, especially those planning to found a new dynasty, studied his life with care. Many consciously emulated him.

Han Gaozu was undoubtedly lucky in being born into a place and time that favored the rise of someone like him. But it is evident that he possessed exceptional ability as an administrator and social engineer, viewing clearly and dealing effectively with such problems as the establishment of order, the assumption of legitimacy, and securing the new dynasty in power.

The views of individuals like Han Gaozu and his advisors, who were in a position to test governmental concepts in the most realistic of laboratories, are of special interest to the student of cross-civilizational political theory. Fortunately, the early Han Dynasty was well recorded in the writings of contemporaries and near-contemporaries. These include several of the greatest of all Chinese historians: Sima Qian (born in *c.* 145 BC) and Ban Gu (AD 32–92). Sima and Ban were deeply interested in the issues of succession and legitimacy. They built on a long-standing tradition of political analysis, exemplified by such already-classic works as the *Book of History* and the *Spring and Autumn Annals*, which made it possible to discuss such issues with surprising frankness.

## Han Dynasty perspectives

Han Gaozu is represented in contemporary sources as a charismatic but uneducated bumpkin, not at all apologetic about having seized the empire by force. He is also depicted, however, as an eager learner who was quick to recognize the need to legitimize his regime by making selective use of tradition, conciliating sections of the old

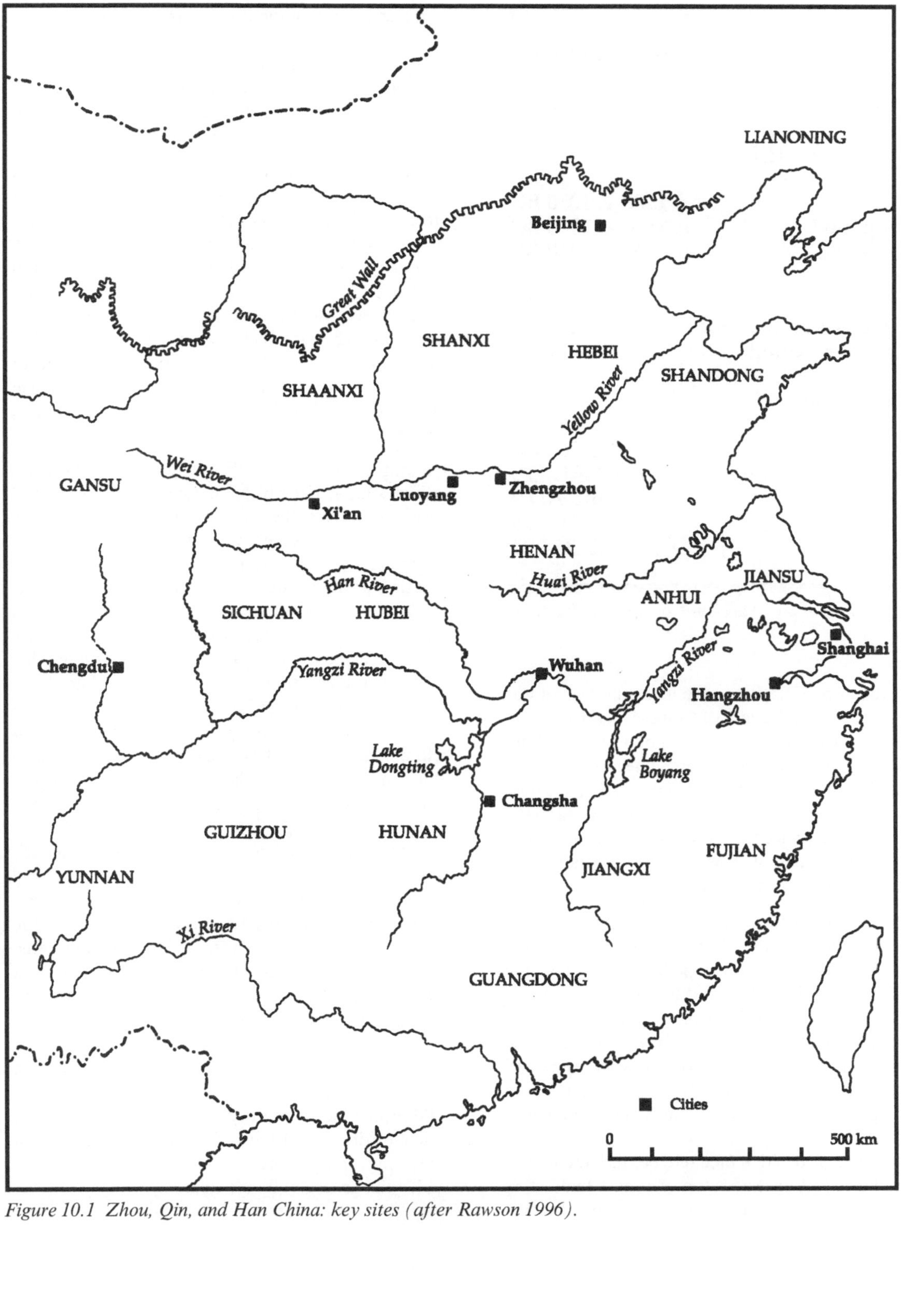


*Figure 10.1 Zhou, Qin, and Han China: key sites (after Rawson 1996).*

| | |
|---|---|
| **Neolithic period** | *c.* 6000–*c.* 1700 BC |
| **Erlitou period** | *c.* 1700–*c.* 1500 BC |
| **Early Historic period:** | |
| Shang | *c.* 1500–*c.* 1050 BC |
| Erligang period | *c.* 1500–*c.* 1300 BC |
| Anyang period | *c.* 1300–*c.* 1050 BC |
| Western Zhou | *c.* 1050–771 BC |
| Eastern Zhou | 770–221 BC |
| Spring and Autumn period | 770–475 BC |
| Warring States period | 475–221 BC |
| **Imperial China:** | |
| Qin | 221–206 BC |
| Han | 206 BC–AD 220 |
| Western Han | 206 BC–AD 9 |
| Xin | AD 9–25 |
| Eastern Han | AD 25-220 |

*Figure 10.2 Chronology of ancient China (after Rawson 1996).*

elite, and acquiring elements of the high culture that was already recognized as the core of Chinese identity.

Sima Qian, who was fond of a good story, relates many about Gaozu. Several of these anecdotes became famous and were often retold by later writers. Those writers seem to have accepted them as substantially accurate. One such anecdote justifies conspicuous consumption in terms that will be familiar to students of other ancient and modern civilizations:

> The Prime Minister Xiao He had been put in charge of the building of the Eternal Palace . . . When Gaozu returned from his expedition and saw the magnificence of the palace and towers, he was extremely angry. "The empire is still in great turmoil," he said to Xiao He, "and though we have toiled in battle these several years, we cannot yet tell whether we will achieve final success. What do you mean by constructing palaces like this on such an extravagant scale?"
>
> Xiao He replied, "It is precisely because the fate of the empire is still uncertain that we must build such palaces and halls. A true Son of Heaven takes the whole world within the Four Seas to be his family. If he does not dwell in magnificence and beauty, he will have no way to manifest his authority, nor will he leave any foundation for his heirs to build upon." With these words, Gaozu's anger turned to delight. (Sima Qian, trans. by Watson 1962, 1: 110–111)

Before this Han Gaozu had not lived luxuriously, but afterward he seems to have gone along with Xiao He's argument. Perhaps he was actually convinced that displaying wealth could reinforce legitimacy and insure order; in any case, he showed few signs of asceticism in later years.

Another anecdote illustrates two themes that may not be often enough considered by interpreters of other ancient civilizations: (1) the deliberate manipulation of tradition for political ends, and (2) the use of ritual in promoting civil rather than cosmic order. Interestingly, the anecdote presents Gaozu in a rather comic light.

> The emperor completely did away with the elaborate and irksome ritual which the Qin had followed and greatly simplified the rules of court. The followers and ministers, however, were given to drinking and wrangling over their respective achievements, some shouting wildly in their drunkenness and hacking at the pillars of the palace so that Emperor Gaozu worried about their behavior. Shusun Tong knew that the emperor was becoming increasingly disgusted by the situation, and so he spoke to him about it. "Confucian scholars," he said, "are not much use when one is marching to conquest, but they can be of help in keeping what has already been won. I beg to summon some of the scholars of Lu who can join with my disciples in drawing up a ritual for the court."
>
> "Can you make one that is not too difficult?" asked the emperor.
>
> "The Five Emperors of antiquity all had different types of court music and dance; the kings of the Three Dynasties by no means followed the same ritual . . . It is my desire to select from a number of ancient codes of ritual, as well as from the ceremonies of Qin, and make a combination of these."
>
> "You may try and see what you can do," replied the emperor. "But make it easy to learn! Keep in mind that it must be the sort of thing I can perform."
>
> [Shusun Tong proceeded to devise an appropriate system of rituals which was first put into practice at a ceremony for the completion of a palace. Officials, nobles and generals all participated.]
>
> At this point the emperor, borne on a litter,

> appeared from the inner rooms . . . Then each of the guests, from the nobles and kings down to the officials of six hundred piculs salary, was summoned in turn to come forward and present his congratulations, and from the nobles down everyone trembled with awe and reverence.
>
> . . . During the drinking which followed the formal audience there was no one who dared to quarrel or misbehave in the least. With this, Emperor Gaozu announced, "Today for the first time I realize how exalted a thing it is to be an emperor." He appointed Shusun Tong his master of ritual and awarded him five hundred catties of gold. (Sima Qian, trans. by Watson 1969: 225–226)

A third anecdote about Han Gaozu relates directly to questions of legitimation. His interlocutor this time is a scholar named Lu Jia.

> In his audiences with the emperor, Master Lu on numerous occasions expounded and praised the [classic] *Book of Odes* and the *Book of Documents* until one day Gaozu began to rail at him. "All I possess I have won on horseback!" said the emperor. "Why should I bother with the *Odes* and *Documents*?"
>
> "Your Majesty may have won it on horseback, but can you rule it on horseback?" asked Master Lu. "Kings Tang and Wu in ancient times won possession of the empire through the principle of revolt, but it was by the principle of obedience that they assured the continuance of their Dynasties . . . The Qin [dynasty] trusted its future solely to punishments and laws, without changing with the times, and thus eventually brought about the destruction of its ruling family. If, after it had united the world under its rule, Qin had practiced benevolence and righteousness and modeled its ways upon the sages of antiquity, how would Your Majesty ever have been able to win possession of the empire?"
>
> The emperor grew embarrassed and uneasy, and finally said to Master Lu, "Try writing something for me on the reasons why Qin lost the empire and I won it, and of the successes and failures of the states of ancient times." (Sima Qian, trans. by Watson 1969: 209–210)

Sima Qian reports that Lu Jia proceeded to write a long treatise which he read to the emperor in installments. Most of the reasons Lu gave for the losing and winning of empires are conventional and moralistic: success and legitimacy, he claimed, stem chiefly from the virtuous character of the ruler.

There is not enough space here to list all of the other justifications offered for changes of dynasty, either as these are sketched by chroniclers of the early Han period or as they were worked out exhaustively in subsequent centuries. Benevolence and righteousness played an important role in claims to legitimacy by incoming dynasts, as did the welfare of commoners and elite, respect for morality, tradition, and family values (see, for example, Sargent 1977: 178).

Signs predicting that a child will become a great man are common to hero myths in many civilizations. In China, as elsewhere, such signs could provide a kind of retrospective legitimation, showing that a new ruler was legitimate because his accession had been predicted. According to Sima Qian, writing well after the fact, there were many such signs in Han Gaozu's early career (Watson 1969: 105–110). His mother dreamed of meeting a god and his father had a vision of a dragon over the place where she was lying; after this she became pregnant with him. In maturity, people continued to see dragons over his bed. He had a dragonlike face and seventy-two black moles on his left thigh. Various seers predicted an extraordinary future for him; one also said that his wife would become "the most important person in the world." No less a personage than his predecessor, Emperor Qin Shi Huangdi, saw signs in the southeastern sky that a Son of Heaven could be found in that direction, and set out on an expedition to suppress this rival. This forced Han Gaozu to flee into the wilderness. However, his wife and other intimates were always able to find him. When he asked how she did this, she replied:

> "There are always signs in the clouds over the place where you are. By following these we manage to find you every time." Gaozu was very pleased in his heart. When word of this circulated among the young men of the district of Pei, many of them sought to become his followers. (Sima Qian, trans. by Watson 1969: 108)

Portents of an impending change in government were essentially of two kinds: an increase in actual troubles like civil strife and natural disasters, and the appearance of more purely symbolic portents such as strange animals, colored auras, significant archaeological finds, comets, prophetic texts, and so forth. As Wechsler (1985: 55–77) points out, political portents were easy to manipulate and indeed were often faked. It is significant that the likelihood of fakery in such matters was widely recognized and, judging by the tone of historical descriptions (i.e., of Wang Mang's usurpation in AD 9 – see Sargent 1977: 140–180), a subject of general skepticism among members of the elite. The fact that political portents continued to be sought and publicized throughout Chinese history indicates that this form of legitimation may have been chiefly aimed at a wider, non-elite audience.

The concept of legitimacy on this level is summarized in the doctrine of the Mandate of Heaven, first recorded in the classic Shu Jing or *Book of Documents*, supposedly compiled by Confucius at about 500 BC. The idea is straightforward: Heaven awards a mandate to rule the world to an exceptionally virtuous individual. This mandate extends to his descendants but only as long as they too are outstandingly virtuous rulers. When the virtue of the lineage begins to diminish and it is no longer capable of providing good government, the Mandate of Heaven is canceled and conferred on another dynasty (Old 1904: 232–236). The main evidence that the Mandate has shifted is the fact that a new dynasty has seized power. The logic involved is saved from being fully circular, but rendered dangerous to established governments, by a persistent belief that shifts in the Mandate are preceded by portents of the kind mentioned above.

### Cross-cultural perspectives

As noted above, Han Gaozu was neither the first nor the last Chinese ruler to face his particular set of problems, and very similar problems have been faced by rulers in many other societies.

### Order

Perhaps the most universal of all such problems is the establishment and maintenance of civil order. Here the overall Han solution seems not to have been greatly different from those chosen by other societies: a judicious mixture of punishment, reward, and propaganda aimed at persuading one's subjects that respect for order is binding and its maintenance justified.

Certain subsystems of the Han solution, however, are more or less unique in the ancient world, except that they were to be retained and extended by later dynasties and imitated by neighboring countries. Those subsystems include land and head taxes based on written census and cadastral records, detailed regulations for controlling population movement, the use of formal recommendations and written examinations to recruit an elite civil service, the promotion of social mobility by opening the examinations to most of the male population, and the establishment of a centralized professional bureaucracy headed by the civil service. Although the full-fledged Chinese imperial civil service system did not emerge until after the Han period, most of its elements were firmly in place well before the end of the dynasty.

An innovation of Han Gaozu's great successor, Han Wudi (140–87 BC) was the establishment of an imperial university aimed at educating future civil servants, not in practical political science but in the high culture as represented by the works of Confucius and other classical literature. By the time of Wang Mang's usurpation in AD 9, the university had 10,000 students. Admission was by recommendation of senior civil servants all over the empire. We may presume that many of the students were the sons either of officials or of important families, but some were talented commoners.

In such a situation, does it make sense to say that the civil order of Han China was appropriated by the elite, as is said to have been the case in ancient Mesopotamia and Egypt? I think only by defining order in a very abstract way. Chinese historiography does not presume that the elite is more committed to the maintenance of order, in the law-and-order sense, than are the common people. Further, Chinese history contains many instances where disturbances of order are initiated by the elite and resisted, passively if not actively, by commoners. It is indeed true that the Chinese elite appropriated the social order, in the sense of social hierarchy, but such a statement is close to being a meaningless tautology.

### Cosmology

Another possible difference between ancient China and many other societies lies in the area of elite versus commoner concerns with the cosmic order. In Pharaonic Egypt, for example, the elite had an effective monopoly of cosmological ritual and did not hesitate to use this in extending its social power. The situation is different, however, in a society like that of traditional China, where the elite was neither in control of nor necessarily involved with the religions of the masses.

The emperor and his agents did promote the worship of Heaven and its personification, Shangdi. As in the case of comparable state rituals in Egypt and Mesopotamia, the so-called Suburban Sacrifices to Heaven were considered not only to reinforce and validate imperial authority but to promote order in the cosmos. The population of China during the Han and later periods seems to have acknowledged that those rituals were important. But the problem is that the worship of Heaven was not the religion of that population, neither of the masses nor, in fact, of the elite as private individuals. In post-Han times, Buddhism and institutional Daoism, both of which had well worked-out cosmologies quite distinct from that of the official Heaven "religion," became the personal faiths of most Chinese. During the Han period, before Buddhism and developed Daoism had become established in popular culture, the religious situation was more diffuse, with numerous proto-Daoist and other cults, notably that of the Queen Mother of the West, competing for the people's favor. The tenets of those popular cults are only imperfectly known. However, it seems clear that few of them had anything to do with the imperial worship of Heaven.

The situation is perhaps analogous to that of classical Greece and Rome, where the official Olympian religion and its associated cosmology were strongly supported as central to state-sustaining ritual even though they evoked little if any fervor from the elite or masses. The personal religions of most Greeks and Romans were either exotic imports from Egypt and the Middle East or home-grown mystery and mother goddess cults. The average Roman was no more likely to make a long, painful pilgrimage to seek the aid of Jupiter than was the average Chinese to dedicate her/his life to the service of Heaven.

The Roman and Chinese cases should make us cautious about accepting the general applicability of Baines and Yoffee's thesis that civilizational collapse can be defined by the eclipse of traditional cosmologies (Baines and Yoffee 1998). Gibbon and his followers, it is true, have long maintained that the conquest by Christianity of the old Roman religion was a major cause of the fall of Rome. But in reality the old Roman religion had become a hollow shell, emptied of all real devotion, long before the reign of Tiberius and the birth of Christ. Similarly, the official Heaven religion of Han and post-Han China may once have been more than a series of splendid and sovereignty-validating ceremonies, but that lay far back in the Bronze Age.

## Wealth

The role of wealth is another area in which Han civilization may have differed somewhat from the civilizations of ancient Egypt and Mesopotamia.

The ancient Chinese did not fail to appreciate the advantages of being rich. In the words of Sima Qian:

> Only when the granaries are full can people appreciate rites and obligations; only when they have enough food and clothing do they think about glory and disgrace. Rites are born of plenty and are abandoned in time of want. When superior men become rich, they delight in practicing virtue; but when mean-minded men are rich, they long only to exercise their power. As fish by nature dwell in the deepest pools and wild beasts congregate in the most secluded mountains, so benevolence and righteousness attach themselves to a man of wealth. (Watson trans. 1969: 336)

Yet wealth in China, unlike Mesopotamia, was not an instrument of legitimation. As the above-quoted anecdote about Han Gaozu's palaces shows, Chinese political theorists maintained that the display of wealth helped in establishing social authority. But being rich was neither a sufficient nor absolutely necessary precondition for the achievement of high social status. In the following passage, Sima Qian implies that a sharp distinction exists between the merely rich and the true nobility:

> A family with a thousand catties of gold may stand side by side with the lord of a city; the man with a hundred million cash may enjoy the pleasures of a king. Rich men such as these deserve to be called the "untitled nobility," do they not? (Watson trans. 1969: 356).

Even though the early Han period was one of exceptional social mobility, Sima evidently does not think that crossing the line and joining the elite was easy in his day. In later centuries, when the merchant class suffered numerous legal disabilities, to cross the line on the basis of wealth alone was in theory, though not always in practice, impossible.

## The inner elite

In Han Gaozu's day, the position of the old inner elite had been severely damaged, first by purges carried out under Qin Shi Huangdi two decades previously and then by a civil war which not only killed many of the old elite but produced a new elite in the form of early adherents of Gaozu's cause. As in the case of successful modern revolutions, the newly installed Han Dynasty found itself burdened with large numbers of former revolutionaries waiting for their reward: an opening in the civil or military service or as a court official. This rebel elite lacked most of the characteristics of inner elites in more stable civilizations: its members had had little contact with the high culture, were unappreciative of ritual and discipline, and had only minimal orientation toward public service.

Within a century, however, Han China had re-developed an inner elite which was closely comparable in most ways to those of Mediterranean and Middle Eastern civilizations. Membership was shared between the nobility (essentially, descendants of emperors and close relatives of empresses and imperial consorts), scholar-officials with their families, certain educated gentry, and a handful of merchants and military individuals. Over the long term, the scholar-official lineages proved to be more stable than other contenders for elite status. They therefore constituted an elite class in most senses of that term even though, as already pointed out, recruitment to the highest official ranks outside the imperial family was by achievement rather than ascription.

The Han and post-Han elite was quite large. In theory and practice, the set of persons qualified to become high-ranking officials included a large percentage of the population, and it is hard to discern a stable inner elite within this broader one. The highest-ranking officials naturally consorted mostly with other high officials, but membership in such cliques was as changeable as the membership of a modern presidential cabinet. Except in the case of imperial princes, the sons of high officials did not inherit their father's positions.

The position of retainer in the inner court or imperial household was often heritable (when having been made a eunuch was not part of the job description) and could be as powerful as that of a high-ranking civil service official. However, the retainers of the inner court were not an inner elite as Baines and Yoffee use that term. They lacked legitimacy in everyone's eyes except insofar as they conveyed the orders of the emperor. And at no time in Chinese history were court retainers conceded to have special authority over or competence in the high culture.

In fact, the tastemakers or cultural gatekeepers of ancient China were scholar-officials on the one hand and intellectuals without official positions on the other. As anecdotes about Han Gaozu and other uncultivated emperors show, power and cultural prestige did not go hand in hand. And as shown by innumerable admiring stories about reclusive intellectuals who became famous although (and because) they refused to serve the government, despite numerous invitations from the emperor himself and sometimes despite personal poverty as well, membership in the inner elite of cultural prestige was by no means confined to the rich and powerful.

Whether a similar pattern ever existed in ancient Mesopotamia or Egypt is not clear to me, but something of the sort – that is, cultural arbiters who do not belong to a political inner elite – can certainly be discerned in the histories of Greece, Rome, India, the Islamic world, and the recent West. Kings, royal scribes, and high priests may have controlled the high cultures of the Egyptians and Sumerians, but their counterparts did not do so in China. I am not sure whether they can validly be said to have had that kind of cultural power in most other ancient and modern civilizations.

**Legitimacy**

China is closely comparable to other ancient civilizations in its preoccupation with establishing and reinforcing the perceived legitimacy of rulers and elite. It may be that early Chinese historians and social philosophers were more up-front about this than most of their peers elsewhere in the ancient world. But the real issues, as understood by the elite and even commoners, were very similar.

Chinese concepts of how authority had to be legitimized were discussed earlier in this chapter. To further illustrate those concepts, we may examine another quotation, this time from the semi-historical thirteenth-century novel, The *Romance of the Three Kingdoms*, which is set in the last years of the Han Dynasty, the early third century AD. In the quotation, Liu Bei is proclaiming that he has established a new dynasty which will preserve the achievements of the Han Dynasty and of Liu's purported ancestor, Gaozu.

> On this twelfth day of the fourth month of the year of "Established Tranquillity" [AD 220], Bei the Emperor makes this solemn announcement to Heaven and Earth. The Dynasty of Han has possessed the empire for years without end . . . Lately Cao Cao, powerful and cruel, slew the Empress, and his crimes cry aloud to Heaven for vengeance. The son, Cao Pei, carrying evils into every quarter, then seized the scepter. My subordinates, regarding the [Han] Dynasty as having been overthrown, think it fitting that I, Bei, should continue the line. As successor to my two warrior ancestors, Gaozu and Guangwu, I will punish as Heaven decrees. Fearing lest my virtue be inadequate to the Imperial throne, I consulted the voices of the people, and all, even the most distant, have said that the Mandate of Heaven may not be disobeyed and the great task of my ancestors may not continue in the hands of another; the land must have a lord, and they aver the cynosure of all eyes is myself. Now I, respecting the Mandate

> of Heaven . . . have reverently selected this auspicious day to ascend the altar, sacrifice and announce my assumption of the imperial seal in order to comfort all the people, rejoice the ancestors of the Dynastic House and bring eternal tranquillity to all the domains." (Brewitt-Taylor trans., n.d., 2: 211)

It will be seen that Liu Bei claims legitimacy on multiple grounds: inheritance, the illegitimacy of a rival (as shown not by his usurpation of power but by his murder of an empress), his own virtue, selection by Heaven, the wishes of the spirits of deceased Han emperors, popular consent (!), and – significantly – the need for domestic order. Connoisseurs of such proclamations, of which there are many in Chinese history, may care to compare this one with those issued by the organizers of modern *coups d'état* (Luttwak 1969: 173–179).

How one begins a dynasty, however, is not necessarily how one keeps it in power. Sweeping public proclamations by would-be dynasts do play a role in carrying out successful rebellions and revolutions. But all such manifestos have an element of unreality about them. They are like corporate mission statements in our own civilization: laboriously produced, vaingloriously pronounced, limitedly relevant, and widely ignored before the brush strokes are dry on the page. In getting started, a successful dynasty may actually have less need for proclamations aimed at the general public than for reassurances and promises of benefits privately conveyed to the outgoing and incoming elites. And to stay in power, a dynasty needs a more practical kind of long-term operating system, one that takes account of the self-interest and capabilities of subjects, the needs and ambitions of rulers, and the availability of wealth and other resources.

Large-scale, legitimacy-promoting ideologies do play a role in keeping things going. If not, then why, Baines and Yoffee might ask, is so much effort devoted by so many civilizations to the artistic and artifactual embodiments of order: big monuments, costly ceremonies, and so forth? And yet in principle a dynasty could survive for some time without much effort being made to convince anyone except an inner core of the elite that its reign was legitimate. Indeed, as the history of recent colonialism shows, it is not impossible to rule for a while entirely by *force majeure* and to pay no attention at all to what any of one's subjects think. Spies and paramilitary police may be expensive, but they are not necessarily more so than costly bribes to local elites and splendid temples dedicated to order-maintaining deities.

The disadvantage of unalloyed coercion, of course, is that the necessary spies and police are too dangerous to the rulers themselves to be considered for long as a sole means of staying in power. Hence, as even the most authoritarian emperors recognized, a stable dynasty needs a degree of unforced consent: perceived legitimacy, consensus about the social order, and enough wealth to persuade key subjects that these things are true. It seems to me that unforced consent has a fourth element as well: the existence of a sociopolitical system that is seen to be functional.

For many early Chinese, elite and commoners alike, it may be that the grand abstractions of political theory and ritual were less essential than the perception that the system did function: that government services were efficient, that the economy was prosperous, that life was secure, and that the emperor was concerned and just. This indeed was what the Mandate of Heaven was all about, a political, social, economic, and environmental system that could be seen by everyone to be reasonably successful. During good times any number of heavenly portents would be cheerfully ignored. During times when the system was not working, the same portents would be collected and publicized as showing that Heaven was about to withdraw its choice and that the Dynasty might fall unless all involved made haste to mend their ways. Here the cosmos is being made to serve very pragmatic ends. As Baines and Yoffee point out, in some civilizations cities, states, and high-cultural artifacts of many other types seem to mimic and even celebrate the cosmos. In China, however, the mimicry seems mostly to have been the other way. The Jade Emperor of the Daoists presided over a court that imitated the courts of earthly emperors. And in a sense, the Mandate of Heaven was no more than the embodiment of a judgment, potentially made by everyone within and on the fringes of Chinese civilization, that the earthly empire was still in working order.

PART III

# Conclusions

# 11
# The politics of high culture: issues of worth and rank

ELIZABETH M. BRUMFIEL

High culture was the focus of archaeological exploration in the mid-nineteenth century. Archaeologists searched for artifacts that embodied the highest artistic and moral standards of ancient civilizations. These objects were incorporated into classroom lectures and museum displays in order to impart the high ideals of "civilization" to the public and to reinforce American institutions of business and government (Hinsley 1985: 56–59). But by the end of the nineteenth century, this humanistic appreciation of high culture had been supplanted by a natural scientific approach to the human past. Archaeologists began to explore questions of biological and social evolution, space–time systematics, cultural reconstruction, and cultural ecology. These scientific studies employed a wide array of mundane artifacts such as ceramic sherds, stone flakes, and charred plant remains. The artifacts of high culture commanded no special respect.

Why, then, do we return to the topic of high culture at this time? What developments within archaeology and American society make high culture interesting once again? Does a renewed interest in high culture necessarily signal the substitution of humanism for science and a return to conservative political and social values?

Several developments, both internal and external to archaeology, probably contribute to our interest in high culture. Foremost among these is the spread of post-modernism across the social sciences. The post-modern emphasis on textual interpretation has fixed our attention on culture and consciousness. In archaeology, the post-modern post-processualists have argued that prehistory was shaped by individuals who acted upon their understanding of the world to negotiate social roles and cultural ideals (Shanks and Tilley 1982; Leone 1984; Hodder 1986: 8). But how do individuals arrive at their ideas about the world? What roles are played by sensation, material culture, ritual, and language? How do these cultural understandings shape plans for action? Questions about order, legitimacy, and wealth are part of this broader interest in culture as it affects all social action.

Outside of archaeology, renewed interest in the cultures of ancient civilizations has several sources. Many Americans, disillusioned with contemporary life, have sought to base their accommodation or social activism in the philosophical ideals of enduring non-Western cultures. Feminists, Greens, and New Agers have looked to the ancients for wisdom and values that seem to address contemporary dilemmas. In addition, the introduction of multiculturalism in American education has stimulated interest in the elite forms of non-Western culture, and reactions against multiculturalism have revitalized efforts to valorize and disseminate the Western cultural heritage (Patterson 1995: 130–131). Many people are interested in knowing more about ancient high cultures, and archaeologists have begun to respond to this interest, as they should.

Baines and Yoffee (1998) provide a series of generalizations about high culture based upon their comparison of Egypt with Mesopotamia. They propose that high culture was a distinctive feature of all ancient civilizations. High culture was formulated by a small body of inner elites and propagated through a variety of cultural media. High culture was largely self-referential. It focused upon symbolic concerns rather than political and economic issues, and it did not diffuse beyond the elite group. Commonly, high culture dealt with questions of cosmic order and the legitimate place of elites within that order. Statements about these issues were communicated and endowed with factuality through the medium of wealth, that is, highly crafted pieces of art. Baines and Yoffee propose that a gap divided high culture from culture in its non-elite forms. At the same time, they suggest that non-elites accepted the postulates of high culture due to a lack of available alternatives. By controling wealth, elites completely monopolized the construction of meaning. Baines and Yoffee observe that the emergence of high culture was rapid; in both Egypt and Mesopotamia state formation was quickly followed by the transformation of art, the development of writing, and the concentration of symbolic structures in central places. This underscores the discontinuity between high culture and culture in its non-elite forms. Finally, Baines and Yoffee suggest that high culture is best studied in its earliest fully developed form. Baines (chapter 2 in this volume) states, "Our interpretations focus on continuing order rather than on periods of formation or of collapse." He distinguishes the high cultures of early civilizations from those of later "successor" empires and states.

Clearly, Baines and Yoffee's formulation stands somewhere between humanism and science. It is humanistic in focusing on the content and not just the function of ancient ideologies. It is scientific in its attempt to generalize about high culture across very different social contexts. Ancient Egypt was rural, agrarian, centralized, and unified, while Mesopotamia was urban, commercial, and politically divided. The proposal that both civilizations shared a concern with order, legitimacy, and wealth as did all early civilizations, seems truly inspired. It also seems courageous, given the current academic retreat from both cross-cultural study and general model-building.

Post-processual archaeologists have criticized comparative study. For example, Hodder (1986: 6) states: "all we can do is come to an understanding of each cultural context in its own right, as a unique set of cultural dispositions and practices." And Shanks and Tilley (1987: 38) ask, "Why must the business of doing science necessarily be equated with the ability, or the will to generalize?" The primary focus of Hodder, Shanks, and Tilley's criticism are the "nomothetic laws" of cultural evolution, regarded by the New Archaeology as the highest goal of archaeological study. Even so, the post-processual rejection of general laws has frequently been extended to all cross-cultural comparison.

But comparison can play a valuable role in archaeology. Discussions among archaeologists in a single region take for granted both familiarity with the data and many shared assumptions about the structure and meaning of the data. At the very least, comparative work forces archaeologists to become aware of their implicitly held assumptions and models and better able to evaluate them. And since archaeologists are always guided by their own frames of interpretation and meaning in studying ancient remains (Shanks and Tilley 1987: 104–106; Johnsen and Olsen 1992), new models that produce new readings of the evidence are welcome.

General formulations such as the Baines and Yoffee proposal have been criticized as "totalizing," i.e., imposing uniformity upon a variable world by reducing all cases to the terms of the model and ignoring the variability that falls outside of it. But such formulations can be used to define precisely those areas where nonconformity and variability exist. In fact, the contributors to this volume seem to have used Baines and Yoffee's essay in just this way. Although the proposal sets the terms of discussion, these authors use their knowledge of specific ancient civilizations to take issue with various aspects of the formulation. But this does not mean that the proposal was wasted effort. Clearly, the proposal prompted contributors to focus upon high culture and to explore aspects of it that they might have ignored in the model's absence.

The contributors to this volume address several aspects of the Baines and Yoffee formulation. These include the purposes of high culture, high culture and earlier symbolic forms, and high culture and the monopoly of meaning.

## The purposes of high culture

According to Baines and Yoffee, high culture was created by a small body of inner elites to deal with questions of cosmic order and the legitimate place of elites within that order. It focused upon symbolic concerns rather than political and economic issues, and it did not diffuse beyond the elite group. Several contributors question the assertion that high culture addressed the elites' concerns about their own legitimacy rather than responding to outside challenges to elite power.

Joyce's view of wealth and legitimacy, for example, is quite different from Baines and Yoffee's. Baines and Yoffee see wealth as a medium of communication; Joyce sees it as a standard of evaluation. For Joyce, objects of skilled craftsmanship are the material instantiation of a system of moral virtue that serves as an argument for social ranking. Baines and Yoffee regard legitimacy as an existential question that elites ponder; Joyce regards it as property which elites acquire through the construction of expensive, exclusive contexts for the enactment of their concepts of order. Although Joyce states that she accepts Baines and Yoffee's assertion that high culture is essentially self-referential and unconcerned with non-elites, the focus of her discussion is how wealth and legitimacy came to be defined, as Mesoamerican elites tried to make their claims to superordinate status stick. Thus, Joyce is fundamentally concerned with questions of political economy, questions that are explicitly ruled irrelevant in Baines and Yoffee's original formulation.

Kenoyer also believes that emerging elites used wealth to validate social distinction. He suggests that items of personal adornment were used to define and legitimate wealth and status differences during the Neolithic and Chalcolithic periods in the Indus Valley. An increased variety of ornaments, using different raw materials and manufacturing technologies, were used to define social difference. But these same ornaments simultaneously played an integrative role. Shared styles of ornamentation served to unite the members of different socioeconomic groups even while ornaments of higher and lower value made visible social distinctions. Kenoyer suggests that emerging social inequality requires both differentiation and integration and that wealth items can promote both of these social processes.

Richards points out that even when high culture originates as an exclusive ideology, inner elites may be tempted to share high culture more widely. This evidently occurred in Egypt during the Middle Kingdom. As political competition intensified, rulers permitted lower and non-elite members of society to share in funerary practices that had been restricted to the inner elite. Richards suggests that this was done to promote a sense of participation among lower and non-elite members of society and to build support for the system of rule.

Exclusion and inclusion can be carried out simultaneously. Kenoyer suggests that even as wealth objects become accessible to lower ranking groups, new forms of wealth are created to maintain social differences. Thus, among the Maya, social distinction was first marked by ornamentation, then by access to restricted spaces and depiction in monumental art, and finally by using writing and calendrical notation. While each of these innovations created new kinds of difference between inner elites and other members of society, the constant stream of innovation enabled rulers to share some elite markers with lower ranking groups without threatening their own superior status.

Bronson affirms that, in China, high culture did not diffuse beyond the elite group; the imperial worship of Heaven was not the religion of the masses. However, even in China, high culture did not grow from the philosophical musings of inner elites, unrelated to political maneuvering. Bronson's sources report that the first Han ruler had no use for high culture until he was convinced that pomp and ceremony would stabilize his rule. Han Gaozu self-consciously manipulated wealth and ritual in order to solidify political relations and allegiances among the political elite and to strengthen his regime.

Thus, high culture is often implicated in the management of social relations as inequality and political centralization develop. We will return to the issue of political power and cultural innovation at the end of this chapter.

### High culture and the monopoly of meaning

Yoffee seeks to substantiate Baines and Yoffee's remarkable claim that elites completely monopolize the construction of meaning in ancient civilizations and that non-elites are forced to accept the postulates of high culture by default, lacking any alternatives. To quote Yoffee, "Even the on-the-ground social and political changes . . . do not threaten the interplay of order, legitimacy, and wealth because there are no alternative cosmologies that could reorient social life." The *nouveau riche* of Old Babylonia endowed positions for their daughters and sisters within existing religious institutions because "There was no thought to challenge Mesopotamian order, no questioning of the legitimate role of temples . . ." However, an alternative explanation might be offered; perhaps, no new cosmologies were necessary. After all, symbols are a malleable idiom, capable of absorbing new meanings and expressing different interests. Perhaps, in the case of Old Babylonia, old symbols could be organized to serve the purposes of newly emerging classes very well.

This conclusion might also be drawn from Alcock's sensitive analysis of the revival of Classical art in Greece under Roman rule. The forms of Classical Greece were not the only ones available to Greek populations under Roman rule; a distinctive imperial Roman style existed. Greek populations chose to revive the Classical style because it best conveyed Greek concepts of order in a Rome-dominated world.[1] Furthermore, Alcock concludes, the existence of distinctive Greek and Roman definitions of order suggests that order and legitimacy were more contested and more fractured concepts than Baines and Yoffee allow. A distinctive interpretation of order and legitimacy can be expected from each segment of each population incorporated in a territorial state or empire.

### High culture and earlier symbolic forms

O'Connor challenges Baines and Yoffee on a related issue: whether the high culture of the inner elite erases broadly distributed earlier symbolic forms. O'Connor examines the few excavated temples and cemeteries from early Egypt and tentatively concludes that local forms do persist.

Van Buren is emphatic on this issue for the Andes. She points out that local shrines continued to be patronized during the Inka empire, and she convincingly demonstrates that Inka imperial culture drew upon a store of pre-existing ideas such as the deification of the sun, the organization of exchanges by an ideology of reciprocity, and the ordering of social relations through the language of kinship. In fact, Van Buren suggests, non-elites played a crucial role in the transmission of Andean civilization, allowing it to survive periods of political and economic collapse. Of course, the Inka were a "successor" empire in the Andean region; they represent the continuity of a long-lived regional tradition.

Richards also focuses on the processes of cultural transmission during periods of collapse. She suggests that elite craftsmen and local rulers played key roles in the transmission process. Local elites became the patrons of elite craftsmen in periods when regional elites were absent. These craftsmen produced the forms of high culture for their local patrons. High culture and craftsmen that survived on the local level during periods of decentralization became resources for the reconstitution of high culture when regional consolidation again occurred.

Richards' analysis raises a question which goes unanswered. As the forms and symbols of high culture diffuse during periods of collapse, do they continue to communicate the ideals of high culture, or are the forms and symbols reinterpreted? Is new wine placed in the old bottles?

### High culture and power-building – an Aztec example

The contributors to this volume agree on several issues. High culture *is* created by the elite for the elite, as Baines and Yoffee assert. But there is more interplay between inner elites and other segments of society than suggested in the original Baines and Yoffee formulation. Moreover, within the elite stratum high culture serves political purposes. This last point emerges clearly from the history of ideological development in the Aztec state.

In the official ideology of the Aztec state at the time of European contact, order, legitimacy, and wealth were very closely linked. According to the Aztecs, the world order depended upon the circulation of *tonalli*, a heat–light–energy force that was indispensable for existence (López Austin 1988: 204–228). Life depended upon the regulated movement of this energy in cycles of day and night, summer and winter, birth and death. But the orderly circulation of *tonalli* was problematic. Day was born only when the sun prevailed over the moon and stars (Sahagún 1950–1982 Bk. 3, ch. 1). Four previous worlds had existed, only to be destroyed as the world order was overwhelmed by chaos (*Leyenda de los Soles* 1945: 119–120).

Aztec rulers claimed to be endowed with greater *tonalli* than their subjects (López Austin 1988: 396–400). Their liberal endowment was said to stem from their noble lineage, carefully guarded from debilitating pollution and sin. It was also enhanced by rigorous education in the temple schools (*calmecac*). This education was intended to impart the moral qualities (piety, diligence, self-restraint, and attention to detail) required for difficult tasks such as public administration. The claim of physiological superiority was used to legitimate the authority of Aztec rulers. The official position was that society flourished under the guidance of leaders infused with vigorous *tonalli* substance.

The ruler's *tonalli* was evident in his royal raiment (Figure 11.3). Rulers were garbed in elite craft products that radiated light. Metal objects and gem stones were polished until they gleamed (Figure 11.4). Feathered headdresses and standards were arranged so that their feathers shimmered (Sahagún 1950–1982 Bk. 9, chs. 16, 17, 21). Even stone sculptures and wooden objects were finished to a high luster. When the ruler donned his royal finery, metal, stone, and feathered objects radiated sparks of divine fire. The strength of the ruler's *tonalli* was manifest.

Thus, order, legitimacy, and wealth were closely interrelated in the official Aztec ideology. But the ideology was not confined to a small circle of inner elites; it had important implications for other segments of the population, especially soldiers who distinguished themselves on the battlefield. Aztec rulers argued that warfare and human sacrifice were necessary to maintain the world order; the forces of order had to be strengthened by *tonalli*-rich human blood (Caso 1958; Conrad and Demarest 1984). Aztec soldiers, who in victory took captives for human sacrifice and in defeat watered the earth with their blood, made an essential contribution to the common good.

The *tonalli* concept thus endowed the activities of Aztec soldiers with transcendental importance. In addition, it conferred value upon the goods that soldiers received from their rulers: richly embroidered capes and loin cloths, earrings, lip plugs, and nose plugs, arm bands, leg bands, feather and gold ornaments for the hair, adornments for the back, and feathered body suits and shields. Not only were such items proof that their bearers had distinguished themselves on the battlefield and enjoyed the ruler's favor, these items also testified to soldiers' vigorous *tonalli*. Just as the glint of elite craft goods lent support to the ruler's claim of superior *tonalli*, they confirmed the strength of the soldiers' *tonalli* as well, and by extension provided

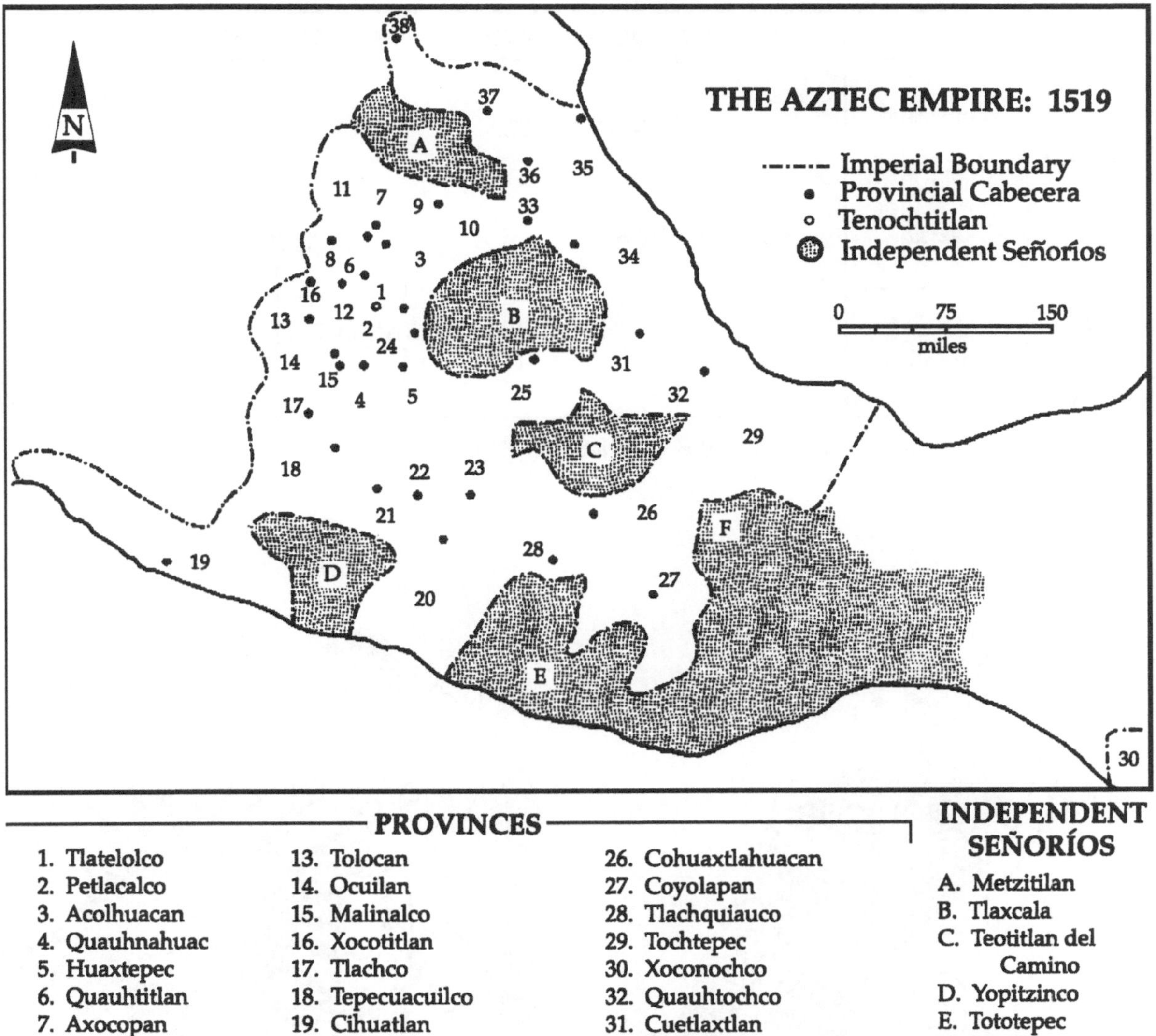


**PROVINCES**

1. Tlatelolco
2. Petlacalco
3. Acolhuacan
4. Quauhnahuac
5. Huaxtepec
6. Quauhtitlan
7. Axocopan
8. Atotonilco de Pedraza
9. Hueypochtlan
10. Atotonilco el Grande
11. Xilotepec
12. Zuahuacan
13. Tolocan
14. Ocuilan
15. Malinalco
16. Xocotitlan
17. Tlachco
18. Tepecuacuilco
19. Cihuatlan
20. Tlapan
21. Tlalcocauhtitlan
22. Quiauhteopan
23. Yoaltepec
24. Chalco
25. Tepeacac
26. Cohuaxtlahuacan
27. Coyolapan
28. Tlachquiauco
29. Tochtepec
30. Xoconochco
32. Quauhtochco
31. Cuetlaxtlan
33. Tlapacoyan
34. Tlatlauhquitepec
35. Tochpan
36. Atlan
37. Tzicoac
38. Oxitipan

**INDEPENDENT SEÑORÍOS**

A. Metzitilan
B. Tlaxcala
C. Teotitlan del Camino
D. Yopitzinco
E. Tototepec
F. Coatlicamao

*Figure 11.1 Map of the extent of the Aztec Empire (after Berdan 1982).*

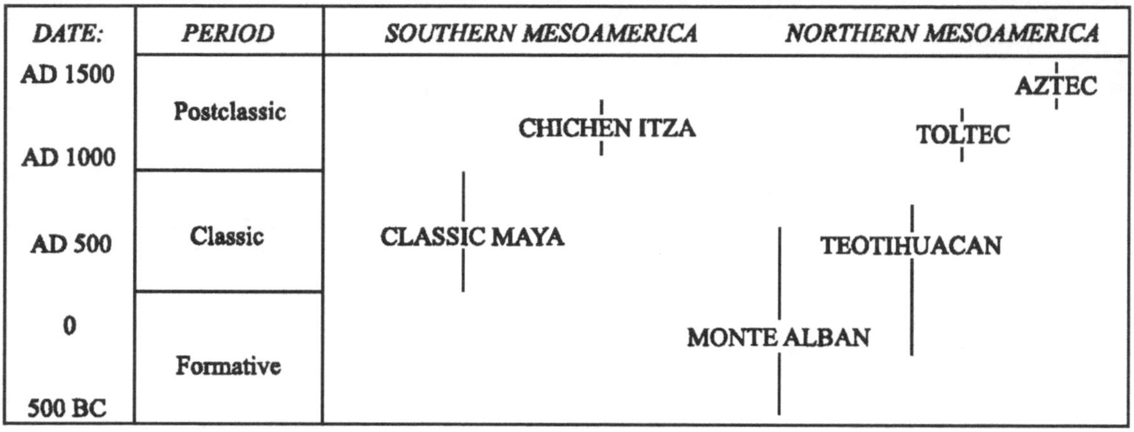


*Figure 11.2 Chronology for central Mexico (after Carmack et al. 1996).*

*Figure 11.3 The Aztec ruler, Moctezuma II, in his royal finery (after the Codex Azcatitlan. Drawing by M. LaNoue.)*

*Figure 11.4 A craftsman polishes a golden object. Gold was polished until "it glistened, it shone, it sent forth rays" (Sahugún 1950–1962, Book 9, Chapter 16). (After the Florentine Codex. Courtesy of the School of American Research and the University of Utah.)*

*Figure 11.5 High-ranking Aztec warriors wear ornate military costumes (after Codex Mendoza 1992, 67r).*

evidence of their noble lineage and virtuous conduct (Figure 11.5).

Thus, the definition of worth and rank contained in the Aztec concepts of cosmic order and disorder, *tonalli* and sacrifice, captured the loyalty of the Aztecs' ablest fighters. The official belief system defined a place of dignity for them in the state's world view, and it established the worth of the material rewards which they received (Brumfiel 1987, 1998). Far from being the unintended outcome of purely philosophical speculation about the cosmic order, the political uses of Aztec ideology were the result of deliberate action. Historical accounts suggest that Aztec rulers elaborated this philosophy over time as a means of strengthening their rule.

The Aztecs won control of central Mexico during the first half of the fifteenth century AD, less than a century before Spanish conquest (Davies 1973; Rounds 1979; Brumfiel 1983). As in the early Han Dynasty discussed by Bronson, the consolidation of power left the Aztecs' first imperial ruler, Itzcoatl, with many disparate groups to satisfy. These included dynastic competitors within his own royal lineage, loyal clients and allies, and the kinsmen of slain enemies. Itzcoatl attempted to satisfy these groups by distributing tribute-producing lands to them (Alva Ixtlilxóchitl 1975–1977 I: 379–80; *Anales de Cuauhtitlan* 1945: 50; Durán 1967 II: 82–83, 98, 113, 130, 151). However, even at this early date, Aztec rulers seem to have understood that the distribution of land was not enough. The distribution of land was accompanied by the distribution of titles (Alva Ixtlilxóchitl 1975–1977 II: 82; Durán 1967 II: 99). These titles (e.g., "He of the Twisted Water" or "He of the House of Darkness") referred to sacred places and forces, and placed the title-bearer in a broader cosmological scheme (Brumfiel 1987: 118).

Itzcoatl's successor, Moctezuma I, altered the composition of rewards, relying upon prizes with more symbolic and less material value. Moctezuma I reduced distributions of tribute-producing land, but he presented his supporters with highly crafted items of personal adornment. The iconography of these items of costume insured that successful warriors would be identified with supernatural powers of various sorts (Anawalt 1992). The worth of these items was further enhanced by a series of sumptuary laws which limited their availability. Moctezuma I restricted many items of dress to accomplished soldiers of specified grades (Durán 1971: 197–198; Sahagún 1950–1982 Bk. 8, ch. 21), and he set aside separate gathering places for individuals of distinction (Durán 1967 II: 236–238). Finally, Moctezuma I made religion more conspicuous in order to heighten the transcendental importance of the behavior and statuses symbolized by the craft items. He substantially enlarged the Aztecs' Great Temple, he commissioned pieces of monumental sculpture to adorn it, and he ordered the first large-scale sacrifices of war captives (Durán 1967 II: 133–135, 171–174, 190–193).

## Conclusions: identity, action, and culture

Moctezuma I seems to have understood that political power depends upon the creation and maintenance of strong coalitions or factions. High culture provides an indispensable tool in this process. Concepts of order enable leaders to engage allies and clients in "projects," actions shaped by "images and ideas of what constitutes goodness – in people, in relationships, and in conditions of life" (Ortner 1984: 152). Elite ideologies capture the commitment of allies and clients by conferring upon them places of dignity within a compelling world view.

Inner elites may consciously favor ideologies where the cosmological, the societal, and the individual coincide. In O'Connor's example, the aspirations and anxieties of the provincial governor Pepyankh centered around a cosmological and personal issue: how to make a successful transition to an afterlife. Loyal service to the ruler provided the means to this end. Carrying out the ruler's commands demonstrated concordance with *Ma'at*, providing the moral standing required for an afterlife. The ruler's largesse financed a proper funeral, the mechanism for entering an afterlife. Thus, in Egypt as in Mexico, the state established transcendental goals for its "key subjects" (Bronson's term) and enabled them to achieve those goals through service to the state. This must have been a crucial step in the history of state formation.

This process was facilitated by the judicious use of wealth. Wealth enabled rulers to "materialize" (i.e., to give physical reality to) concepts of cosmic order, worth, and rank (DeMarrais *et al.* 1996), so that cosmic goals were accepted as worthy goals. Conversely, concepts of cosmic order, worth, and rank conferred value upon items of wealth. Wealth items are rarely intrinsically rewarding; they must be imbued with cultural meaning in order to be made desirable. Once their meaning was established, wealth items could be distributed to the members of coalitions, conferring honor and securing loyalty.

In summary, then, concepts of order, legitimacy, and wealth are closely linked in the high cultures of ancient states. High cultures *are* essentially created by the elite, as Baines and Yoffee assert. But there is considerably more cultural exchange between inner elites and other segments of society than envisioned in the original Baines and Yoffee formulation. High culture often builds upon existing concepts of order, legitimacy, and wealth, and it does not clear the field of other cultural forms. Far from focusing on the concerns of a tiny inner elite, the categories and forms of high culture are often deployed to alter social and political alignments. The categories and forms of high culture can be used to orient and motivate key social segments, and these same categories and forms can be appropriated by non-elite segments of society to legitimate their claims from below. The symbolic forms and meanings created by high culture are too powerful to be left to the self-absorbed musings of a tiny inner elite. High culture is typically as concerned with political and economic issues as it is with abstract cosmology. Bruce Trigger (1993) reaches a similar conclusion in his cross-cultural study of early civilizations.

These forms and meanings still exercise their power, energizing the current culture wars debates. High culture has provided the criteria by which civilizations are defined, and with these criteria have come debates about the worthiness of different cultures and the proper content of general studies curricula at American universities (Patterson 1997). A reconsideration of both the substance and the operation of high cultures in their original settings may help to clarify the cultural issues currently being debated within academia. The past and present importance of high culture makes us truly grateful to Baines and Yoffee for having undertaken an extensive, serious consideration of the topic, and to Richards and Van Buren for having produced this volume.

## Notes

These comments were written when I was a fellow at the Center for Advanced Study in the Behavioral Sciences in Stanford, California. I am grateful for financial support provided by the Andrew W. Mellon Foundation and the National Endowment for the Humanities, which made my stay at the CASBS possible.

1 Alcock's analysis reminded me of Elijah Anderson's (1990) exploration of how inner-city youth develop a world view and value system which accords them a position of respect in a society that denies them the material and cultural resources that are the criteria for respect in middle-class culture. Both Alcock's and Anderson's work provide examples of culture-building at levels below the elite stratum.

# References


Abel, R. 1973. The comparative study of dispute institutions in society. *Law and Society Review* 8: 217–347.

Abercrombie, T. A. 1998. *Pathways of Memory and Power: Ethnography and History Among an Andean People*. Madison: University of Wisconsin Press.

Adams, M. 1992. Community and societal organization in early historic Egypt: introductory report on 1991–92 fieldwork conducted at Abydos Settlement Site. *Newsletter of the American Research Center in Egypt* 158/159: 1–9.

Adams, R. McC. 1981. *Heartland of Cities*. Chicago: University of Chicago Press.

Alcock, S. E. 1993. *Graecia Capta: The Landscapes of Roman Greece*. Cambridge: Cambridge University Press.

1994. Landscapes of memory and the authority of Pausanias. In J. Bingen (ed.) *Pausanias historien*, pp. 241–276. Entretiens sur l'antiquité classique 41. Geneva: Fondation Hardt.

Allen, J. 1988. *Genesis in Egypt. The Philosophy of Ancient Egyptian Creation Accounts*. Yale Egyptological Studies 2. New Haven: Yale Egyptological Seminar.

Almazan, M. A. 1994. *The Northern Mesoamerican States-System, 1350–1524 A. D.: Structure and Dynamics: A Thesis*. Ph.D. dissertation. Cambridge, MA: Harvard University.

Altekar, A. S. 1984. *State and Government in Ancient India*. Reprint of 3rd edn. Delhi: Motilal Banarsidass 1958.

Alva Ixtlilxochitl, F. de 1975–1977. *Obras Históricas*. E. O'Gorman (ed.) Mexico City: Universidad Nacional Autonoma de Mexico.

*Anales de Cuauhtitlan* 1945. In P. Velázquez (ed.) *Codice Chimalpopoca*, pp. 1–118. Mexico City: Universidad Nacional Autonoma de Mexico.

Anawalt, P. R. 1981. *Indian Clothing Before Cortes: Mesoamerican Costumes from the Codices*. Norman: University of Oklahoma Press.

1992 A comparative analysis of the costumes and accoutrements of the Codex Mendoza. In F. F. Berdan and P. R. Anawalt (eds.) *The Codex Mendoza*. Vol. I, pp. 103–150. Berkeley: University of California Press.

Anderson, E. 1990. *Streetwise: Race, Class and Change in an Urban Community*. Chicago: University of Chicago Press.

Anderson, G. 1993. *The Second Sophistic: A Cultural Phenomenon in the Roman Empire*. London: Routledge.

Anderson, R. L. 1989. *Art in Small-Scale Societies*. Englewood Cliffs, NJ: Prentice Hall.

Andrews, C. 1994. *Amulets of Ancient Egypt*. London: British Museum Press.

Andrews, E. W., V. 1986. Olmec jades from Chacsinkin, Yucatán, and Maya ceramics from La Venta, Tabasco. In E. W. Andrews V (ed.) *Research and Reflections in Archaeology and History: Essays in Honor of Doris Stone*, pp. 11–49. New Orleans: Tulane University, Middle American Research Institute Publication 57.

Appadurai, A. 1986a. Introduction: commodities and the politics of value. In A. Appadurai (ed.) *The Social Life of Things: Commodities in Cultural Perspective*, pp. 3–63. Cambridge: Cambridge University Press.

Appadurai, A. (ed.) 1986b. *The Social Life of Things: Commodities in Cultural Perspective*. Cambridge: Cambridge University Press.

Arnaud, D. 1986. *Recherches au Pays d'Aštata. Emar*. Vol. VI, pt. 3, pp. 7–33. Paris: Editions Recherche sur les Civilisations, Synthèse 18.

Arnold, D. 1996. Hypostyle halls of the Old and Middle Kingdom? In P. der Manuelian (ed.) *Studies in Honor of William Kelly Simpson*. Vol. I, pp. 39–45. Boston: Museum of Fine Arts.

Arriaga, P. J. de 1968. *The Extirpation of Idolatry in Peru*. L. C. Keating (trans. and ed.) Lexington: University of Kentucky Press.

Assmann, J. 1989. *Maat, l'Egypte pharaonique et l'idée de justice sociale*. Paris: Julilard.

1995. *Egyptian Solar Religion in the New Kingdom: Re, Amun and the Crisis of Polytheism*. London: Kegan Paul International.

Bagby, P. 1958. *Culture and History*. London: Longmans, Green.

Baines, J. 1983. Literacy and ancient Egyptian society. *Man* 18: 572–599.

1985. *Fecundity Figures: Egyptian Personification and the Iconology of a Genre*. Warminster: Aris and Phillips; Chicago: Bolchazy-Carducci.

1988. An Abydos list of gods and an Old Kingdom use of texts. In J. Baines, T. G. H. James, M. A. Leahy, and A. F. Shore (eds.) *Pyramid Studies*, pp. 124–133. London: Egypt Exploration Society.

1989. Ancient Egyptian concepts and uses of the past: third to second millennia BCE. In R. Layton (ed.) *Who Needs the Past? Indigenous Values and Archaeology*, pp. 131–149. London: Unwin Hyman.

1991. Society, morality, and religious practice. In B. Shafer (ed.) *Religion in Ancient Egypt*, pp. 123–200. Ithaca: Cornell University Press.

1994. On the status and purposes of ancient Egyptian art. *Cambridge Archaeological Journal* 4 (1): 67–94.

1995. Kingship, definition of culture, and legitimation of rule. In D. O'Connor and D. Silverman (eds.) *Ancient Egyptian Kingship*, pp. 3–47. Leiden: Brill.

Baines, J. and N. Yoffee 1998. Order, legitimacy, and wealth in ancient Egypt and Mesopotamia. In G. Feinman and J. Marcus (eds.) *The Archaic State: A Comparative Perspective*, pp. 199–260. Santa Fe: School of American Research Press.

Barlow, R. H. 1949. Codex Azcatitlan. *Journal de la Société des Americanistes* New Series 38: 101–135.

Barthélémy de Saizieu, B. 1990. Le cimetière néolithique de Mehrgarh (Balouchistan Pakistanais) apport de l'analyse factorielle. *Paléorient* 16 (1): 23–43.

1992. Stabilité et évolution des pratiques funéraires néolithiques à Mehrgarh (Période I: *c.* 7000–5800 B.C.). *Paléorient* 17 (2): 21–50.

Barthélémy de Saizieu, B. and A. Bouquillon 1994. Steatite working at Mehrgarh during the Neolithic and Chalcolithic periods: quantitative distribution, characterization of material and manufacturing process. In A. Parpola and P. Koskikallio (eds.) *South Asian Archaeology, 1993*, pp. 47–60. Helsinki: Suomalainen Tiedeakatemia.

Baudez, C. and P. Becquelin 1973. *Archéologie de los Naranjos, Honduras*. Études mesoaméricaines 2. Mexico, D. F. : Mission Archéologique et Ethnologique Française au Mexique.

Bauer, B. 1996. Legitimization of the state in Inca myth and ritual. *American Anthropologist* 98 (2): 327–337.

Beckman, G. 1982. The Hittite assembly. *Journal of the American Oriental Society* 102: 435–442.

Bennett, W. 1948. The Peruvian co-tradition. In W. Bennett (ed.) *A Reappraisal of Peruvian Archaeology*, pp. 1–7. Memoirs of the Society for American Archaeology 4. Menasha, WI: The Society for American Archaeology and the Institute of Andean Research.

Benson, E. and B. de la Fuente 1996. *Olmec Art of Ancient Mexico*. Washington DC: National Gallery of Art.

Berdan, F. 1982. *The Aztecs of Central Mexico: An Imperial Society*. New York: Holt, Rinehart and Winston.

Berdan, F., R. Blanton, E. H. Boone, M. Hodge, M. Smith, and E. Umberger (eds.) 1996. *Aztec Imperial Strategies*. Washington, DC: Dumbarton Oaks.

Berthelot, J. 1986. The extraction of precious metals at the time of the Inka. In J. Murra, N. Wachtel, and J. Revel (eds.) *Anthropological History of Andean Polities*, pp. 69–88. Cambridge: Cambridge University Press.

Bhan, K. K., M. Vidale, and J. M. Kenoyer 1994. Harappan technology: methodological and theoretical issues. *Man and Environment* 19 (1–2): 141–157.

Bietak, M. 1996. *Avaris: The Capital of the Hyksos*. London: British Museum.

Bintliff, J. (ed.) 1991. *The Annales School and Archaeology*. New York: New York University Press.

Black, D. 1976. *The Behavior of Law*. New York: Academic Press.

Blackman, A. 1924. *The Rock Tombs of Meir, Part IV*. London: Egypt Exploration Society.

Blackman, A. and M. Apted 1953. *The Rock Tombs of Meir, Part V*. London: Egypt Exploration Society.

Blanton, R., G. Feinman, S. Kowalewski, and P. Peregrine 1996. A dual-processual theory for the evolution of Mesoamerican civilization. *Current Anthropology* 37 (1): 1–14.

Bolshakov, A. 1997. *Man and His Double in Egyptian Ideology of the Old Kingdom*. Ägypten und Altes Testament 37. Wiesbaden: Harassowitz Verlag.

Bourdieu, P. 1973. The Berber house. In M. Douglas (ed.) *Rules and Meanings: The Anthropology of Everyday Knowledge*, pp. 98–110. Harmondsworth: Penguin Books.

1977. *Outline of a Theory of Practice*. Cambridge: Cambridge University Press.

Bourriau, J. 1988. *Pharaohs and Mortals: Egyptian Art*

*in the Middle Kingdom*. Cambridge: Cambridge University Press.

1991. Patterns of change in burial customs during the Middle Kingdom. In S. Quirke (ed.) *Middle Kingdom Studies*, pp. 3–20. New Malden: SIA Publishing.

Bowersock, G. 1969. *Greek Sophists in the Roman Empire*. Oxford: Clarendon Press.

1974. *Approaches to the Second Sophistic*. University Park, PA: American Philological Association.

Bowie, E. L. 1974. The Greeks and their past in the Second Sophistic. In M. I. Finley (ed.) *Studies in Ancient Society*, pp. 166–209. London: Routledge and Kegan Paul.

Bowman, A. and G. Woolf (eds.) 1994. *Literacy and Power in the Ancient World*. Cambridge: Cambridge University Press.

Braudel, F. 1994. *A History of Civilizations*. New York: Penguin Press.

Brewitt-Taylor, C. H. n. d. *Lo Kuan-Chung's Romance of the Three Kingdoms*. Taipei: Chinese Classics in English.

Broda de Casas, J. 1969. *The Mexican Calendar as Compared to Other Mesoamerican Systems*. Acta Ethnologica et Linguistica Number 15, Series Americana 4. Vienna: Engelbert Stiglmayr.

Brovarski, E. 1980–1982. Naga (Nag')-ed-Der. In W. Helck and W. Westendorf (eds.) *Lexikon der Ägyptologie*. Vol. VI, pp. 296–317. Wiesbaden: Harrassowitz.

Brumfiel, E. M. 1983. Aztec state making: ecology, structure and the origin of the state. *American Anthropologist* 85: 261–284.

1987. Elite and utilitarian crafts in the Aztec state. In E. Brumfiel and T. Earle (eds.) *Specialization, Exchange and Complex Societies*, pp. 676–686. Cambridge: Cambridge University Press.

1989. Factional competition in complex society. In D. Miller, M. Rowlands, and C. Tilley (eds.) *Domination and Resistance*, pp. 127–139. London: Unwin Hyman.

1992. Breaking and entering the ecosystem: gender, class, and faction steal the show. *American Anthropologist* 94: 551–567.

1996. Quality of tribute cloth: the place of evidence in archaeological argument. *American Antiquity* 61 (3): 453–462.

1997. Tribute cloth production and compliance in Aztec and colonial Mexico. *Museum Anthropology* 21 (2): 55–71.

1998. Huitzilopochtli's conquest: Aztec ideology in the archaeological record. *Cambridge Archaeological Journal* 8: 3–13.

Brumfiel, E. M. (ed.) 1994. *The Economic Anthropology of the State*. Monographs in Economic Anthropology 11. Lanham, MD: University Press of America.

Brumfiel, E. M. and T. Earle (eds.) 1987. *Specialization, Exchange and Complex Societies*. Cambridge: Cambridge University Press.

Brunton, G. 1927. *Qau and Badari*. Vols. I and II. British School of Archaeology in Egypt 44 and 45. London: British School of Archaeology in Egypt.

1937. *Mostagedda and the Tasian Culture*. London: Bernard Quaritch.

1948. *Matmar*. London: Bernard Quaritch.

Butzer, K. 1976. *Early Hydraulic Civilization in Egypt: A Study In Cultural Ecology*. Chicago: University of Chicago Press.

Campbell, L. 1976. Middle American languages. In L. Campbell and M. Mithun (eds.) *The Languages of Native America: Historical and Comparative Assessment*, pp. 902–1000. Austin: University of Texas Press.

Campbell, L., T. Kaufman and T. C. Smith-Stark 1986. Meso-America as a linguistic area. *Language* 62 (3): 530–570.

Carlson, J. B. 1981. Olmec concave iron-ore mirrors: the aesthetics of a lithic technology and the Lord of the Mirror (with an illustrated catalogue of mirrors). In E. Benson (ed.) *The Olmec and Their Neighbors*, pp. 117–148. Washington, DC: Dumbarton Oaks.

Carmack, R. M., J. Gasco, and G. H. Gossen (eds.) 1996. *The Legacy of Mesoamerica: History and Culture of a Native American Civilization*. New Jersey: Prentice Hall.

Cartledge, P. and A. Spawforth 1989. *Hellenistic and Roman Sparta: A Tale of Two Cities*. London: Routledge.

Caso, A. 1958. *The Aztecs: People of the Sun*. L. Dunham (trans.). Norman: University of Oklahoma Press.

1965. Lapidary work, goldwork, and copperwork from Oaxaca. In R. Wauchope and G. R. Willey (eds.) *Handbook of Middle American Indians*. Vol. III, pp. 896–930. Austin: University of Texas Press.

Ch'Å, T'ung-tsu 1972. *Han Social Structure*. Seattle: University of Washington Press.

Champion, T. C. (ed.) 1989. *Centre and Periphery*. London: Unwin Hyman.

Charpin, D. 1986. Transmission des titre de propriété et constitution des archives privées en Babylonie ancienne. In K. Veenhof (ed.) *Cuneiform Archives and Libraries*, pp. 121–140. Leiden: Nederlands Historisch-Archaeologisch Instituut te Istanbul.

Chase, D. Z. and A. F. Chase 1992. Mesoamerican elites: assumptions, definitions and models. In D. Z. Chase and A. F. Chase (eds.) *Mesoamerican Elites: An Archaeological Assessment*, pp. 3–17. Norman: University of Oklahoma Press.

Chase-Dunn, C. and T. D. Hall 1995. Cross-world-system comparisons: similarities and differences. In S. Sanderson (ed.) *Civilizations and World Systems: Studying World-Historical Change*, pp. 109–121. Walnut Creek, CA: Altamira Press.

Chattopadhyaya, B. (ed.) 1987. *Essays in Ancient Indian Economic History*. New Delhi: Munshiram Manoharlal.

Childe, V. G. 1936. *Man Makes Himself*. London: Watts and Co.

1944. *Progress and Archaeology*. London: Watts and Co.

1950. The urban revolution. *The Town Planning Review* 21 (1): 3–17.

1951. *Social Evolution*. London: Watts and Co.

Cieza de León, P. 1959. *The Incas of Pedro de Cieza de León*. H. de Onis (trans.), V. W. von Hagen (ed.) Norman: University of Oklahoma Press.

Civil, M. 1969. *The Series lú=ša and Related Texts*. Materials for the Sumerian Lexicon 12. Rome: Pontificium Institutum Biblicum.

Clark, J. E. 1983. A preclassic Mesoamerican society: analysis of Francesca-Phase burials from Chiapa de Corzo, Mexico. Unpublished paper provided courtesy of the author.

1987. Politics, prismatic blades, and Mesoamerican civilization. In J. Johnson and C. Morrow (eds.) *The Organization of Core Technology*, pp. 259–284. Boulder and London: Westview Press.

Clark, J. E. (ed.) 1994. *Los Olmecas en Mesoamérica*. Mexico: El Equilibrista; Madrid: Turner Libros.

Clark, J. E. and M. Blake 1994. The power of prestige: competitive generosity and the emergence of rank societies in lowland Mesoamerica. In E. Brumfiel and J. Fox (eds.) *Factional Competition and Political Development in the New World*, pp. 17–30. Cambridge: Cambridge University Press.

Clark, J. E. and W. Parry 1990. Craft specialization and cultural complexity. *Research in Economic Anthropology* 12: 289–346.

Cobo, B. 1990. *Inca Religion and Customs*. R. Hamilton (trans. and ed.). Austin: University of Texas Press.

Cock, C. G. and M. E. Doyle 1979. Del culto solar a la clandestinidad de Inti y Punchao. *Historia y Cultura* 12: 51–73.

*Codex Mendoza* 1992. F. F. Berdan and P. R. Anawalt (trans. and eds.). Berkeley: University of California Press.

Coe, M. 1957. Cycle 7 monuments in Middle America: a reconsideration. *American Anthropologist* 59: 597–611.

1966. *An Early Stone Pectoral from Southeastern Mexico*. Washington, DC: Dumbarton Oaks Studies in Pre-Columbian Art and Archaeology 1.

1976. Early steps in the evolution of Maya writing. In H. Nicholson (ed.) *Origins of Religious Art and Iconography in Preclassic Mesoamerica*, pp. 107–122. Los Angeles: UCLA Latin American Center Studies 31.

Coe, S. D. 1994. *America's First Cuisines*. Austin: University of Texas Press.

Cohen, D. 1995. *Law, Violence, and Community in Classical Athens*. Cambridge: Cambridge University Press.

Conrad, G. 1992. Inca imperialism: the great simplification and the accident of empire. In A. Demarest and G. Conrad (eds.) *Ideology and Pre-Columbian Civilizations*, pp. 159–174. Santa Fe: School of American Research Press.

Conrad, G. and A. Demarest 1984. *Religion and Empire: The Dynamics of Aztec and Inca Expansionism*. Cambridge: Cambridge University Press.

Costin, C. and T. Earle 1989. Status distinction and legitimation of power as reflected in changing patterns of consumption in Late Prehispanic Peru. *American Antiquity* 54 (4): 691–714.

Cowgill, G. 1992a. Social differentiation at Teotihuacan. In D. Z. Chase and A. F. Chase (eds.) *Mesoamerican Elites: An Archaeological Assessment*, pp. 206–220. Norman: University of Oklahoma Press.

1992b. Toward a political history of Teotihuacan. In A. Demarest and G. Conrad (eds.) *Ideology and Pre-Columbian Civilizations*, pp. 87–114. Santa Fe: School of American Research Press.

Dales, G. F. 1965. A suggested chronology for Afghanistan, Baluchistan and the Indus Valley. In R. W. Ehrich (ed.) *Chronologies in Old World Archaeology*, pp. 257–284. Chicago: University of Chicago Press.

Dales, G. F. and J. M. Kenoyer 1986. *Excavations at Mohenjo Daro, Pakistan: The Pottery*. Philadelphia: University Museum Press.

1990. Excavation at Harappa – 1989. *Pakistan Archaeology* 25: 241–280.

1991. Summaries of five seasons of research at Harappa (District Sahiwal, Punjab, Pakistan) 1986–1990. In R. H. Meadow (ed.) *Harappa Excavations 1986–1990*, pp. 185–262. Madison: Prehistory Press.

Dalley, S. 1980. Old Babylonian dowries. *Iraq* 42: 53–74.

D'Altroy, T. 1992. *Provincial Power in the Inka Empire*. Washington, DC: Smithsonian Institution Press.

Dandamaev, M. 1981. The Neo-Babylonian citizens. *Klio* 63: 45–49.

1982. The Neo-Babylonian elders. In M. Dandamaev *et al.* (eds.) *Societies and Languages of the Ancient Near East: Studies in Honour of I. M. Diakonoff*, pp. 38–41. Warminster: Aris and Phillips.

1988. The Neo-Babylonian popular assembly. *Šulmu* 3: 63–71.

D'Auria, S., P. Lacovara, and C. Roehrig (eds.) 1988. *Mummies and Magic: The Funerary Arts of Ancient Egypt*. Boston: Museum of Fine Arts.

Davies, N. 1973. *The Aztecs: A History*. London: Macmillan.

Davis, W. 1992. *Masking the Blow: The Scene of Representation in Late Prehistoric Egyptian Art*. Berkeley: University of California Press.

Dean, C. S. 1990. Painted images of Cuzco's Corpus Christi: social conflict and cultural strategy in Viceregal Peru. Ph.D. dissertation. Ann Arbor: University Microfilms International.

Demarest, A. 1981. *Viracocha: The Nature and Antiquity of the Andean High God*. Peabody Museum Monographs No. 6. Cambridge: Harvard University.

De Marrais, E., L. J. Castillo, and T. Earle 1996. Ideology, materialization, and power strategies. *Current Anthropology* 37 (1): 15–31.

Diakonoff, I. M. 1969. The rise of the despotic state in Ancient Mesopotamia. In I. M. Diakonoff (ed.) *Ancient Mesopotamia*, pp. 173–203. Moscow: Nauka.

1982. The structure of Near Eastern society before the middle of the 2nd millennium B.C. *Oikumene* 3: 7–100.

Dombradi, E. 1996. *Die Darstellung des Rechtsaustrags in den altbabylonischen Prozessurkunden*. Freiburger Altorientalische Studien 20/1 and 2. Stuttgart: Franz Steiner Verlag.

Drennan, R. 1976. Ritual and ceremonial development at the early village level. In K. Flannery and J. Marcus (eds.) *The Cloud People: Divergent Evolution of the Zapotec and Mixtec Civilizations*, pp. 46–50. New York: Academic Press.

Driver, G. R. and J. C. Miles 1935. *The Assyrian Laws*. Oxford: Oxford University Press.

1952–1955. *The Babylonian Laws*. 2 vols. Oxford: Clarendon Press.

Drucker, R. D. 1987. Mexican ("Aztec") and Western Yucatec (Landa) Maya 365-day calendars: a perpetual relation. *American Antiquity* 52 (4): 816–819.

Dubs, H. H. (trans. and ed.) 1938, 1944, 1955. *The History of the Former Han Dynasty by Pan Ku*. Baltimore: Waverly Press.

Duell, P. 1938. *The Mastaba of Mereruka*. Vol. II. Chicago: University of Chicago Press.

Dunham, D. 1937. *Naga ed Der Stelae of the First Intermediate Period*. Boston: Museum of Fine Arts.

Durán, D. 1967. *Historia de las Indias de Nueva España*. Mexico City: Porrua.

1971 *Book of the Gods and Rites and the Aztec Calendar*. F. Horcasitas and D. Heyden (trans.). Norman: University of Oklahoma Press.

Durand, J.-M. 1989. L'assemblé en Syrie à l'époque préamorite. In P. Fronzaroli (ed.) *Miscellanea Eblaitica* 2, pp. 27–44. Florence: Università di Firenze.

Durand-Forest, J. de 1967. El cacao entre los Aztecas. *Estudios de Cultura Nahuatl* 7: 155–181.

1971. Cambios económicos y moneda entre los Aztecas. *Estudios de Cultura Nahuatl* 9: 105–124.

1980. Aperçu de l'économie azteque. In *Matricula de Tributos (Códice de Moctezuma)*, pp. 12–26. Graz: Akademische Druck- und Verlagsanstalt.

Durkheim, E. 1954. *The Elementary Forms of the Religious Life*. Joseph Ward Swain (trans.). Reprint of 1915 edition. London: Allen and Unwin.

Durrani, F. A. 1988. Excavations in the Gomal Valley: Rehman Dheri excavation report No. 1. *Ancient Pakistan* 6: 1–232.

Duviols, P. 1977. *La destrucción de las religiones andinas: conquista y la colonia*. Mexico City: Universidad Nacional Autonoma de México.

Eigner, D. 1996. A palace of the early 13th Dynasty at Tell el-Dab'a. In M. Bietak (ed.) *Haus und Palast in alten Ägypten*, pp. 73–80. Vienna: Verlag der Osterreichischen Akademie der Wissenschaften.

Eisenstadt, S. N. (ed.) 1986. *The Origins and Diversity of Axial Age Civilizations*. Albany: State University of New York Press.

Elsner, J. 1995. *Art and the Roman Viewer: The Transformation of Art from the Pagan World to Christianity*. Cambridge: Cambridge University Press.

Englund, R. 1994. *Archaic Administrative Texts from Uruk: The Early Campaigns*. Archaische Texte aus Uruk V. Berlin: Gebr. Mann.

Erim, K. 1986. *Aphrodisias, City of Venus Aphrodite*. New York: Facts on File.

Evans, G. 1958. Ancient Mesopotamian assemblies. *Journal of the American Oriental Society* 78: 1–11.

Fairservis, W. A. 1967. The origin, character and decline of an early civilization. *Novitates* No. 2302: 1–48.

1989. An epigenetic view of the Harappan culture. In C. C. Lamberg-Karlovsky (ed.) *Archaeological Thought in America*, pp. 205–217. New York: Cambridge University Press.

Feinman, G. and J. Marcus (eds.) 1998. *Archaic States*. Santa Fe: School of American Research Press.

Fields, V. M. 1991. Iconographic heritage of the Maya jester god. In M. G. Robertson and W. Fields (eds.) *Sixth Palenque Round Table, 1986*, pp. 167–174. The Palenque Round Table Series 8. Norman: University of Oklahoma Press.

Figulla, H. H. 1967. *Old-Babylonian Nadītu Records*. Cuneiform Texts in the British Museum 47. London: British Museum.

Finkelstein, J. J. 1970. *šilip rēmim* and related matters. In B. Eichler (ed.) *Kramer Anniversary Volume: Cuneiform Studies in Honor of Samuel Noah Kramer*, pp. 187–194. Alter Orient und Altes Testament 25. Neukirchen-Vluyn: Kuvelaer.

Fischer, H. G. 1961. The Nubian mercenaries of Gebelein during the First Intermediate Period. *Kush* 9: 44–80.

1989. The origin of Egyptian hieroglyphs. In W. Senner (ed.) *The Origins of Writing*, pp. 59–77. Lincoln: University of Nebraska Press.

Flannery, K. V. 1976. Contextual analysis of ritual paraphernalia from Formative Oaxaca. In K. Flannery (ed.) *The Early Mesoamerican Village*, pp. 333–345. New York: Academic Press.

Flannery, K. V. and J. Marcus 1983. *The Cloud People: Divergent Evolution of the Zapotec and Mixtec Civilizations*. New York: Academic Press.

Flores Galindo, A. 1987. *Buscando un Inca: Identidad y utopia en los Andes*. Lima: Instituto de Apoyo Agrario.

Forman, W. and S. Quirke 1996. *Hieroglyphs and the Afterlife in Ancient Egypt*. Norman: University of Oklahoma Press.

Fortner, J. D. 1996. Adjudicating entities and levels of legal authority in lawsuit records of the Old Babylonian Era. Ph.D. dissertation. Cincinnati: Hebrew Union College.

Foucault, M. 1977. *Discipline and Punish*. Vintage: New York.

Fowler, W. 1989. *The Cultural Evolution of Ancient Nahua Civilizations*. Norman: University of Oklahoma Press.

Franke, D. 1995. The Middle Kingdom in Egypt. In J. Sasson (ed.) *Civilizations of the Ancient Near East*. Vol. II, pp. 735–748. New York: Scribners.

Freidel, D. 1993. Jade ahau: toward a theory of commodity value in Maya civilization. In F. Lange (ed.) *Precolumbian Jade: New Geological and Cultural Interpretations*, pp. 149–165. Salt Lake City: University of Utah Press.

Freidel, D. and J. Sabloff. 1984. *Cozumel: Late Maya Settlement Patterns*. New York: Academic Press.

Freidel, D. and L. Schele 1988a. Kingship in the Late Preclassic Maya Lowlands: the instruments and places of ritual power. *American Anthropologist* 90 (3): 547–567.

1988b. Symbol and power: a history of the Lowland Maya cosmogram. In E. Benson and G. Griffin (eds.) *Maya Iconography*, pp. 44–93. Princeton: Princeton University Press.

Fuente, B. de la 1992. Order and nature in Olmec art. In R. Townsend (ed.) *Ancient Americas: Art from Sacred Landscapes*, pp. 120–133. Chicago: Art Institute of Chicago; Munich: Prestel-Verlag.

Garcia, J. 1997. Administration territoriale et organisation de l'espace en Egypte au troisième millénaire avant J. C. II: *swnw*. *Zeitschrift für Ägyptische Sprache* 24: 116–130.

Gardiner, Sir A. 1964. *Egypt of the Pharaohs*. Reprint of 1961 edition. London: Oxford University Press 1964.

Garstang, J. 1901. *Mashasna and Bet Khallaf*. London: B. Quariteh.

1904. *Tombs of the Third Egyptian Dynasty at Reqaqna and Beth Khallaf*. Westminster.

1909. Excavations at Abydos 1909: preliminary description of the principal finds. *Liverpool Annals of Archaeology and Anthropology* 2: 125–129.

Gelb, I. J. 1969. On the alleged temple and state economies in Ancient Mesopotamia. *Studi in Onore di Edoardo Volterra* 6: 137–154.

1979. Household and family in early Mesopotamia. In E. Lipinski (ed.) *State and Temple Economy in the Ancient Near East*. Vol. I, pp. 1–97. Orientalia Lovaniensia analecta 5. Louvain: Departement Orientalistiek.

1984. *Šībūt kušurrā'im*, "witnesses of the indemnity." *Journal of Near Eastern Studies* 43: 263–276.

Gelb, I. J., P. Steinkeller, and R. Whiting 1991. *Earliest Land Tenure Systems in the Near East: Ancient Kudurrus*. Chicago: Oriental Institute.

Geniére, J. de la and K. Erim (eds.) 1987. *Aphrodisias de Carie*. Paris: Editions recherches sur les civilisations.

Gillespie, S. D. 1993. Power, pathways, and appropriations in Mesoamerican art. In N. Whitten and D. Whitten (eds.) *Imagery and Creativity: Ethnoaesthetics and Art Worlds in the Americas*, pp. 67–107. Tucson: University of Arizona Press.

Gillespie, S. D. and R. A. Joyce 1997. Gendered goods: the symbolism of Maya hierarchical exchange relations. In C. Claassen and R. Joyce (eds.) *Women in Prehistory: North America and Mesoamerica*, pp. 189–207. Philadelphia: University of Pennsylvania Press.

Gisbert, T. 1994. *Iconografía y mitos indígenas en el arte*. La Paz, Bolivia: Linea Editorial, Fundación BHN and Editorial Gisbert y CIA.

Gleason, M. 1995. *Making Men: Sophists and Self-Presentation in Ancient Rome*. Princeton: Princeton University Press.

Gluckman, M. 1973. Limitations of the case-method in the study of tribal law. *Law and Society Review* 7: 643–666.

Goody, J. 1986. *The Logic of Writing and the Organization of Society*. Cambridge: Cambridge University Press.

Graham, I. 1975. *Corpus of Maya Hieroglyphic Inscriptions*. Vol. II, pt. 1, *Naranjo*. Cambridge: Peabody Museum Press.

Greengus, S. 1995. Legal and social institutions of ancient Mesopotamia. In J. Sasson with J. Baines, G. Beckman, and K. Rubinson (eds.) *Civilizations of the Ancient Near East*. Vol. I, pp. 469–484. New York: Scribners.

Griffith, F. L. 1898. *The Petrie Papyri: Hieratic Papyri from Kahun and Gurob*. London: B. Quaritch.

Grove, D. C. 1970. *The Olmec Paintings of Oxtotitlan Cave, Guerrero, Mexico*. Washington, DC: Dumbarton Oaks Studies in Pre-Columbian Art and Archaeology 6.

1973. Olmec altars and myths. *Archaeology* 26 (2): 128–135.

1981. Olmec monuments: mutilation as a clue to meaning. In E. Benson (ed.) *The Olmec and Their Neighbors*, pp. 49–68. Washington, DC: Dumbarton Oaks.

1999. Public monuments and sacred mountains: observations on three Formative Period sacred landscapes. In D. C. Grove and R. A. Joyce (eds.) *Social Patterns in Pre-Classic Mesoamerica*, pp. 255–299. Washington, DC: Dumbarton Oaks.

Grove, D. C. (ed.) 1987. *Ancient Chalcatzingo*. Austin: University of Texas Press.

Grove, D. C. and S. D. Gillespie 1992. Archaeological indicators of Formative Period elites: a perspective from Central Mexico. In D. Z. Chase and A. F. Chase (eds.) *Mesoamerican Elites: An Archaeological Assessment*, pp. 191–205. Norman: University of Oklahoma Press.

Habicht, C. 1997. Roman citizens in Athens (228–31 B.C.). In M. Hoff and S. Rotroff (eds.) *The Romanization of Athens*, pp. 9–17. Oxford: Oxbow Books.

Hall, T. D. and C. Chase-Dunn 1996. Comparing world-systems: concepts and hypotheses. In P. N. Peregrine and G. M. Feinman (eds.) *Pre-Columbian World Systems*, pp. 11–25. Madison, WI: Prehistory Press.

Hammond, N. 1999. The genesis of hierarchy: mortuary and offertory ritual in the Preclassic at Cuello, Belize. In D. C. Grove and R. A. Joyce (eds.) *Social Patterns in Pre-Classic Mesoamerica*, pp. 49–66. Washington, DC: Dumbarton Oaks.

Hansen, R. D. 1992. El proceso cultural de Nakbe y el área del Peten nor-central: las épocas tempranas. In J. P. Laporte, H. L. Escobedo A., and S. Villagrán de Brady (eds.) *V Simposio de investigaciones arqueológicas en Guatemala*, pp. 81–87. Museo Nacional de Arqueologa y Etnologa, 15–18 de Julio de 1991. Guatemala City: Ministerio de Cultura y Deportes, Instituto de Antropologa e Historia, y Asociación Tikal.

Harris, O. 1980. The power of signs: gender, culture and the wild in the Bolivian Andes. In C. MacCormack and M. Strathern (eds.) *Nature, Culture and Gender*, pp. 70–94. Cambridge: Cambridge University Press.

1989. The earth and the state: the sources and meanings of money in Northern Potosí, Bolivia. In J. Parry and M. Bloch (eds.) *Money and the Morality of Exchange*, pp. 232–268. Cambridge: Cambridge University Press.

Harris, R. 1964. The nadītu woman. In J. A. Brinkman (ed.) *Studies Presented to A. L. Oppenheim*, pp. 106–135. Chicago: Oriental Institute.

1969. Notes on the Babylonian cloister and hearth: a review article. *Orientalia* 38: 133–145.

1975. *Ancient Sippar: A Demographic Study of an Old Babylonian City, c. 1894–1595 B.C.* Leiden: Istanbul/Nederlands Historisch-Archaeologisch Instituut.

Hassan, F. 1993. Town and village in ancient Egypt: ecology, society and urbanization. In T. Shaw, P. Sinclair, B. Andah, and A. Okpoko (eds.) *The*

*Archaeology of Africa: Food, Metal and Towns*, pp. 551–569. New York: Routledge.

Hawass, Z. and M. Lehner 1994. Who built the Sphinx and why? *Archaeology* 47 (5): 30–47.

Hayes, W. C. 1953. *The Scepter of Egypt: A Background for the Study of the Egyptian Antiquities in The Metropolitan Museum of Art*. Vol. I. New York: Harper, in cooperation with The Metropolitan Museum of Art.

1971. The Middle Kingdom in Egypt. *Cambridge Ancient History*, 3rd edn. Vol. I, pt. 2. Cambridge: Cambridge University Press.

Helms, M. 1981. Precious metals and politics: style and ideology in the Intermediate Area and Peru. *Journal of Latin American Lore* 7 (2): 215–238.

1993. *Craft and the Kingly Ideal: Art, Trade and Power*. Austin: University of Texas Press.

Hendon, J. 1999. The Pre-Classic Maya compound as the focus of social identity. In D. C. Grove and R. A. Joyce (eds.) *Social Patterns in Pre-Classic Mesoamerica*, pp. 97–125. Washington, DC: Dumbarton Oaks.

Henshaw, R. 1994. *Female and Male: The Cultic Personnel. The Bible and the Rest of the Ancient Near East*. Allison Park, PA: Pickwick Publications.

Heyer, P. 1988. *Communications and History: Theories of Media, Knowledge and Civilization*. New York: Greenwood Press.

Hicks, F. 1991. Gift and tribute: relations of dependency in Aztec Mexico. In H. J. M. Claessen and P. van de Velde (eds.) *Early State Economics*, pp. 199–213. Political and Legal Anthropology Series 8. New Brunswick: Transaction Publishers.

1994. Cloth in the political economy of the Aztec State. In M. Hodge and M. Smith (eds.) *Economies and Polities in the Aztec Realm*, pp. 89–111. Albany: Institute of Mesoamerican Studies, State University of New York.

Hinsley, C. 1985. From shell-heaps to stelae: early anthropology at the Peabody Museum. In G. W. Stocking Jr. (ed.) *Objects and Others: Essays on Museums and Material Culture*, pp. 49–74. Madison: University of Wisconsin Press.

Hirth, K. 1992. Interregional exchange as elite behavior: an evolutionary perspective. In D. Z. Chase and A. F. Chase (eds.) *Mesoamerican Elites: An Archaeological Assessment*, pp. 18–29. Norman: University of Oklahoma Press.

Hodder, I. 1982. *Symbols in Action: Ethnoarchaeological Studies of Material Culture*. Cambridge and New York: Cambridge University Press.

1986. *Reading the Past: Current Approaches to Interpretation in Archaeology*. New York: Cambridge University Press.

Hodder, I. (ed.) 1987. *Archaeology as Long-Term History*. Cambridge: Cambridge University Press.

Hoebel, E. A. 1954. *The Law of Primitive Man*. New York: Atheneum.

Hoepfner, W. and E. L. Schwander 1986. *Haus und Stadt im klassischen Griechenland*. Berlin: Deutscher Kunst Verlag.

Hoff, M. 1989. Civil disobedience and unrest in Augustan Athens. *Hesperia* 59: 267–276.

1997. Laceratae Athenae: Sulla's siege of Athens in 87/6 B.C. and its aftermath. In M. Hoff and S. Rotroff (eds.) *The Romanization of Athens*, pp. 33–51. Oxford: Oxbow Books.

Huertas Vallejos, L. 1981. *La religión en una sociedad rural andina (siglo XVII)*. Ayacucho, Peru: Universidad Nacional de San Cristóbal de Huamanga.

Ilan, D. 1995. The dawn of internationalism – the Middle Bronze Age. In T. Levy (ed.) *The Archaeology of Society in the Holy Land*, pp. 297–319. New York: Facts on File.

Imparati, F. 1991. Autorità centrale e istituzioni collegiali nel regno Ittita. In A. Ciani and G. Dirurni (eds.) *Exercizio del Potere e Prassi della Consultazione*, pp. 161–181. Rome: Libraria Edetrice Vaticana.

Jacobsen, T. 1943. Primitive democracy. *Journal of Near Eastern Studies* 2: 159–172.

1957. Political development in Mesopotamia. *Zeitschrift für Assyriologie* 52: 91–140.

1959. An ancient Mesopotamian trial for homicide. *Analecta Biblica at Orientalia* 12: 130–150.

1978–1979. Iphur-Kishi and his times. *Archiv für Orientforschung* 26: 1–14.

Janssen, C. 1991. Samsu-iluna and the hungry *nadītums*. *Mesopotamian History and Government, Series I, Northern Akkad Project Reports* 5: 3–39.

Jarrige, C. 1988. Les figurines humaines au Baluchistan. In J.-F. Jarrige (ed.) *Les Cités oubliées de l'Indus*, pp. 65–70. Paris: Musée National des Arts Asiatiques Guimet.

Jarrige, C., J.-F. Jarrige, R. H. Meadow, and G. Quivron (eds.) 1995. *Mehrgarh Field Reports 1975 to 1985 – From the Neolithic to the Indus Civilization*. Karachi: Department of Culture and Tourism, Government of Sindh and the French Foreign Ministry.

Jarrige, J.-F. 1982. Excavations at Mehrgarh: their significance for understanding the background of the Harappan civilization. In G. L. Possehl (ed.) *Harappan Civilization*, pp. 79–84. New Delhi: Oxford and IBH Publishing Co.

1984. Chronology of the earlier periods of the Greater Indus as seen from Mehrgarh, Pakistan. In B. Allchin (ed.) *South Asia Archaeology 1981*, pp. 21–28. Cambridge: Cambridge University Press.

1988. Excavations at Nausharo. *Pakistan Archaeology* 23: 149–203.

1990. Excavation at Mehrgarh-Nausharo 1987–88. *Pakistan Archaeology* 24: 21–67.

1995. Introduction. In C. Jarrige, J.-F. Jarrige, R. H. Meadow, and G. Quivron (eds.) *Mehrgarh Field Reports 1975 to 1985 – From the Neolithic to the Indus Civilization*, pp. 51–95. Karachi: Department of Culture and Tourism, Goverment of Sindh and the French Foreign Ministry.

Johnsen, H. and B. Olsen 1992. Hermeneutics and archaeology. *American Antiquity* 57: 419–436.

Johnson, A. and T. Earle 1987. *The Evolution of Human Societies: From Foraging Group to Agrarian State*. Stanford: Stanford University Press.

Joyce, R. A. 1992a. Innovation, communication and the archaeological record: a reassessment of Middle Formative Honduras. *Journal of the Steward Anthropological Society* 20 (1/2): 235–256.

1992b. The social construction of power in Formative Period Honduras. A paper presented at the annual meeting of the American Anthropological Association, San Francisco.

1996. Social dynamics of exchange: changing patterns in the Honduran archaeological record. In H. Langebaek and F. Cardenas-Arroyo (eds.) *Chieftains, Power, and Trade: Regional Interaction in the Intermediate Area of the Americas*, pp. 31–45. Bogota, Columbia: Departamento de Antropología, Universidad de los Andes.

1999. Social dimensions of Preclassic burials. In D. C. Grove and R. A. Joyce (eds.) *Social Patterns in Pre-Classic Mesoamerica*, pp. 15–47. Washington, DC: Dumbarton Oaks.

Joyce, R. A., R. Edging, K. Lorenz, and S. D. Gillespie 1991. Olmec bloodletting: an iconographic study. In M. G. Robertson and V. M. Fields (eds.) *Sixth Palenque Round Table, 1986*, pp. 143–150. Norman: University of Oklahoma Press.

Joyce, R. A. and D. C. Grove 1999. Asking new questions about the Mesoamerican Preclassic. In D. C. Grove and R. A. Joyce (eds.) *Social Patterns in Pre-Classic Mesoamerica*, pp. 1–14. Washington, DC: Dumbarton Oaks.

Julien, C. 1982. Inca decimal administration in the Lake Titicaca region. In G. Collier, R. Rosaldo, and J. Wirth (eds.) *The Inca and Aztec States, 1400–1800: Anthropology and History*, pp. 119–154. New York: Academic Press.

Justeson, J. 1986. Origin of writing systems: Preclassic Mesoamerica. *World Archaeology* 17 (3): 437–458.

1988. Non-Maya calendars of southern Veracruz-Tabasco and the antiquity of the civil and agricultural years. *Journal of Mayan Linguistics* 6: 1–21.

Kamrin, J. 1992. Monument and microcosm: the 12th Dynasty tomb chapel of Khnumhotep II at Beni Hasan. Ph.D. dissertation. Michigan: University Microfilms International.

Kapferer, B. 1997. *The Feast of the Sorcerer: Practices of Consciousness and Power*. Chicago: University of Chicago Press.

Katz, D. 1993. *Gilgamesh and Akka*. Groningen: Styx.

1995. Enmebaragesi, king of kish, a sister of Gilgamesh? *Nouvelles Assyriologiques Brèves et Utilitaires* 1995 (2): 24.

Kemp, B. 1989. *Ancient Egypt. Anatomy of a Civilization*. London: Routledge.

1995. How religious were the ancient Egyptians? *Cambridge Archaeological Journal* 5/1: 25–54.

Kennedy, N. 1981. The Formative Period ceramic sequence from Playa de los Muertos, Honduras. Ph.D. dissertation. Ann Arbor: University Microfilms International.

Kenoyer, J. M. 1983. *Shell Working Industries of the Indus Civilization: An Archaeological and Ethnographic Perspective*. Berkeley: University of California-Berkeley.

1986. The Indus bead industry: contributions to bead technology. *Ornament* 10 (1): 18–23.

1989. Socio-economic structures of the Indus Civilization as reflected in specialized crafts and the question of ritual segregation. In J. M. Kenoyer (ed.) *Old Problems and New Perspectives in the Archaeology of South Asia*, pp. 183–192. Madison: Department of Anthropology, University of Wisconsin. Wisconsin Archaeological Reports, Vol. 2.

1991a. The Indus Valley Tradition of Pakistan and Western India. *Journal of World Prehistory* 5 (4): 331–385.

1991b. Urban process in the Indus Tradition: a preliminary model from Harappa. In R. H. Meadow (ed.) *Harappa Excavations* 1986–1990, pp. 29–60. Madison: Prehistory Press.

1992a. Harappan craft specialization and the question

of urban segregation and stratification. *Eastern Anthropologist* 45 (1/2): 39–54.

1992b. Ornament styles of the Indus Tradition: evidence from recent excavations at Harappa, Pakistan. *Paléorient* 17 (2): 79–98.

1994a. The Harappan state: was it or wasn't it? In J. M. Kenoyer (ed.) *From Sumer to Meluhha: Contributions to the Archaeology of South and West Asia in Memory of George F. Dales, Jr.*, pp. 71–80. Madison: Department of Anthropology, University of Wisconsin.

1994b. Faience from the Indus Valley Civilization. *Ornament* 17 (3): 36–39, 95.

1994c. Experimental studies of Indus Valley technology at Harappa. In A. Parpola and P. Koskikallio (eds.) *South Asian Archaeology, 1993*, pp. 245–262. Helsinki: Suomalainen Tiedeakatemia.

1995a. Interaction systems, specialized crafts and culture change: the Indus Valley Tradition and the Indo-Gangetic Tradition in South Asia. In G. Erdosy (ed.) *The Indo-Aryans of Ancient South Asia: Language, Material Culture and Ethnicity*, pp. 213–257. Berlin: W. DeGruyter.

1995b. Ideology and legitimation in the Indus State as revealed through symbolic objects. *The Archaeological Review. Journal of Pakistan Archaeologists Forum* 4 (1–2): 87–131.

1995c. Shell trade and shell working during the Neolithic and Early Chalcolithic at Mehrgarh. In C. Jarrige, J.-F. Jarrige, R. H. Meadow, and G. Quivron (eds.) *Mehrgarh Field Reports 1975 to 1985 – From the Neolithic to the Indus Civilization*, pp. 566–581. Karachi: Department of Culture and Tourism, Government of Sindh and the French Foreign Ministry.

1997a. Trade and technology of the Indus Valley: new insights from Harappa, Pakistan. *World Archaeology* 29 (2): 262–280.

1997b. Early city-states in South Asia: comparing the Harappan Phase and the Early Historic period. In D. L. Nichols and T. H. Charlton (eds.) *The Archaeology of City-States: Cross Cultural Approaches*, pp. 51–70. Washington, DC: Smithsonian Institution Press.

Khatri, J. S. and M. Acharya 1995. Kunal: a new Indus-Saraswati site. *Puratattva* 25: 84–86.

Kidder, A. V., J. Jennings, and E. Shook 1946. *Excavations at Kaminaljúyú, Guatemala.* Washington, DC: Carnegie Institution of Washington Publication 561.

Kirchhoff, P. [1952] 1968. Meso-America: its geographic limits, ethnic composition, and cultural characteristics. In Sol Tax and members of the Viking Fund Seminar on Middle American Ethnology (eds.) *Heritage of Conquest*, pp. 17–30. Reprint, New York: Cooper Square Publishers, Inc.

Klengel, H. 1960. Zu den *šībūtum* in altbabylonischer Zeit. *Orientalia* 24: 357–375.

1965. Die Rolle der Ältesten (LÚ$^{\text{meš}}$ŠU.GI) im Kleinasien der Hethiterzeit. *Zeitschrift für Assyriologie* 23: 223–236.

1989. "Älteste" in den Texten aus Ebla und Mari. In M. LeBeau and P. Talon (eds.) *Reflets de deux fleuves. Volume de mélanges offerts à André Finet*, pp. 61–5. Leuven: Uitgeverij Peeters en Departement Orientalistik.

Knapp, A. B. (ed.) 1992. *Archaeology, Annales, and Ethnohistory*. Cambridge: Cambridge University Press.

Korošec, V. 1964. Keilschriftrecht. In E. Sidl, V. Korosec, E. Pritsch, (eds.) *Orientalisches Recht*, pp. 49–219. Handbuch der Orientalistik. Erste Abteilung, Nahe und er Mittlere Osten, supp. vol. III. Leiden: Brill.

Koschaker, P. 1917. *Rechtsvergleichende Studien zur Gesetzgebung Hammurapis*. Leipzig: Verlag von Veit & Comp.

1923. *Hammurabi's Gesetz* (with Arthur Ungnad). Band 6. Leipzig: Eduard Pfeiffer.

Koshurnikov, S. 1984. An Old Babylonian family archive from the city of Dilbat. *Vestnik Drevnej Istorii*, pp. 123–141 (in Russian).

Kowalewski, S., G. Feinman, and L. Finsten 1992. The elite and assessment of social stratification in Mesoamerican archaeology. In D. Z. Chase and A. F. Chase (eds.) *Mesoamerican elites: An Archaeological Assessment*, pp. 259–277. Norman: University of Oklahoma Press.

Kraus, F. R. 1982. *Kārum*, ein organ städtischer Selbstverwaltung der altbabylonischen Zeit. In A. Finet (ed.) *Les pouvoirs locaux en Mésopotamia et dans les régions adjacentes*, pp. 29–42. Brussels: Institut des Hautes Etudes de Belgique.

Kroeber, A. 1957. *Style and Civilizations.* Ithaca: Cornell University Press.

1962. *A Roster of Civilizations and Culture.* New York: Viking Fund Publications.

Kuhrt, A. 1995. *The Ancient Near East*. Vol. I. London: Routledge.

Kümmel, H. 1979. *Familie, Beruf und Amt im spätbabylonischen Uruk*. Berlin: Gebr. Mann.

Kus, S. 1982. Matters material and ideal. In I. Hodder (ed.) *Symbolic and Structural Archaeology*, pp. 47–62. Cambridge: Cambridge University Press.

1989. Sensuous human activity and the state: towards an archaeology of bread and circuses. In D. Miller, M. Rowlands, and C. Tilley (eds.) *Domination and Resistance*, pp. 140–154. London: Unwin Hyman.

LaFont, B. 1985. Le sâbum du roi de Mari au temps de Yasmah-Addu. In J.-M. Durand (ed.) *Miscellanea Babyloniaca: Mélanges offerts à Maurice Birot*, pp. 161–180. Paris: Editions Recherches sur les civilisations.

Lambert, W. G. 1992. Prostitution. In V. Haas (ed.) *Aussenseiter und Randgruppen*, pp. 127–158. Xenia: Konstanzer Althistorische Vorträge und Forschungen 32. Konstanz: Universitätsverlag.

Larsen, M. T. 1976. *The Old Assyrian City-State and its Colonies*. Copenhagen: Akademisk Forlag.

Lasswell, H., D. Lerner and H. Speier (eds.) 1979. *Propaganda and Communication in World History*. Vol. I, *The Symbolic Instrument in Early Times*. Honolulu: University of Hawaii.

Lautner, J. G. 1922. *Die richterliche Entscheidung und die Streitbeendigung in altbabylonischen Prozessrechte*. Leipzig: Verlag Theodor Weicher.

Layton, R. 1988. *Conflict in the Archaeology of Living Traditions*. London: Unwin.

Leahy, A. 1989. A protective measure at Abydos in the Thirteenth Dynasty. *Journal of Egyptian Archaeology* 75: 41–60.

Lechtman, H. 1996. Cloth and metal: the culture of technology. In E. H. Boone (ed.) *Andean Art at Dumbarton Oaks*. Vol. I, pp. 33–43. Washington, DC: Dumbarton Oaks Research Library and Collection.

Leone, M. P. 1984. Interpreting ideology in historical archaeology: using the rules of perspective in the William Paca Garden in Annapolis, Maryland. In D. Miller and C. Tilley (eds.) *Ideology, Power and Prehistory*, pp. 25–35. Cambridge: Cambridge University Press.

*Leyenda de los Soles* 1945. In P. Velazquez (trans.) *Codice Chimalpopoca*, pp. 119–142. Mexico City: Universidad Nacional Autónoma de México.

Lichtheim, M. 1973. *Ancient Egyptian Literature*. Vol. I, *The Old and Middle Kingdoms*. Berkeley: University of California Press.

1988. *Ancient Egyptian Autobiographies Chiefly of the Middle Kingdom*. Freibourg: Biblical Institute of the University of Freibourg.

Liverani, M. 1990. *Prestige and Interest: International Relations in the Near East, c.* 1600–1100 B.C. Padua: Sargon srl.

1993a. Model and actualization: the kings of Akkad in the historical tradition. In M. Liverani (ed.) *Akkad: The First World Empire*, pp. 41–68. Padua: Sargon srl.

1993b. Nelle pieghi del despotismo. Organismi rappresentativi nell'Antico Oriente. *Studi Storici* 34 (1): 7–33.

Loat, W. 1923. A Sixth Dynasty cemetery at Abydos. *Journal of Egyptian Archaeology* 9: 161–163.

López Austin, A. 1988. *The Human Body and Ideology: Concepts of the Ancient Nahuas*. T. Ortiz de Montellano and B. Ortiz de Montellano (trans.). Salt Lake City: University of Utah Press.

Love, M. 1992. Material culture and social practice in Preclassic Pacific Guatemala. A paper presented at the annual meeting of the American Anthropological Association, San Francisco.

1999. Ideology, material culture, and daily practice in the Pre-Classic Mesoamerica: a Pacific coast perspective. In D. C. Grove and R. A. Joyce (eds.) *Social Patterns in Pre-Classic Mesoamerica*, pp. 127–153. Washington, DC: Dumbarton Oaks.

Lustig, J. 1997. Kinship, gender, and age in Middle Kingdom tomb scenes and texts. In J. Lustig (ed.) *Anthropology and Egyptology*, pp. 43–65. Monographs in Mediterranean Archaeology 8. Sheffield: Sheffield Academic Press.

Luttwak, E. 1969. *Coup d'État, A Practical Handbook*. Greenwich, CN: Fawcett Publications.

McCarthy, B. and P. B. Vandiver 1990. Ancient high-strength ceramics: fritted faience bangle manufacture at Harappa (Pakistan), *c.* 2300–1800 B.C. In P. B. Vaniver, J. Druzik, and G. S. Wheeler (eds.) *Materials Issues in Art and Archaeology*. Vol. II, pp. 495–510. Pittsburgh: Materials Research Society.

MacCormick, S. 1991. *Religion in the Andes: Vision and Imagination in Early Colonial Peru*. Princeton: Princeton University Press.

McDowell, A. 1989. *Jurisdiction in the Workmen's Community at Deir el-Medina*. Leiden: Nederlands Instituut voor het Nabije Oosten.

Machinist, P. 1986. On self-consciousness in Mesopotamia. In S. Eisenstadt (ed.) *The Origins and Diversity of Axial Age Civilizations*, pp. 193–202. Albany: State University of New York Press.

McNamara, J. K. 1996. *Sisters in Arms: Catholic Nuns Through Two Millennia*. Cambridge, MA: Harvard University Press.

Malek, J. 1986. *In the Shadow of the Pyramids*. Norman: University of Oklahoma Press.

Malpass, M. (ed.) 1993. *Provincial Inca: Archaeological and Ethnohistorical Assessment of the Inca State*. Iowa City: University of Iowa Press.

Mann, M. 1986. *The Sources of Social Power*. Vol. I, A History of Power from the Beginning to A.D. 1760. Cambridge: Cambridge University Press.

Marcus, G. 1992. The concern with elites in archaeological reconstructions: Mesoamerican materials. In D. Z. Chase and A. F. Chase (eds.) *Mesoamerican Elites: An Archaeological Assessment*, pp. 292–302. Norman: University of Oklahoma Press.

Marcus, J. 1976. *Emblem and State in the Classic Maya Lowlands*. Washington, DC: Dumbarton Oaks.

1989. Zapotec chiefdoms and the nature of Formative religions. In R. Sharer and D. Grove (eds.) *Regional Perspectives on the Olmec*, pp. 148–197. Cambridge: Cambridge University Press.

1992a. *Mesoamerican Writing Systems: Propaganda, Myth and History in Four Ancient Civilizations*. Princeton: Princeton University Press.

1992b. Royal families, royal texts: examples from the Zapotec and Maya. In D. Z. Chase and A. F. Chase (eds.) *Mesoamerican Elites: An Archaeological Assessment*, pp. 221–241. Norman: University of Oklahoma Press.

Marcus, J. and K. V. Flannery 1996. *Zapotec Civilization: How Urban Society Evolved in Mexico's Oaxaca Valley*. London: Thames and Hudson.

Marshall, S. J. 1931. *Mohenjo-daro and the Indus Civilization*. London: A. Probsthain.

Martin-Pardey, E. 1976. *Untersuchungen zur Ägyptischen Provinzialverwaltung bis zum Ende des Alten Reiches*. Hildesheim: Verlag Gerstenberg.

Matos Moctezuma, E. 1996. Catalogue entry 94: deity mask. In E. P. Benson and B. de la Fuente (eds.) *Olmec Art of Ancient Mexico*, p. 252. Washington, DC: National Gallery of Art.

Meadow, R. H. and J. M. Kenoyer 1993. Excavations at Harappa 1992 and 1993. *Pakistan Archaeology* 28: 55–107.

1997. Excavations at Harappa 1994–1995: new perspectives on the Indus script, craft activities and city organization. In B. Allchin (ed.) *South Asian Archaeology 1995*. Bombay: Oxford and IBH, in press.

1999. Harappa excavations 1996–1997. In M. Taddei (ed.) *South Asian Archaeology 1997*. Rome: IsIAO, in press.

Meadow, R. H., J. M. Kenoyer and R. P. Wright 1998. *Harappa Excavations 1998*. Madison: Harvard University and the University of Wisconsin.

Meskell, L. 1998. *Archaeology Under Fire: Nationalism, Politics, and Heritage in the Eastern Mediterranean and the Middle East*. London: Routledge.

Michalowski, P. 1976. The Royal correspondence of Ur. Ph.D. dissertation. New Haven: Yale University.

1983. History as charter: some observations on the Sumerian King List. *Journal of the American Oriental Society* 103: 237–248.

Miller, D. 1989. The limits of dominance. In D. Miller, M. Rowlands, and C. Tilley (eds.) *Domination and Resistance*, pp. 63–79. London: Unwin Hyman.

Miller, D., M. Rowlands, and C. Tilley (eds.) 1989a. *Domination and Resistance*. London: Unwin Hyman.

1989b. Introduction. In D. Miller, M. Rowlands, and C. Tilley (eds.) *Domination and Resistance*, pp. 1–26. London: Unwin Hyman.

Miller, H. M.-L. 1997. Status and imitation in the Indus Valley: social implications in the changing technologies of white and blue bead production. Paper presented at the annual meeting of the Society for American Archaeology, Nashville, TN, April 1997.

1999. Reassessing the urban structure of Harappa: evidence from craft production location. In M. Taddei (ed.) *South Asian Archaeology 1997*. Rome: IsIAO, in press.

Mishkin, B. 1963. The contemporary Quechua. In J. Steward (ed.) *Handbook of South American Indians*. Vol. II, pp. 411–470. New York: Cooper Square Publishers.

Molina, F. A. de 1970. *Vocabulario en lengua castellana y mexicana, y mexicana u castellana*. 4th edn. Originally published as *Vocabulario en lengua castellana y mexicana*, 1571. Reprint of Leipzig: B. Teubner 1880. Mexico, D. F. : Editorial Porrua.

Monaghan, J. 1990. Sacrifice, death, and the origins of agriculture in the Codex Vienna. *American Antiquity* 55 (3): 559–569.

Moore, S. 1978. *Law as Social Process: An Anthropological Approach*. London: Routledge and Kegan Paul.

Moorey, P. R. S. 1994. *Ancient Mesopotamian Materials and Industries*. Oxford: Clarendon.

Morris, C. 1982. The infrastructure of Inka control in the Peruvian Central Highlands. In G. Collier, R. Rosaldo, and J. Wirth (eds.) *The Inca and Aztec States, 1400–1800: Anthropology and History*, pp. 153–171. New York: Academic Press.

Morris, C. and D. Thompson 1985. *Huánuco Pampa: An*

*Inca City and its Hinterland*. London: Thames and Hudson.

Morris, I. 1992. *Death-Ritual and Social Structure in Classical Antiquity*. Cambridge: Cambridge University Press.

1997. An archaeology of equalities? The Greek city-states. In D. Nichols and T. H. Charlton (eds.) *The Archaeology of City-States: Cross-Cultural Approaches*, pp. 91–105. Washington, DC: Smithsonian Institution Press.

Moseley, M. 1978. *Peru's Golden Treasures: An Essay on Five Ancient Styles*. Chicago: Field Museum of Natural History.

Mughal, M. R. 1974. New evidence of the Early Harappan culture from Jalilpur, Pakistan. *Archaeology* 27: 106–113.

1982. Recent archaeological research in the Cholistan desert. In G. L. Possehl (ed.) *Harappan Civilization*, pp. 86–95. New Delhi: Oxford and IBH Publishing.

1990. The protohistoric settlement patterns in the Cholistan desert. In M. Taddei and P. Callieri (eds.) *South Asian Archaeology 1987*, pp. 143–156. Rome: IsMEO.

1997. A preliminary review of archaeological surveys in Punjab and Sindh: 1993–1995. *South Asian Studies* 13: 241–249.

Munn, N. 1986. *The Fame of Gawa*. Durham, NC: Duke University Press.

Murra, J. 1980. *The Economic Organization of the Inka State*. Greenwich: JAI Press.

Murra, J. and C. Morris 1976. Dynastic oral tradition, administrative records, and archaeology in the Andes. *World Archaeology* 7: 269–279.

Nash, June 1979 *We Eat the Mines, and the Mines Eat Us*. New York: Columbia University Press.

Nichols, D. and T. H. Charlton (eds.) 1997. *The Archaeology of City-States: Cross-Cultural Approaches*. Washington, DC: Smithsonian Institution Press.

Nissen, H., P. Damerow, and R. Englund 1990. *Frühe Schrift und Techniken der Wirtschaftsverwaltung im alten Vorderen Orient: Informationsspeicherung und -verarbeitung vor 5000 Jahren*. Translated as *Archaic Bookkeeping: Early Writing and Techniques of Economic Administration in the Ancient Near East*. Chicago: University of Chicago Press, 1993.

Ocaña, D. de 1969. *Un viaje fascinant e por la América hispana del siglo XVI*. Fr. A. Alvarez (ed.) Madrid: STVDIVM ediciones.

Ochoa, P. 1996. Catalogue entry 25: acrobat effigy vessel. In E. P. Benson and B. de la Fuente (eds.) *Olmec Art of Ancient Mexico*, p. 189. Washington, DC: National Gallery of Art.

O'Connor, D. 1983. New Kingdom and Third Intermediate Period, 1552–664 BC. In B. Trigger, B. J. Kemp, D. O'Connor, and A. B. Lloyd (eds.) *Ancient Egypt: A Social History*, pp. 183–278. Cambridge: Cambridge University Press.

1985. The "cenotaphs" of the Middle Kingdom at Abydos. In P. Posener-Krieger (ed.) *Mélanges Gamal Eddin Mokhtar*, pp. 162–177. Cairo: Institut français d'archéologie orientale.

1989. City and palace in New Kingdom Egypt. *Cahier de Recherches de l'Institut de Papyrologie et d'Égyptologie de Lille* 11: 73–87.

1993. Urbanism in Bronze Age Egypt and Northeast Africa. In T. Shaw *et al.* (eds.) *The Archaeology of Africa: Food, Metals, and Towns*, pp. 570–586. New York: Routledge.

1996. Sexuality, statuary, and the afterlife: scenes in the tomb-chapel of Pepyankh (Heny the Black). An interpretive essay. In P. der Manuelian (ed.) *Studies in Honor of William Kelly Simpson*. Vol. II, pp. 621–633. Boston: Museum of Fine Arts.

1997. Egyptian architecture. In D. Silverman (ed.) *Searching for Ancient Egypt: Art, Architecture and Artifacts from the University of Pennsylvania Museum of Archaeology and Anthropology*, pp. 155–161. Dallas: Dallas Museum of Art; Philadelphia: University of Pennsylvania Museum; Ithaca: Cornell University Press.

Old, W. G. (trans. and ed.) 1904. *The Shu King of the Chinese Historical Classic*. London and Benares: Theosophical Publishing Society.

Oppenheim, A. L. 1967. A new look at the structure of Mesopotamian society. *Journal of the Economic and Social History of the Orient* 10: 1–16.

Ortner, S. B. 1984. Theory in anthropology since the sixties. *Comparative Studies in Society and History* 26: 126–166.

Parkinson, R. 1991. *Voices from Ancient Egypt*. London: British Museum Press.

1997. *The Tale of Sinuhe and other Ancient Egyptian Poems, 1940–1640 BC*. Oxford: Clarendon Press.

1999. Imposing words: the entrapment of language in "The Tale of the Eloquent Peasant." *Lingua Aegyptiaca*, in press.

Parpola, A. 1990. Bangles, sacred trees and fertility: interpretation of the Indus script relating to the cult of Skanda-Kumara. In M. Taddei and P. Callieri (eds.) *South Asian Archaeology 1987*, pp. 263–284. Rome: IsMEO.

1994. *Deciphering the Indus Script*. Cambridge: Cambridge University Press.

Parry, J. and M. Bloch (eds.) 1989. *Money and the Morality of Exchange*. Cambridge: Cambridge University Press.

Patterson, T. C. 1985. Exploitation and class formation in the Inca state. *Culture* 5 (1): 35–42.

1986. Ideology, class formation, and resistance in the Inca state. *Critique of Anthropology* 6 (1): 75–85.

1991. *The Inca Empire: The Formation and Disintegration of a Pre-Capitalist State*. New York and Oxford: Berg.

1995. *Toward a Social History of Archaeology in the United States*. Fort Worth: Harcourt Brace.

1997. *Inventing Western Civilization*. New York: Monthly Review Press.

Paynter, R. 1989. The archaeology of equality and inequality. *Annual Review of Anthropology* 18: 369–399.

Paynter, R. and R. McGuire 1991. The archaeology of inequality: material culture, domination and resistance. In R. McGuire and R. Paynter (eds.) *The Archaeology of Inequality*, pp. 1–27. Oxford: Blackwell.

Peet, T. 1914. *The Stela of Sebek-khu, the Earliest Record of an Egyptian Campaign in Asia*. Manchester: Sherratt and Hughes.

Peet, T. and W. Loat 1914. *Cemeteries of Abydos II*. London: Egypt Exploration Fund Memoirs No. 34.

Peregrine, P. N. 1996. Introduction: world-systems theory and archaeology. In P. Peregrine and G. Feinman (eds.) *Pre-Columbian World Systems*, pp. 1–10. Monographs in World Archaeology 26. Madison, WI: Prehistory Press.

Peregrine, P. N. and G. Feinman (eds.) 1996. *Pre-Columbian World Systems*. Monographs in World Archaeology 26. Madison, WI: Prehistory Press.

Petrie, W. M. F. 1923. *Lahun II*. British School of Archaeology in Egypt and Egyptian Research Account Vol. 33. London: Quaritch.

Pettinato, G. 1977. Fondazione della città UNKEN$^{ki}$. *Oriens Antiquus* 16: 173–176.

Petrochilos, N. K. 1974. *Roman Attitudes to the Greeks*. Athens: National and Capodistrian University of Athens, Faculty of Arts.

Piña Chan, R. 1971. Preclassic or Formative pottery and minor arts of the Valley of Mexico. In R. Wauchope, G. Ekholm, and I. Bernal (eds.) *Handbook of Middle American Indians*. Vol. X, pp. 157–178. Austin: University of Texas.

Pires-Ferreira, J. W. 1976. Shell and iron-ore mirror exchange in Formative Mesoamerica, with comments on other commodities. In K. V. Flannery (ed.) *The Early Mesoamerican Village*, pp. 311–328. New York: Academic Press.

Pizarro, P. 1921. *Relation of the Discovery and Conquest of the Kingdoms of Peru*, Vol. I. P. A. Means (trans.) New York: The Cortes Society.

Pollitt, J. J. 1986. *Art in the Hellenistic Age*. Cambridge: Cambridge University Press.

Popenoe, D. 1934. Some excavations at Playa de los Muertos, Ulua River, Honduras. *Maya Research* 1: 62–86.

Pospisil, L. 1978. *The Ethnology of Law*. Menlo Park: Cummings.

Postgate, J. N. 1992. *Early Mesopotamia: Society and Economy at the Dawn of History*. London: Routledge.

Powers, E. E. 1922. *Medieval English Nunneries*. Cambridge: Cambridge University Press.

Prasad, K. D. 1984. *Cities, Crafts and Commerce under the Kusanas*. Delhi: Agam Kala Prakashan.

1987. *Taxation in Ancient India: From the Earliest Times up to the Guptas*. Delhi: Mittal Publications.

Proskouriakoff, T. 1974. *Jades from the Cenote of Sacrifice, Chichen Itza, Yucatan*. Cambridge: Peabody Museum of Archaeology and Ethnology Memoirs 10 (1).

Quirarte, J. 1977. Early art styles of Mesoamerica and Early Classic Maya art. In R. E. W. Adams (ed.) *The Origins of Maya Civilization*, pp. 249–284. Albuquerque: University of New Mexico Press.

Quirke, S. 1991a. "Townsmen" in the Middle Kingdom. *Zeitschrift für Ägyptische Sprache* 118: 141–149.

1991b. Royal power in the 13th Dynasty. In S. Quirke (ed.) *Middle Kingdom Studies*, pp. 123–139. New Malden: SIA Publishing.

Ragaranjan, L. N. 1992. *Kautilya: The Arthashastra*. Reprint of 1987 edition. New Delhi: Penguin Books.

Rands, R. 1965. Jades of the Maya lowlands. In R. Wauchope and G. R. Willey (eds.) *Handbook of Middle American Indians*. Vol. III, pp. 561–580. Austin: University of Texas.

Rawson, J. (ed.) 1996. *Mysteries of Ancient China*. London: British Museum Press.

Redfield, R. 1953. *The Primitive World and Its Transformations*. Ithaca: Cornell University Press.

1956. *Peasant Society and Culture: An Anthropological Approach to Civilization*. Chicago: The University of Chicago Press.

Reilly, F. K., III 1991. Olmec iconographic influences

on the symbols of Maya rulership: an examination of possible sources. In M. G. Robertson and V. Fields (eds.) *Sixth Palenque Round Table, 1986*, pp. 151–166. The Palenque Round Table Series, Volume 8. Norman: University of Oklahoma Press.

1994. Cosmología, soberanismo y espacio ritual en la Mesoamérica del Formativo. In J. Clark (ed.) *Los olmecas en Mesoamérica*, pp. 239–259. Mexico: El Equilibrista; Madrid: Turner Libros.

Reisner, G. 1932. *A Provincial Cemetery of the Pyramid Age. Naga-ed-Der, Part III*. Oxford: Oxford University Press.

Reiter, K. 1996. Haushaltsgegenstände in altbabylonischen Texten unter besonderer Berücksichtigung der Kessel und Metalgeräte. In K. Veenhof (ed.) *Houses and Households in Ancient Mesopotamia*, pp. 261–272. Leiden: Nederlands Instituut voor het Nabije Oosten.

Renfrew, C. 1985. *The Archaeology of Cult*. London: British School of Archaeology.

Renfrew, C. and J. Cherry (eds.) 1986. *Peer Polity Interaction and Socio-Political Change*. Cambridge: Cambridge University Press.

Renger, J. 1967. Untersuchungen zum Priestertum in der altbabylonischen Zeit. *Zeitschrift für Assyriologie* 58: 110–188.

Reynolds, J. 1982. *Aphrodisias and Rome*. London: Society for the Promotion of Roman Studies.

Richards, J. 1992. Mortuary variability and social differentiation in Middle Kingdom Egypt. Ph.D. dissertation. Ann Arbor: University Microfilms International.

1998. Ancient Egyptian mortuary practice and the study of socio-economic differentiation. In J. Lustig (ed.) *Egyptology and Anthropology: A Developing Dialogue*, pp. 33–42. Monographs in Mediterranean Archaeology 8. Sheffield: Sheffield Academic Press.

1999. Conceptual landscapes in the Egyptian Nile Valley. In W. Ashmore and B. Knapp (eds.) *Archaeologies of Landscape: Contemporary Perspectives*, pp. 83–100. Oxford: Blackwell.

Richards, J. and T. Wilfong (eds.) 1995. *Preserving Eternity: Modern Goals, Ancient Intentions*. Ann Arbor: Kelsey Museum of Archaelogy.

Ringle, W. 1999. Pre-classic cityscapes: ritual politics among the Early Lowland Maya. In D. C. Grove and R. A. Joyce (eds.) *Social Patterns in Pre-Classic Mesoamerica*, pp. 183–223. Washington, DC: Dumbarton Oaks.

Rissman, P. C. 1989. The organization of seal production in the Harappan civilization. In J. M. Kenoyer (ed.) *Old Problems and New Perspectives in the Archaeology of South Asia*, pp. 159–170. Madison: Wisconsin Archaeological Reports.

Roberts, S. 1979. *Order and Dispute*. Harmondsworth: Penguin Books.

Robins, G. 1990. Problems in interpreting Egyptian art. *Discussions in Egyptology* 17: 45–58.

1994. Some Principles of Compositional Dominance and Gender Hierarchy in Ancient Egyptian Art. *Journal of the American Research Center in Egypt* 31: 33–40.

1997. *The Art of Ancient Egypt*. Cambridge, MA: Harvard University Press.

Roemer, W. Ph. 1980. *Das sumerische Kurzepos "Bilgameš und Akka": Versuch einer Neubearbeitung*. Alter Orient und Altes Testament 209. Kevelaer: Butzon & Becker; Neukirchen-Vluyn: Neukirchner Verlag.

Roth, A. 1988. The organization of royal cemeteries at Saqqara in the Old Kingdom. *Journal of the American Research Center in Egypt* 25: 201–214.

1993. Social change in the Fourth Dynasty: the spatial organization of pyramids, tombs, and cemeteries. *Journal of the American Research Center in Egypt* 30: 33–55.

1994. The practical economies of tomb building in the Old Kingdom: a visit to the necropolis in a carrying chair. In D. Silverman (ed.) *For His Ka: Essays Offered in Memory of Klaus Bauer*, pp. 235–248. Chicago: Oriental Institute.

1995. *A Cemetery of Palace Attendants*. Giza Mastabas 6. Boston: Museum of Fine Arts.

Roth, M. 1988. Women in transition and the *bīt mār banî*. *Revue d'Assyriologie* 82: 131–138.

1989. A case of contested status. In H. Behrens, D. Loding, and M. Roth (eds.) *DUMU-E$_2$-DUB-BA-A: Studies in Honor of Åke W. Sjøberg*, pp. 481–489. Philadelphia: Samuel Noah Kramer Fund, University Museum.

1995. *Law Collections from Mesopotamia and Asia Minor*. Atlanta: Scholars Press.

Roueché, C. and K. Erim (eds.) 1990. *Aphrodisias papers*. Ann Arbor: Journal of Roman Archaeology Supplement 1.

Rounds, J. 1979. Lineage, class, and power in the Aztec state. *American Ethnologist* 6: 73–86.

Rowe, J. 1967. Colonial portraits of Inca nobles. In Sol Tax (ed.) *The Civilizations of Ancient America*, pp. 258–268. New York: Cooper Square Publishers.

Rowlands, M., M. Larsen, and K. Kristiansen (eds.)

1987. *Centre and Periphery in the Ancient World.* Cambridge: Cambridge University Press.

Ruhlmann, G. 1981. Zur sozialen Funktion der Beamtengrabdarstellungen im ägyptischen alten Reich. *Hallesche Beitrage Zur Orientwissenschaft* 3: 28–45.

Runciman, W. G. 1990. Doomed to extinction: the polis as an evolutionary dead-end In O. Murray and S. Price (eds.) *The Greek City: From Homer to Alexander*, pp. 347–367. Oxford: Clarendon Press.

Sahagún, B. de 1950–1982. *Florentine Codex: General History of the Things of New Spain.* 14 vols. A. J. O. Anderson and C. E. Dibble (trans.) Monographs of the School of American Research and the Museum of New Mexico, No. 14. Santa Fe: The School of American Research Press; Salt Lake City: The University of Utah Press.

1954. *Florentine Codex: General History of the Things of New Spain, Book 8 – Kings and Lords.* A. J. O. Anderson and C. E. Dibble (trans.) Monographs of the School of American Research and the Museum of New Mexico, No. 14, Part IX. Santa Fe: School of American Research Press; Salt Lake City: The University of Utah Press.

1961. *Florentine Codex: General History of the Things of New Spain, Book 10 – The People.* A. J. O. Anderson and C. E. Dibble (trans.) Monographs of the School of American Research and the Museum of New Mexico, No. 14, Part XI. Santa Fe: School of American Research Press; Salt Lake City: The University of Utah Press.

Salles-Reese, V. 1997. *From Virococha to the Virgin of Copacabana: Representation of the Sacred at Lake Titicaca.* Austin: University of Texas Press.

Sallnow, M. 1989. Precious metals in the Andean moral economy. In J. Parry and M. Bloch (eds.) *Money and the Morality of Exchange*, pp. 209–231. Cambridge: Cambridge University Press.

Salomon, F. and G. L. Urioste 1991. *The Huarochirí Manuscript: A Testament of Ancient and Colonial Andean Religion.* Austin: University of Texas Press.

Samzun, A. 1988. Le chalcolithique ancien à Mehrgarh. In J.-F. Jarrige (ed.) *Les Cités oubliées de l'Indus*, pp. 53–55. Paris: Musée National des Arts Asiatiques Guimet.

Samzun, A. and P. Sellier 1983. Découverte d'une nécropole Chalcolithique à Mehrgarh, Pakistan. *Paléorient* 9 (2): 69–79.

Sanderson, S. K. (ed.) 1995. *Civilizations and World Systems: Studying World-Historical Change.* Walnut Creek, CA: Altamira Press.

Sargent, C. B. 1977. *Wang Mang.* Reprint of 1947 edition. Westport, CN: Hyperion Press.

Sasson, J. (ed.) 1995. *Civilizations of the Ancient Near East.* 4 vols. New York: Scribner.

Scharfe, H. 1989. *The State in Indian Tradition.* Leiden: E. J. Brill.

Schele, L. and M. E. Miller 1986. *The Blood of Kings: Dynasty and Ritual in Maya Art.* Fort Worth: Kimball Art Museum.

Schneider, H. K. 1974. *Economic Man: The Anthropology of Economics.* New York: The Free Press.

Schorr, M. 1913. *Urkunden des altbabylonischen Zivil- und Prozessrechts.* Leipzig: J. C. Hinrichs.

Scott, J. 1985. *Weapons of the Weak: Everyday Forms of Peasant Resistance.* New Haven: Yale University Press.

Seidlmayer, S. J. 1990. *Gräberfelder aus dem Übergang vom Alten zum Mittleren Reich.* Heidelberg: Heidelberger Orientverlag.

1996 Town and state in the Early Old Kingdom: a view from Elephantine. In J. Spencer (ed.) *Aspects of Early Egypt*, pp. 108–127. London: British Museum Press.

Sellier, P. 1988. La nécropole néolithique de Mehrgarh. In J.-F. Jarrige (ed.) *Les Cités oubliées de l'Indus*, pp. 59–64. Paris: Musée National des Arts Asiatiques Guimet.

Shaffer, A. 1983. Gilgamesh, the cedar forest, and Mesopotamian history. *Journal of the American Oriental Society* 103: 307–313.

Shaffer, J. G. 1982. Harappan culture: a reconsideration. In G. L. Possehl (ed.) *Harappan Civilization*, pp. 41–50. New Delhi: Oxford and IBH Publishing.

1992. The Indus Valley, Baluchistan and Helmand traditions: Neolithic through Bronze Age. In R. Ehrich (ed.) *Chronologies in Old World Archaeology.* 3rd edn., pp. 441–464. Chicago: University of Chicago Press.

Shanks, M. and C. Tilley 1982. Ideology, symbolic power and ritual communication: a reinterpretation of Neolithic mortuary practices. In I. Hodder (ed.) *Symbolic and Structural Archaeology*, pp. 129–154. Cambridge: Cambridge University Press.

1987. *Re-constructing Archaeology.* Cambridge: Cambridge University Press.

Sharer, R. J. and D. C. Grove, eds. 1989 *Regional Perspectives on the Olmec.* Cambridge University Press, Cambridge.

Sharer, R. J. and D. W. Sedat 1973. Monument I, El Portón, Guatemala and the development of Maya calendrical and writing systems. In J. Graham (ed.) *Studies in Ancient Mesoamerica*, pp. 177–194. Berkeley: University of California-Berkeley, Archaeological Research Facility, Contributions No. 18.

Shear, T. L. 1981. Athens: from city-state to provincial town. *Hesperia* 50: 356–377.

Shulman, A. R. 1964. *Military Rank, Title, and Organization in the Egyptian New Kingdom*. Münchener Ägyptologische Studien 6. Berlin: B. Hessling.

Silverblatt, I. 1988. Imperial dilemmas, the politics of kinship, and Inca reconstructions of history. *Comparative Studies in Society and History* 30 (1): 83–102.

Simpson, W. K. 1974. *The Terrace of the Great God at Abydos*. Publications of the Pennsylvania–Yale Expedition to Egypt 5. New Haven and Philadelphia: Peabody Museum of Natural History of Yale University and University of Pennsylvania Museum of Archaeology and Anthropology.

1997. *Inscribed Material from the Pennsylvania–Yale Excavations at Abydos*. Publications of the Pennsylvania–Yale Expedition to Egypt No. 6. New Haven and Philadelphia: Peabody Museum and University of Pennsylvania Museum.

Small, D. 1997. City-State dynamics through a Greek lens. In D. Nichols and T. H. Charlton (eds.) *The Archaeology of City-States: Cross-Cultural Approaches*, pp. 107–118. Washington, DC: Smithsonian Institution Press.

Smith, A. 1996. Imperial archipelago: the making of the Urartian landscape in Southern Transcaucasia. Ph.D. dissertation. Tucson: University of Arizona.

Smith, C. S. 1976. On art, invention and technology. *Technology Review* 79: 36–41.

Smith, M. 1987. Household position and wealth in agrarian states: implications for archaeology. *Journal of Anthropological Archaeology* 6: 297–335.

Smith, R. R. R. 1987. The imperial reliefs from the Sebasteion at Aphrodisias. *Journal of Roman Studies* 77: 88–138.

1988. Simulacra gentium: the ethne from the Sebasteion at Aphrodisias. *Journal of Roman Studies* 78: 50–77.

1993. *Aphrodisias I: The Monument of C. Julius Zoilos*. Mainz: von Zabern.

Smith, R. R. R. and K. Erim (eds.) 1991. *Aphrodisias Papers 2*. Ann Arbor: Journal of Roman Archaeology Supplement 2.

Smith, R. R. R. and C. Ratté 1995. Archaeological research at Aphrodisias in Caria, 1993. *American Journal of Archaeology* 99: 33–58.

1996. Archaeological research at Aphrodisias in Caria, 1994. *American Journal of Archaeology* 100: 5–33.

1997. Archaeological research at Aphrodisias in Caria, 1995. *American Journal of Archaeology* 101: 10–14.

1998. Archaeological research at Aphrodisias in Caria, 1996. *American Journal of Archaeology* 102: 225–250.

Smith, W. S. 1981. *The Art and Architecture of Ancient Egypt*. 2nd edn., revised with additions by W. K. Simpson. New York: Penguin Books.

Snodgrass, A. M. 1986. Interaction by design: the Greek city state. In C. Renfrew and J. F. Cherry (eds.) *Peer Polity Interaction and Socio-Political Change*, pp. 47–58. Cambridge: Cambridge University Press.

Spalding, K. 1984. *Huarochirí: An Andean Society under Inca and Spanish Rule*. Stanford: Stanford University Press.

Spawforth, A. J. S. 1997. The early reception of the imperial cult in Athens: problems and ambiguities. In M. Hoff and S. Rotroff (eds.) *The Romanization of Athens*, pp. 183–201. Oxford: Oxbow Books.

Spencer, A. 1982. *Death in Ancient Egypt*. Harmondsworth: Penguin Books.

Spengler, O. 1922. *The Decline of the West*. New York: Alfred Knopf.

Stol, M. 1976. *Studies in Old Babylonian History*. Leiden/Istanbul: Nederland Historisch-Archaeologisch Instituut.

Stone, E. 1982. The social role of the *nadītu* women in Old Babylonian Nippur. *Journal of the Economic and Social History of the Orient* 25: 50–70.

Strong, W. D., A. V. Kidder II, and A. J. Drexel Paul 1938. *Preliminary report of the Smithsonian Institution–Harvard University Archaeological Expedition to Northwestern Honduras, 1936*. Washington, DC: Smithsonian Institution Miscellaneous Collections 97.

Swain, S. 1996. *Hellenism and Empire: Language, Classicism and Power in the Greek World, AD 50–250*. Oxford: Clarendon Press.

Taube, K. 1985. The Classic Maya maize god: a reappraisal. In M. G. Robinson and V. Fields (eds.) *Fifth Palenque Round Table, 1983*, pp. 171–181. San Francisco: Pre-Columbian Art Research Institute.

1989. Maize tamale in Classic Maya diet, epigraphy, and art. *American Antiquity* 54 (1): 31–51.

Toren, C. 1989. Drinking cash: the purification of

money through ceremonial exchange in Fiji. In J. Parry and M. Bloch (eds.) *Money and the Morality of Exchange*, pp. 142–164. Cambridge: Cambridge University Press.

Toynbee, A. J. 1934–61 *A Study of History*. 12 vols. London: Oxford University Press.

Trigger, B. 1979. Egypt and the comparative study of early civilizations. In K. Weeks (ed.) *Egyptology and the Social Sciences*. Cairo: American University in Cairo Press.

1989. *A History of Archaeological Thought*. Cambridge: Cambridge University Press.

1993. *Early Civilizations: Ancient Egypt in Context*. Cairo: American University in Cairo Press.

1998. *Sociocultural Evolution*. Oxford: Blackwell.

Tschopik, H. 1963. The Aymara. In J. Steward (ed.) *Handbook of South American Indians*. Vol. II, pp. 501–573. New York: Cooper Square Publishers.

Urton, G. 1998. From knots to narratives: reconstructing the art of historical record keeping in the Andes. *Ethnohistory* 45 (3): 409–438.

van den Brink, E. 1986. A geo-archaeological survey of the northeastern delta, Egypt: the first two seasons, a preliminary report. *Mitteilungen des deutschen archäologischen Institut Kairo Abteilung* 43: 7–31.

Vanzetti, A. and M. Vidale 1994. Formation processes of beads: defining different levels of craft skill among the early beadmakers of Mehrgarh. In A. Parpola and P. Koskikallio (eds.) *South Asian Archaeology 1993*, pp. 763–776. Helsinki: Suomalainen Tiedeakatemia.

Veenhof, K. 1995. Kanesh: an Assyrian colony in Anatolia. In J. Sasson *et al.* (eds.) *Civilizations of the Ancient Near East*. Vol. II, pp. 859–872. New York: Scribner.

1994. Two *šilip rēmim* adoptions from Sippar. In H. Gasche *et al.* (eds.) *Cinquante-deux réflexions sur le prôche-orient ancien offerts à Léon De Meyer*, pp. 143–155. Mesopotamian History and Environment Occasional Publications 2. Leuven: Uitgeverÿ Peeters en Departement Orientalistik.

Vernus, P. 1970. Quelques exemples du type de parvenu en ancienne egypte. *Bulletin de la societé française d'égyptologie* 59: 31–47.

Vidale, M. 1989a. Specialized producers and urban elites: on the role of craft industries in mature Harappan urban contexts. In J. M. Kenoyer (ed.) *Old Problems and New Perspectives in the Archaeology of South Asia*, pp. 171–182. Madison: Wisconsin Archaeological Reports.

1989b. Early Harappan steatite, faience and paste beads in a necklace from Mehrgarh-Nausharo (Pakistan). *East and West* 39 (1–4): 291–300.

1995. Early beadmakers of the Indus tradition: the manufacturing sequence of talc beads at Mehrgarh in the 5th millenium B.C. *East and West* 45 (1–4): 45–80.

Wachtel, N. 1977. *The Vision of the Vanquished: The Spanish Conquest of Peru through Indian Eyes, 1530–1570*. New York: Harper and Row.

Walker, S. 1997. Athens under Augustus. In M. Hoff and S. Rotroff (eds.) *The Romanization of Athens*, pp. 67–80. Oxford: Oxbow Books.

Wallerstein, I. 1974. *The Modern World-System I: Capitalist Agriculture and the Origins of the European World-Economy in the Sixteenth Century*. New York: Academic Press.

Walther, A. 1917. *Das altbabylonische Gerichtswesen*. Leipzig Semitische Studien 6, bd. 4–6. Leipzig: J. C. Hinrichs.

Wardman, A. 1976. *Rome's Debt to Greece*. London: Paul Elek.

Watson, B. (trans. and ed.) 1962. *Records of the Grand Historian, Translated from the Shih Chi of Ssu-ma Ch'ien*. 2nd edn. New York: Columbia University Press.

1969. *Records of the Historian, Chapters from the Shih Chi of Ssu-ma Ch'ien*. New York: Columbia University Press.

Webster, G. 1980. Labor control and emergent stratification in prehistoric Europe. *Current Anthropology* 31 (4): 337–366.

Wechsler, H. J. 1985. *Offerings of Jade and Silk: Ritual and Symbol in the Legitimation of the T'ang Dynasty*. New Haven: Yale University Press.

Westbrook, R. 1988. *Old Babylonian Family Law*. Graz: Archiv für Orientforschung Beiheft 23.

1989. Cuneiform law codes and the origins of legislation. *Zeitschrift für Assyriologie* 79: 201–222.

Westenholz, A. 1984. The Sargonic period. In A. Archi (ed.) *Circulation of Goods in Non-palatial Context in the Ancient Near East*, pp. 17–30. Rome: Edizioni dell'Ateneo.

Whiting, R. 1987. *Old Babylonian Letters from Tell Asmar*. Chicago: Oriental Institute.

Wilcke, C. 1970. Drei Phases des Niedergangs des Reiches von Ur III. *Zeitschrift für Assyriologie* 60: 54–69.

1974. Zum Königtum in der Ur III Zeit. In P. Garelli (ed.) *Le palais et la royauté: compte rendu de la XIX^ème^ Rencontre assyriologique internationale*, pp. 177–232. Paris: Librairie Orientaliste Paul Geuthner.

1975. Politische Opposition nach sumerischen Quellen: der Konflikt zwischen Königtum und Ratsversammlung. Literaturwerke als politische Tendenzschriften. In A. Finet (ed.) *La voix de l'opposition*, pp. 37–65. Bruxelles: L'Institut des Hautes Etudes de Belgique.

1992. Diebe, Räuber und Mörder. In V. Haas (ed.) *Aussenseiter und Randgruppen: Beiträge zu einer Sozialgeschichte des Alten Orients*, pp. 53–78. Konstanzer Althistorische Vorträge und Forschungen 32. Konstanz: Universitätsverlag.

Willems, H. O. 1996. *The Coffin of Heqata (Cairo JdE 36418): A Case Study of Egyptian Funerary Culture of the Early Middle Kingdom*. Orientalia Lovaniensia Analecta 70. Leuven: Uitgeverij Peeters en Departement Oriëntalistiek.

1988. *Chests of Life: A Study of the Typology and Conceptual Development of Middle Kingdom Standard Class Coffins*. Leuven: Uitgeverij Peeters en Departement Orientalistiek.

Willey, G. R. 1966. *An Introduction to American Archaeology*. Vol. I, *North and Middle America*. Englewood Cliffs, NJ: Prentice-Hall.

Willey, G. R. and P. Phillips 1958. *Method and Theory in American Archaeology*. Chicago: University of Chicago Press.

1975 Population, Exchange, and Early State Formation in Southwestern Iran. *American Anthropologist* 77: 267–289.

Wink, A. 1986. *Land and Sovereignty in India: Agrarian Society and Politics under the Eighteenth-century Maratha Svarajya*. Bombay: Orient Longman/-Cambridge University Press.

Woodbury, R. 1965. Artifacts of the Guatemalan highlands. In R. Wauchope and G. R. Willey (eds.) *Handbook of Middle American Indians*. Vol. II, pp. 163–179. Austin: University of Texas.

Woolf, G. 1994. Becoming Roman, staying Greek: culture, identity and the civilizing process in the Roman East. *Proceedings of the Cambridge Philological Society* 40: 116–143.

Woolley, S. L. 1955. *Excavations at Ur*. London: Ernest Benn Ltd.

Wright, H. and G. Johnson 1975. Population, exchange, and early state formation in Southwestern Iran. *American Anthropologist* 77: 267–289.

Yoffee, N. 1977. *The Economic Role of the Crown in the Old Babylonian Period*. Bibliotheca Mesopotamica 5. Malibu: Undena Publications.

1988a. Aspects of Mesopotamian land sales. *American Anthropologist* 90: 119–130.

1988b. The collapse of ancient Mesopotamian states and civilization. In N. Yoffee and G. Cowgill (eds.) *The Collapse of Ancient States and Civilizations*, pp. 44–68. Tucson: University of Arizona Press.

1988c. Context and authority in early Mesopotamian law. In R. Cohen and J. Tolen (eds.) *State Formation and Political Legitimacy*, pp. 95–113. New Brunswick: Transaction Books of Rutgers University Press.

1993a. The late great tradition in ancient Mesopotamia. In M. Cohen, D. Snell, and D. Weisberg (eds.) *The Tablet and the Scroll: Near Eastern Studies in Honor of William W. Hallo*, pp. 300–308. Bethesda, MD: CDL Press.

1993b. Too many chiefs? (or safe texts for the '90s). In N. Yoffee and A. Sherratt (eds.) *Archaeological Theory: Who Sets the Agenda?* pp. 60–78. Cambridge: Cambridge University Press.

1995a. Political economy in early Mesopotamian states. *Annual Review of Anthropology* 24: 281–311.

1995b. Review of Mario Liverani *Prestige and Interest. Journal of Near Eastern Studies* 54: 54–55.

1997. Robert McCormick Adams: an archaeological biography. *American Antiquity* 62: 349–413.

Yoffee, Norman and George Cowgill (eds.) 1988 *The Collapse of Ancient States and Civilizations*. Tucson: University of Arizona Press.

Zadok, R. 1979. *The Jews in Babylonia during the Chaldean and Achaemenian Periods according to the Babylonian Sources*. Haifa: Haifa University Press.

Zanker, P. 1988. *The Power of Images in the Age of Augustus*. Ann Arbor: University of Michigan Press.

# Index